# HOMESPUN CERAMICS

A Study of Spatterware

by

Arlene and Paul H. Greaser

Fourth Edition—Enlarged

Published By
Wallace-Homestead Book Co.
Des Moines, Iowa 50305

Library of Congress Card Number 67-31449
ISBN No. 0-87069-075-2



2638 TILGHMAN ST.
ALLENTOWN, PA. — 18104

dedicated to

EILEEN PATRICIA HOOK
AND MICHAEL CHARLES HOOK

*with appreciation*
*to Thelma and John R. Yeager,*
*and Mrs. Viola L. Neiman*
*for their valuable assistance.*

# DATE OF PRODUCTION

WHEN, in the course of undirected or aimless collecting, one purchases a piece of Spatterware for the appeal and color it adds to a collection and for the reason that it seems to show a somewhat direct association to other somewhat similar specimens he seems to have taken a tremendous step toward confusion. Confusion of body or biscuit, of period, of production and anything else that he wants to know about his purchase. He secures answers that are dis-similar, that are not substantiated and generally unsatisfactory.

One dealer will tell him that it is Soft Paste, another that it is Soft Paste Porcelain, another that it is Pearlware, another that he shall be alert because the term Soft Paste used in this country is a different usage than that referred to in England and in studying it he may get confused, another will tell him that it is Regular Staffordshire, another Ironstone and another Graniteware until he knows quite well that before he is finished studying it he will need expert assistance and guidance.

One will tell him that it was made in the 18th Century, another the 19th Century, and one can give up at this point and accept the confusion as an unsolvable mystery or try his hand at what will be a very involved and almost hopeless task.

There are of course a number of facts known, and from here, he must reach a logical conclusion since this subject has never to the best of our knowledge been fully covered.

The most full and accurate description has been given to us by Prof. Cornelius Weygandt in his entertaining and accurate Red Hills, in his book so beautifully and understandingly written about the Pennsylvania Dutch and their country, their customs and their possessions.

He tells us that he had a collection of perhaps a hundred pieces, which he has the opportunity to study thoroughly and frequently, that all of the Spatterware that he has seen is Soft Paste or Stoneware. In Soft Paste he has found it sponged in blue, pink, lake, deep red, green, yellow, purple, brown and black, and with several combinations of two and even three of these colors. He has, also, in Soft Paste found Spatterware not sponged but daubed on with the open spaces between the bits of color, etc.

He also tells us both sorts are early, from 1790 to 1840. He continues to tell us of his collection, why he likes them and describes them so thoroughly and accurately that he seems to give to each a personality and he ends one chapter by inviting those who have pursued this recital of crudities of yesterday so far as this—if there are any such—I can only say: Come and see my Spatter, all of it, in the Dutch cupboard in my back room, and you will understand why I like it. There are people, we all know, who love reading in bed, and pug dogs, and salt on cantaloupes. As the sage says: Human nature being what it is, anything is possible.

This remarkable and humane volume published in 1929 by the University of Pennsylvania Press—Philadelphia should be a must on the list of any one who has any interest in Spatterware or really anything Pennsylvania Dutch. He was one of us and understood us thoroughly.

Varying authors, since that time, have referred to this product and they all concede that it was made primarily for the Pennsylvania Dutch, and then it seems that they proceed to Ohio and Illinois to inspect and secure examples for illustrating or for securing marks to be found on Spatterware and to fix the date of production. They furthermore refer to it as a relatively heavy, whitish earthenware and at the same time repeat Professor Weygandt's reference to Soft Paste, but did not take advantage of his offer to—Come and see my Spatter, all of it, in the Dutch cupboard in my back room.

Forgetting history, forgetting when Soft Paste faded from the picture, forgetting that the Western movement started after the Revolution and about the time that Pearlware was introduced originally, they could find very little elsewhere about the Pennsylvania Dutch, their ceramics or their culture. These authors then set the starting date of production of this primarily 18th Century ceramic to a mid-19th Century era.

It is and has been felt for a long time that the Soft Paste period of Spatterware was in the 18th Century as the good Professor has indicated and we realized that it required a broad study of the subject and an intimate knowledge from living with them as well, to study as we read and we attach a partial listing of books we have and study regularly on this subject.

We read in various areas and hear that research and discovery in antiques is never ending—new found facts and opinions are constantly being recorded which is what makes study and collecting so interesting. This is true and correct but for some strange reason we find no change or correction on Spatterware recorded in the last 34 years although we find that generally new opinions are advanced verbally—nor can we find a fairly complete listing of patterns known to exist.

While the good Professor had the collection, the time, the knowledge, and the ability to prove his statements, he told all and sundry what he found. He gave them a chance, if they desired to view, to question, to check, to seek, to find, to settle for all time, to correct.

At this late date we no longer had this opportunity and had to create our own collection for this purpose.

Spatterware is but the name of a ceramic that has been decorated in some manner with Spatter work, possibly on the border, possibly all over and as we study it so many more come to our attention that it is difficult to tell exactly, as a style or pattern, what form or type it could and did take, but the first thing to remember is that it is only a designation of the type of decoration.

In order, then, to determine the date of potting the next thing to consider is the paste or body of the ceramic on which this decoration was applied.

First, we should call attention to FIGURES 1, 2, 113, 114, 115 and 116. These are pictures of plates that we have been able to secure of Creamware. They are of a uniform size similar to Leed's type, they are 8¼ inches in diameter, they come in a single color Spatter border, both fine and coarse

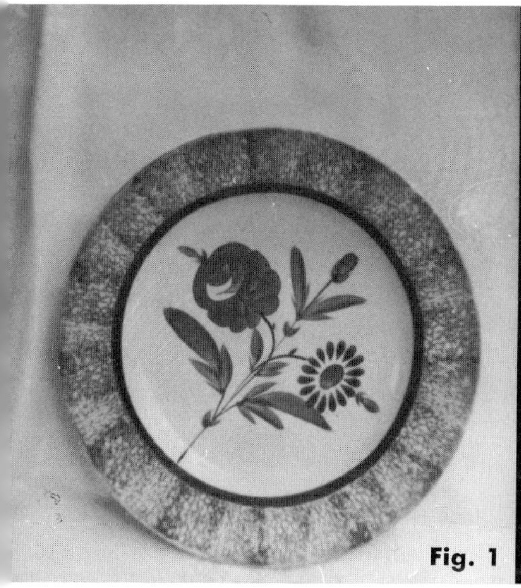

Fig. 1

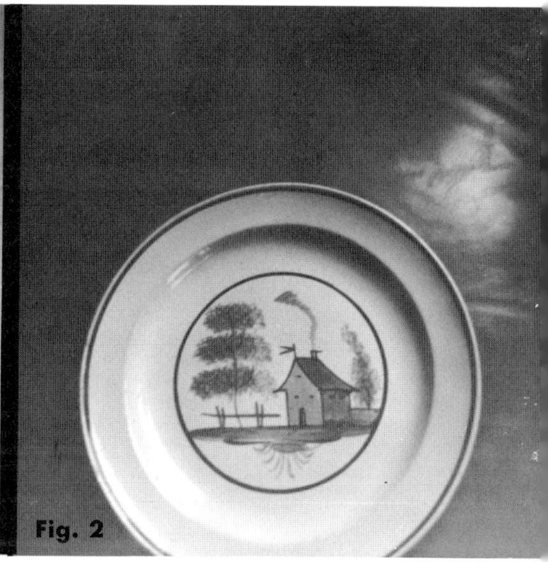

Fig. 2

Spatter type, in a two color Rainbow type, in a plain border with only circular lines around as commonly found on Delft and while the other colors are similar to the Spatterware we are studying, the red colors are usually of the rust shade generally used on Delft and on King's Rose.

Whereas a Leed's plate 8-inch size will weigh 8½ ounces this Creamware plate in an 8¼-inch size weighs 11 ounces. They have the bob or shragger marks on the back as found on Delft and in order to learn the date of potting we found it necessary to secure expert advice. We approached three museums and an antiquarian with our find. Two of the museums are among the largest and most exacting in America, the other a very unique specializing type with a vast fund of knowledge of their specific product and a reliable and early established antiquarian who was recommended to us very highly because of their knowledge of ceramics of this apparent period and their reliability. We found that these plates were of an 1785 to 1790 period, Creamware and of a Wedgwood shape. Further it was admitted that these were the first examples of Creamware Spatterware called to their attention and it was this that secured for us the opportunity for their expert opinion.

Just why these are of a heavier body than the Leed's type with which we are acquainted we do not know, but we are aware that as a result of the French Revolution, when the Napoleonic Wars were in progress it affected business generally in England and it probably caused the body to receive less attention than previously and caused it to become heavier, or possibly through the use by some potters of Growan Stone and Cornish Kaolin in Creamware as a result of the patent rights granted Champion of Bristol in 1775.

We learn from Therle and Bernard Hughes, page 86, English Painted Enamels that after the Revolution (1799) Napoleon prohibited some products completely and imposed such heavy duties that trade decreased so alarmingly that England was faced with a commercial panic, in fact by the end of the 18th Century the majority of enamellers had been forced out of business.

Having found authoritatively the date of potting of our Creamware examples and the weight, we were next interested in finding how early, our Soft Paste, our Pearlware plates compared and were delighted to find that they were the exact same weight, an 8¼-inch plate weighing also 11 ounces. We had these identified as Pearlware, perfected in 1775 and introduced in 1779 by Wedgwood and to find that they compared exactly to our Creamware examples in weight was indeed interesting.

We turned next to page 39, a Living Tradition, by John Meredith Graham II and Hensleigh Cecil Wedgwood, The Brooklyn Museum and found that Pearlware came as a result of complaints from customers about the varying shades of Creamware, as a result of variations in raw materials and firing techniques, the hues varying from a pale cream to straw or saffron but these variations were in the glaze and not in the body. As a result the demand became so great for a white body that Pearlware was introduced.

Pearlware contains a greater proportion of flint and white clay than does the Creamware and a small percentage of Cobalt oxide was added to the glaze to give the same effect as blueing does in the laundry.

This then explains why the Pearlware (Soft Paste) early type is the same weight as the Creamware examples above referred to, and the approximate date of the start of production. A natural question would next be for what period of time did this Soft Paste Pearlware then continue and once more we are up against a difficult answer. In the first place when the English had a winner they would continue to produce it, as they should, until demand slackened, and when this demand stopped they discontinued it but they, with their small potteries, could still make it when requested on a small or special order without upsetting their schedules or plans too much, so that any date may be only general, they did not stop as one pulls down a shade, but possibly, gradually.

To find this date we possibly had better refer to page 21, William Adams—The Old English Potter by William Turner where we find that in judging (Benjamin Adams) the son it must be remembered that, at the time he lived, a period of decadence had set in throughout all the centers of Art-production in the Kingdom and the continent. The prolonged wars had very much reduced the resources of these nations, and the population could buy only the necessaries of life, even the printed ware of the son was neither as light in weight, nor had it the fine finish of the productions created by his father. Books available indicate that this was in 1809.

In other words, in 1809 the early soft paste had become heavier in the Adams factory and since this was a general national condition, it did the same in the Staffordshire district and in the whole of England as well. Your light weight Pearlware, Soft Paste Pearlware had a period of possibly 30 years—1779 to 1809 and then the heavier paste or as some call it, the Regular Paste or Regular Staffordshire started to be manufactured, not as a new item, but as a continuation of Pearlware but under the existing conditions, as explained.

Of Ironstone we have very little knowledge having found one that is so marked in the Pennsylvania markets up to the present time, and only three or four that were heavy, possibly Graniteware.

We learn, however, that Ironstone was patented in 1813 by Charles James Mason and that his Ironstone jugs took on a new form, being octagonal so that the corners would not be easily broken (page 79—chats on old Earthenware—Arthur Hayden) and since all through the chronicles of this subject we find that these potters copied one another mercilessly it is quite possible that upon the basis of this new shape his competitors started to copy this from the outset and that a lot of the Spatterware of this shape is of an early 19th Century potting as well.

Since all collections vary each collector must, from the above, determine to which group his pieces should be assigned, since very few are marked.

It may be well to add that about one in a hundred is marked with the name of a potter and about two in each hundred is marked with the mark of a worker in the Dr. Wall or the Caughley potteries.

In FIGURE 3 we show a semi-circle band depressed with W Adams & Sons, in FIGURE 4 we show a Capital C as used by Caughley, and in FIGURE 5 a dot under a semi-circle, resembling an eye as used by a Dr. Wall worker. We learn that in 1783 Spode got two men from the Caughley works and knowing how easily these men transferred from one employer to another this is quite understandable, in the 1779-1785 period.

## WHO WERE THESE ARTISTS?

If we refer to America's Arts and Skills by Time, Inc. we find that the Port of Philadelphia was in 1750 the largest Port in the thirteen Colonies and the City of Philadelphia was the largest city in the British Empire at that time. This then was naturally the area that came first to the

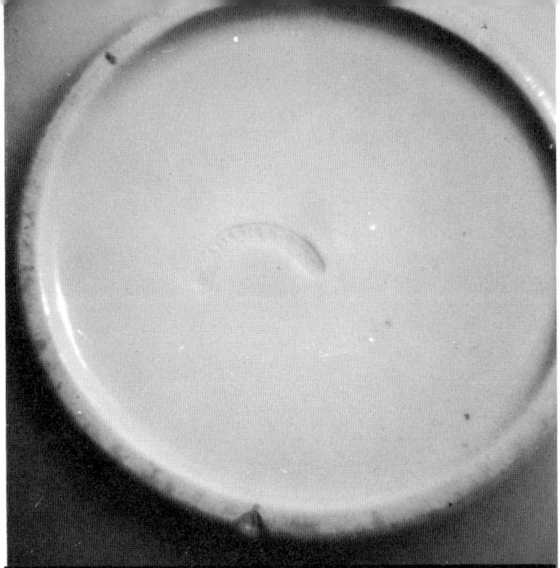

Fig. 3

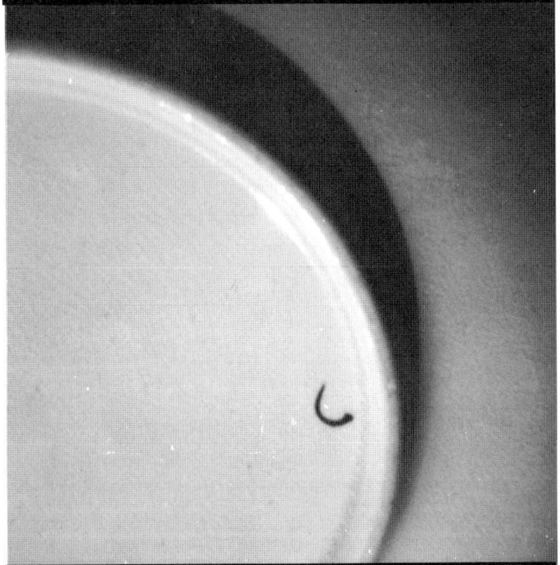

Fig. 4

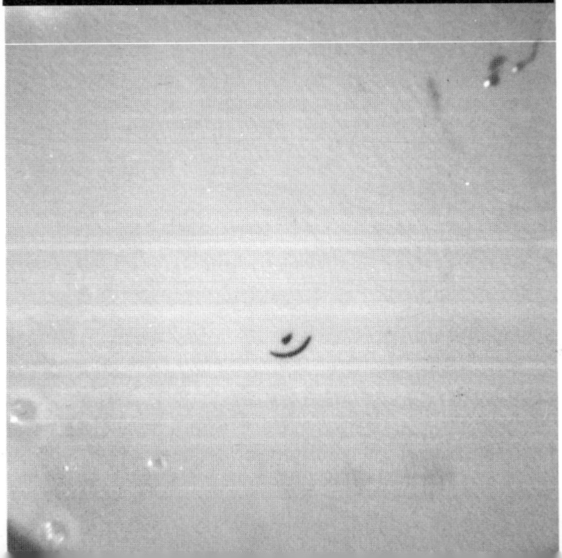

Fig. 5

mind of shippers and skippers when they had a shipment to make. The standard of living was the highest of that of any comparable area in the world. The Pennsylvania Dutch therefore had the earliest opportunity to secure this ware, and the most natural, and it was quickly accepted by them because it resembled somewhat their own sgraffito in its bold conception and execution, the colors appealed to them and who could resist the price. It appealed to their sense of thrift and beauty.

When in 1765 a Staffordshire potter opened a pottery in South Carolina this alarmed the English potters and at that time Wedgwood wrote "We cannot make anything too rich and costly" when referring to the markets that they had in the 13 colonies.

While records seem to indicate Sgraffito being made in 1773 it seems to have had its greatest period in about 1785 to 1825 with very little being made after 1830 and it seems that, like Tole, to have about this time started reverting to the Chinese design whenever done so that the Peafowl were part of the foliage and design, instead of the bold exotic individualistic type, as previously. The design now seemed to want to cover the entire tray or object decorated.

From time to time, no doubt, the shippers tried the other thirteen colonies with their Spatterware because it is indeed found along the entire Eastern Seaboard, but the area where the greatest sales were made was in the Philadelphia area, and from the small amount of the heavier or Ironstone type found in Pennsylvania compared with that we understand is found in Ohio and Illinois and because it appears that there are more specimens marked with the name of a manufacturer in Western States than seems to be found in Pennsylvania it appears that the peak of our acceptance was reached about 1825.

The outbreak of the Revolution in this country put a speedy end to the importation of goods from Great Britain and at its end the English manufacturers made a desperate attempt to recover this large and productive American market. In fact we learn from John Spargo—Early American Pottery and China that the Revolution had greatly stimulated the manufacture of pottery in this country and that at its end the English manufacturers sent cargoes of wares to Philadelphia to be sold at prices which the local factory could not meet. This brought disaster and ruin to Bonnin & Morris, a manufacturer who was trying to establish a pottery in Philadelphia at about that time. He also tells us that this was not an isolated case.

If at that time a queen's ware plate was selling in England for 14 shillings per dozen or 30 cents each and they had to pay shipping costs, and consider an allowance for breakage as well, how could they compete against our prices even if our standard of living was higher than theirs?

Also, how is it that this ceramic is not listed among the patterns of any manufacturer, how is it that this ceramic of so much color and decorative appeal and for which there was such a desire and demand among the Pennsylvania Dutch has been so studiously and seriously disowned? That it is unheralded and unsung?

The introduction of Pearlware in 1779, the end of the Revolution, the start of Spatter decoration on ceramics and the sudden flooding of our markets with ceramics at greatly reduced prices all seem to start at approximately the same time and it seems to be too much of a coincidence to be accidental. The English would have to take a loss on such a repeated or regular practice as we understand this became, but instead, in spite of the Napoleonic Wars which followed and which stopped their market on the continent and made us their main and most important customer, these potters became more wealthy and affluent, not less so.

It is a matter of record, we believe, that plates of Spatterware were selling at 9½ cents each and we have seen one with such a marking on it. How then could a conventionally decorated Queen's ware plate sell in excess of 30 cents and a Spatterware plate for 9½ cents at the same margin of profit? How could other decorated patterns sell at comparable prices and these Spatterware plates sell so comparatively inexpensive?

We learn on page 17—English Delftware by Professor F H Garner that in the latter part of the 17th Century the English copied from the continent the use of a form of instruction known as TREK—a method whereby dark blue lines were used to form outlines of leaves and scenery and then the space between was filled in by less expert craftsmen or apprentices.

About 1776 Saddler and Green of Liverpool started to print outlines of designs and then had the designs filled in by young girls where they desired uniform results, and we know that a similar practice was followed previously but in hand outlines to teach pupils and apprentices the art of drawing and coloring.

On page 192—Old Bristol Potteries by W J Pountney we learn that in 1750 and 1751 a Bristol manufacturer advertised—That if the parents, or guardians of any young lads above the age of fourteen are inclined that they shall learn the Art of Pottery, as practiced in Staffordshire and will find them lodging and all the necessaries during the term of apprenticement, no money will be required for learning them in the best manner, and, particularly children of either sex, not under the above age, may be learned to draw and paint by persons appointed for that purpose, that they may be qualified to paint the said ware, whereby they may acquire a genteel subsistance. The consideration expected for such instruction, being the perquisite of the painters, it is left to them and the persons to agree.

On page 74 Mr Pountney tells us that in an old filled in quarry on Brandon Hill were found fragments showing many birds, their legs formed by a single stroke of the brush, without middle joint. In some cases these quaintly drawn legs are bent in the wrong direction. This seems to indicate the acquaintance of these artists with our Peafowl, where a similar condition exists. It seems to indicate that these efforts to paint and draw were not recognized as having any specific or salable value and were discarded early during the era of instruction, feeling that no market existed for it.

While the decorative art work on the creamware plates in our collection show the firm hand of an accomplished artist, one who no longer possibly could find work on the Delft which he had formerly been decorating, the decorative work on Pearlware Soft Paste is with very little doubt the work of children. It was with very few, if any, exceptions done at one place as a comparison will show—the school house is always the same view, the trees may change, the foreground may change slightly, but the school house itself is the same regardless of the shape of the rim around the plate. Very few pieces are marked but when you find a cup and a saucer that are marked, while the decoration is the same it is rare to find that the two pieces have similar markings. It is not rare to find a light weight cup and a heavier saucer. A thorough study of your own pieces at your home will tell many things that do not show up at a casual glance in someone elses home or shop. And the more pieces that you have and study the more convinced you will become.

If these Spatterware ceramics were produced at schools by children the decorative labor would have been free and this would have the advantage of lowering the cost of production.

A study of the Creamware plates in our collection shows their uniformity, they are all 8¼ inches in diameter, and a study of Leeds and Leeds type plates indicates a similar general uniformity, but, in Spatterware we do not find this to exist. The sizes of the plates vary considerably and the cups, while of a similar shape generally, are never alike—they vary in height, they vary in diameter, they vary in the degree of the angle of the sides, some are convex, some are concave, some are straight. These all look to us to be seconds or rejects. And it is our opinion that these teachers secured bodies to decorate, without charge, to teach the children, thus permitting the teachers to take over the job of flooding the colonies with their pseudo art at prices that the American potters could not meet and permit the potters in England to secure their profits, so sorely needed to operate. The freight did not cost too much by comparison, and having no costs they could be sold for 9½ cents profitably and at the same time build up the maritime powers of England and permit the potters to enjoy the profitable market they relished, more especially since in a short time, Napoleon would cut down their markets for them.

While the schools accepted the customary shaped saucer from the potter, it seems that, they would accept one shape of cup only to secure uniformity or possibly because the teacher had one shape of holder to secure the cup to outline for the pupil.

We find on page 171—Staffordshire Pottery and its History by Josiah C Wedgwood that the throwers and pressers were paid by the piece but only for those pieces that were good. They were not paid for those pieces that left their hands in good condition, but for those that ultimately came from the oven in good condition. In other words, they suffered for other peoples breakages and carelessness. They could get no proof that the ware was bad at all. They had no appeal. Some masters were said even to refuse to pay for what they themselves afterwards sold as seconds. Under such conditions it would be easy to supply the schools practically all of the bodies they needed at no, or little cost, to further the cutting into our American potters markets.

They could get rid of their seconds, not worry about the American competition, secure apprentices cheaper, secure lower rates by the increased shipping, cut into the markets that we were now starting to look toward China to secure, secure more return for the teachers—They were a Canny lot.

They, no doubt, decided to see if we would buy their by-product with a highly colored and bold design or picture which compared somewhat with our Sgraffito if popularly priced, and if this assumption is correct it will explain also why we have never seen, or learned of any one who did, a British Registry mark on any of this Spatterware supposed to have been made after 1842. Schools would possibly be exempt.

The dealers will delight in showing you a specimen that is unusual, how it seems to have started out as one thing and turned out to be something of an entirely different nature as though this was a childish prank, but you will realize that this was fostered by the teacher to see their inventive ability.

How many different patterns were produced by these prolific artists we have no idea, we are aware of at least one hundred and the list swells almost every week, but we have been asked to list and to illustrate the known specimens to facilitate study and especially to designate or describe them. There is a need for uniformity of name for each pattern so as to speak the same language and have the same descriptive reference, to avoid misunderstandings and it is, with the demand for Spatterware so large and with mail offers to sell frequent, indeed lamentable that for all these years these were not reported and recorded, passing them off as unrecorded patterns—nameless— and permitting a different name in one area from that used in another area for the same pattern, more especially where there are so many patterns known.

The most popular and most frequently found pattern seems to be the Peafowl. A pattern where the outline is drawn most noticably and more frequently. This in our opinion is the one which pupils were given a chance to prove their merit and talent. By the great number of Peafowl compared with the next runnerup it seems that a great number of students must have been eliminated quickly. The work is generally very poorly done, paint sometimes covering the lines given as guides, sometimes not meeting the lines, sometimes the paint is over the glaze to touch it up, almost any kind of poor work is to be found on this pattern.

After this weeding out process the teachers had their pupils, in our opinion try the School House pattern. This, then, was their opportunity to show their skill in free hand drawing, or better, painting without outline assistance. He, however, was given no latitude. They were all of one type, one view. Generally a left side and front view with chimney at rear. The trees may vary, the foreground may vary, there may be birds, but the view is the same with very few exceptions. The colors or the combination of colors may vary but not the view. These more or less indicate that the articles attributed to varying potters were potted only by them but the decorating was not, in our opinion. Again the size of the school will vary, showing the lack of skill, the lack of judgment, the lack of perspective. A small object will have a large School House and a large object will have a small School House. The door will be too small, or it may be too large and shows that it was corrected. The sill will be too high or the header over the door too low. But it shows the trial and error of the students and the results. It is indeed, a colorful and cheerful ceramic.

Our great grandparents in their sturdy homespun clothes, with their frugal manner and love of color actually made this by-product the cradle of the decorating art in England, which, looking backward to the Farm-yard series of John Niglett and the West Indian influence of Thomas and Richard Frank for their inspiration, at the same time created by their originality and charm, effects which would have a later and far flung influence on the ceramics to follow.

# EXAMPLES SHOULD TELL THE STORY

Peafowl ceramics with Spatter work decoration are usually found in about 4 different patterns.

FIGURE 6 Regular or usual type

FIGURE 7 Open body type

FIGURE 8 Peafowl on a bar

FIGURE 9 Rooster Peafowl

Since the color of the neck may be blue, the body yellow, the tail red, the rim green on one plate, and just the reverse on another and since there are so many opportunities to change combinations, it is possible to have hundreds of the Peafowl and have no two alike, then again it must be remembered that there are additionally black, purple and infrequently grey —sometimes shadings of these colors are found and to top it all, of course, is the frequent rainbow effects where any two or three of these colors are alternated around the rim of the plate. We are dealing with a very imaginative and resourceful group of pupils and teachers.

Attached are FIGURES 10 and 11 to indicate the workmanship on Leed's type ceramics and it will be observed how much more subdued in coloring and how altogether better handled this type appears, although not as colorful and decorative in design. It appears to have been done by experts by comparison.

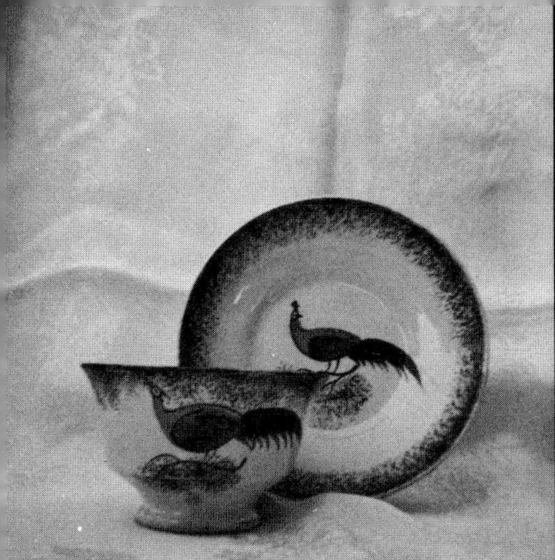

Fig. 6

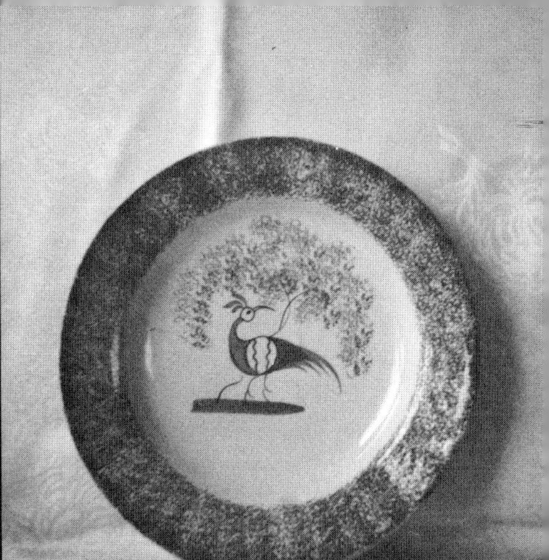

Fig. 7

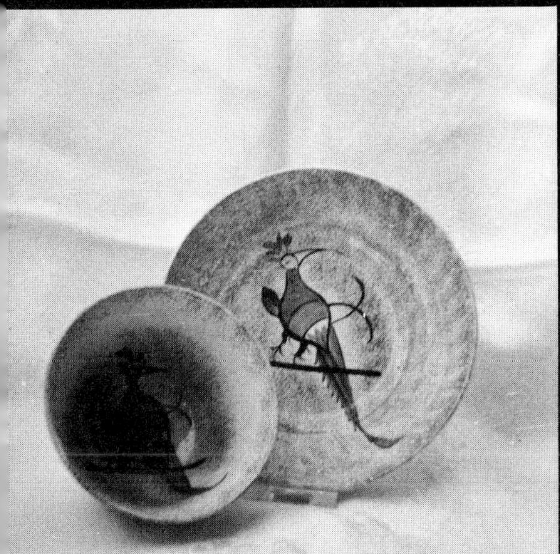

Fig. 8

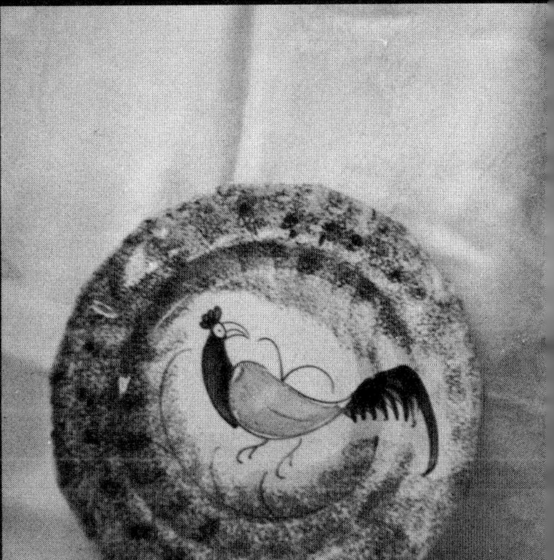

Fig. 9

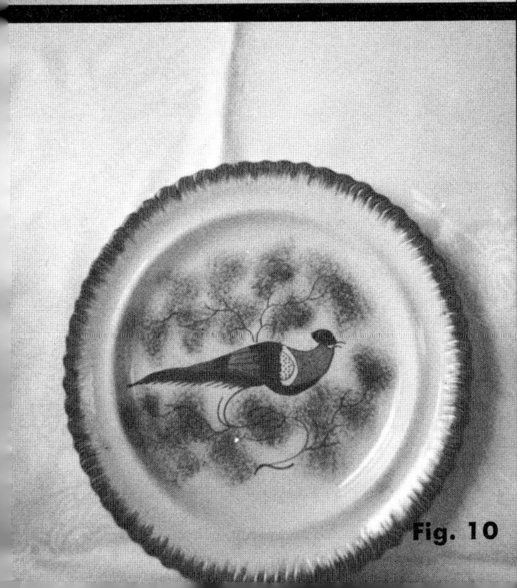

Fig. 10

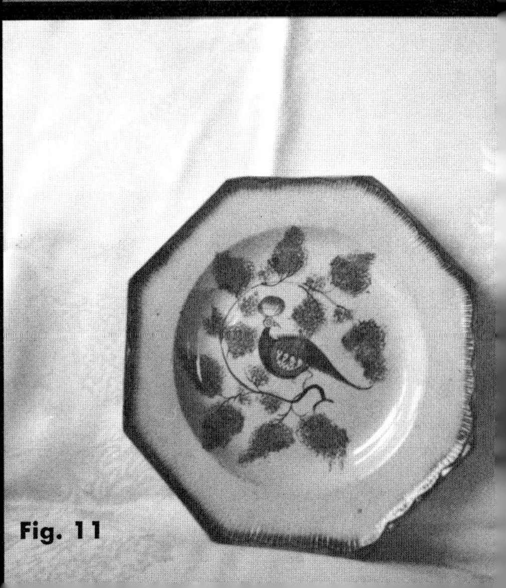

Fig. 11

It is impossible to imagine any one but a child as responsible for the effort on FIGURE 12, one of the crudest peafowl that we have ever seen.

How, however, we shall explain the effort in FIGURE 13 might be even more difficult. The teacher, in a humorous vein may have drawn such a monstrosity, or he may have given another student the assignment to see how he was advancing with his brush work and, to see if he could handle a thin lettering brush. Of only one thing are we certain, this never started or was planned as being a Peafowl.
It turned out to be a Guinea Hen, and the chances of finding additional pieces to complete a set or part of one are extremely remote.

FIGURE 14 is the Gooney Bird. How it ever received this name we have no knowledge. We understand that the Albatross has been referred to as a Gooney Bird, but this is a far cry from the Albatross. But, as stated, this is the Gooney Bird.

FIGURE 15 is the Parrot, a rather unavailable fellow.

FIGURE 16 is Peacock at the Fountain in a transfer design, usually available in blue, not colorful, but available in soft paste as well as in the later and heavier paste, indicating production over an extended period.

FIGURE 17 is the Dove pattern, possibly one of the least colorful designs produced.

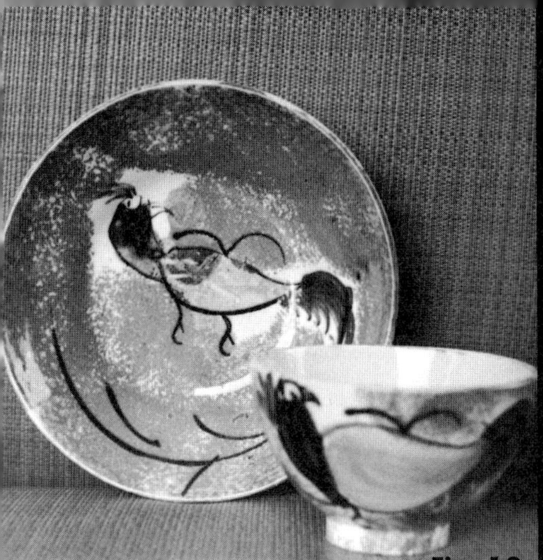
Fig. 12

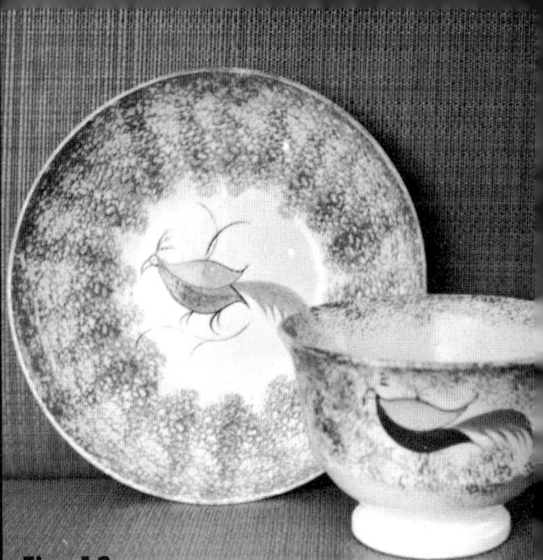
Fig. 13

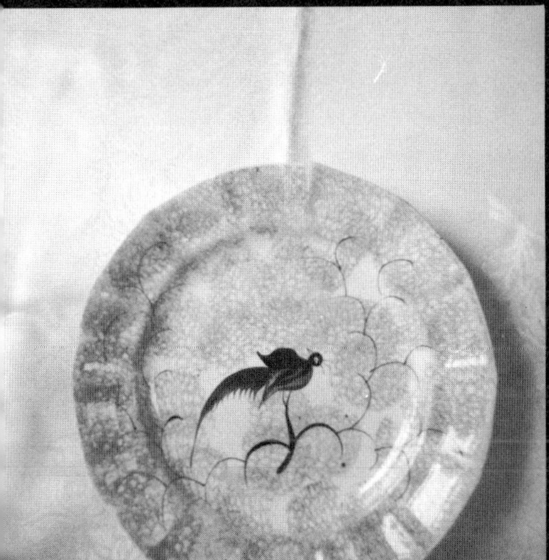
Fig. 14

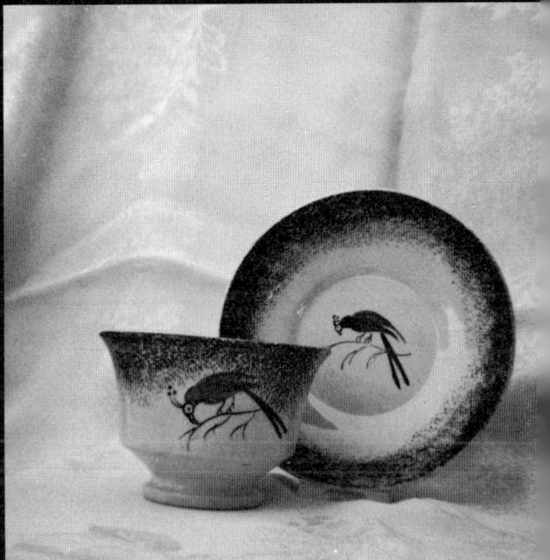
Fig. 15

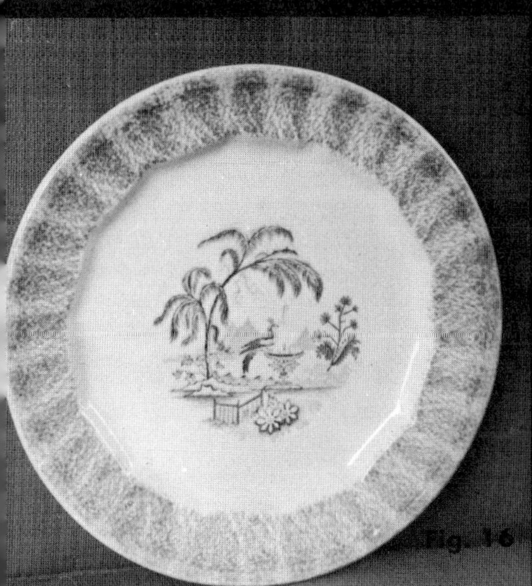
Fig. 16

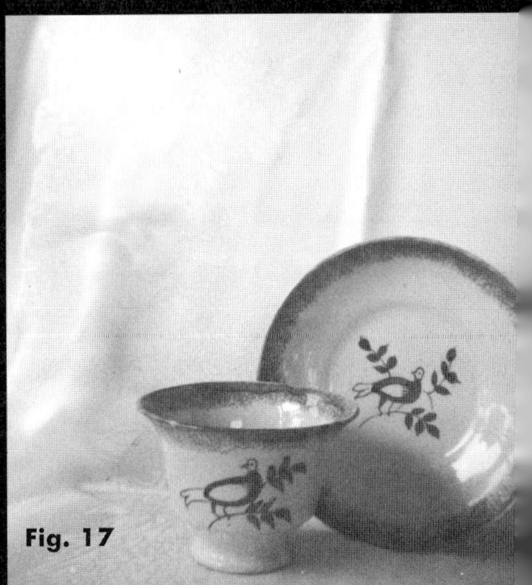
Fig. 17

In order, however, to show the versatility of these students we will show several illustrations of Roses, first to show the latitude given, second to show how these interpretations varied and the liberties taken with the subject.

FIGURE 18 is the Red Rose and Criss Cross, a beautiful and Dainty miniature with the rose bud appearing in the inside of the cup, a very unusual item.

FIGURE 19 is the early three color Rainbow plate with the three colors circling the rim—red on the outside, blue in the center and green the inner of the three colors, center pattern is a rose although this is probably found more often with no center pattern than with one. These plates as a rule are very light in weight indicating an early potting date.

FIGURE 20 is the conventional rose but this time with a large blue bud, much larger and more blue than the Cornflower and a very unusual specimen.

FIGURE 21 is a cup and saucer in a rose decoration and on a body impressed in an unrecorded semi-circular band W ADAMS & SONS. It is of a lighter weight body and seems to have been done early in their potting.

FIGURE 22 indicates a rose with Cornflower and a two color Rainbow border where the colors were spattered across the border in a radial manner, each color about one-inch wide with alternating red and green stripes.

FIGURE 23 is of a similar type rose with a design border, the design around the rim resembling daisies made entirely with lines and, we suggest that these roses be observed since they seem to have teeth on the inside of the rose.

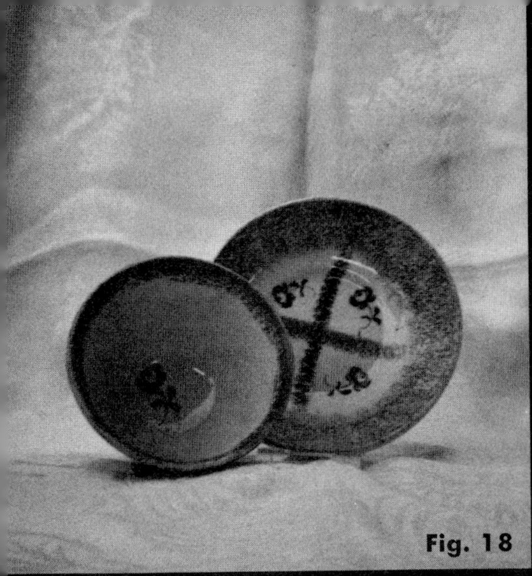

Fig. 18

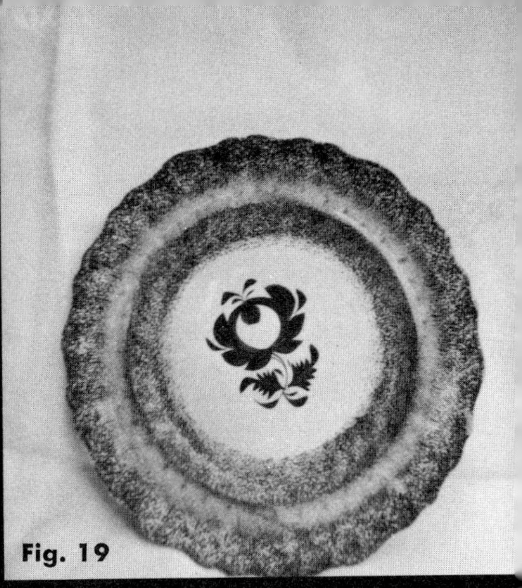

Fig. 19

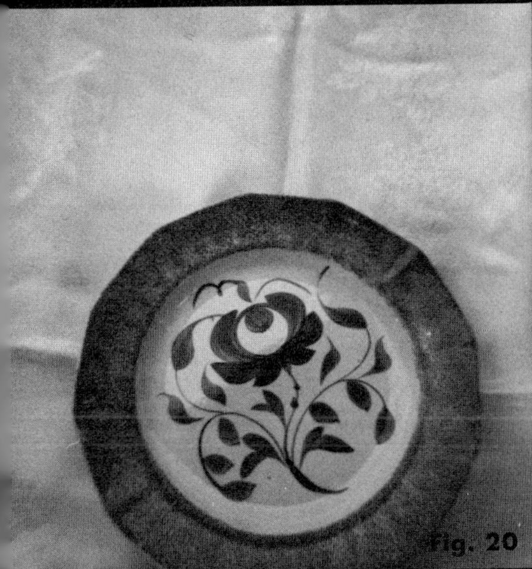

Fig. 20

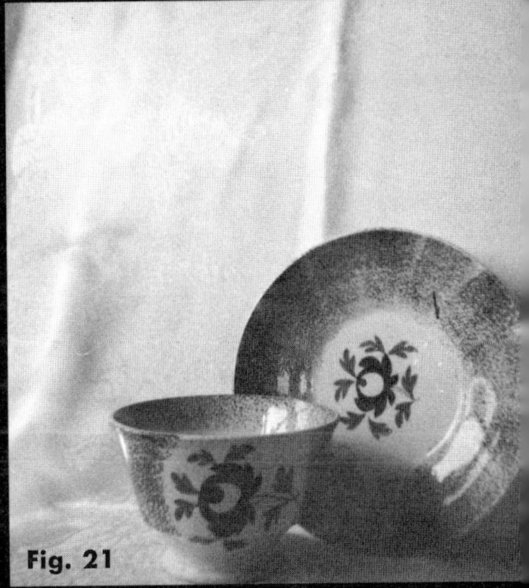

Fig. 21

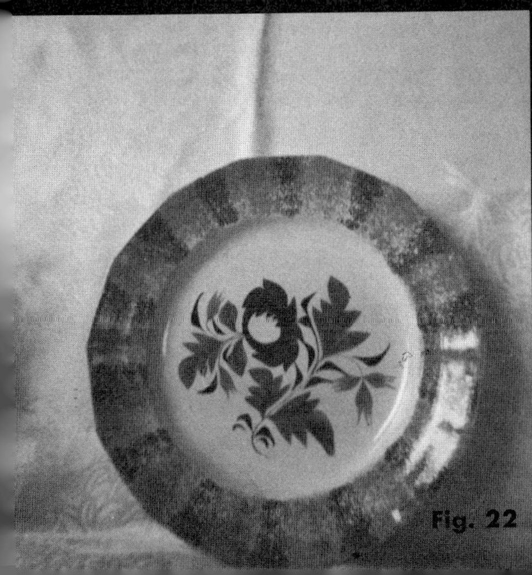

Fig. 22

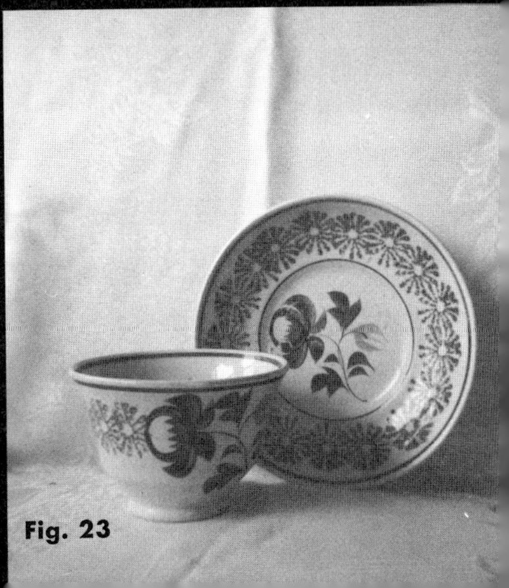

Fig. 23

FIGURE 24 is a rose and blue daisy-type flower with a red design border that is very colorful and again entirely different from any of those illustrated above. This gives a good idea of the several types of roses depicted by these embryo artists.

FIGURE 25 is one of a more nightmarish type and we can assume that the perpetrator of this masterpiece was probably a victim of Rose Fever and did not relish his assignment. It seems to have been planned this way and does not seem to have been an accident as some of these atrocities seem to have been.

But then again, we should probably refer to FIGURE 26 and try to determine what caused this type of decoration. It is likewise called a rose but it takes a lot of imagination to see a rose in this plate. However, a Rose it is, and we are sure that a rose by any other name will look just as lovely and smell just as sweet.

This, then will give you an idea of the large amount of latitude given the students in the freehand class in the second try, but now we should possibly return to the first class in freehand, the School House and give a few examples of that.

The School House is by far the most primitive and the most carelessly done of all the Spatter patterns and readily shows where it stands in the field of ceramics, but they are mainly of one style and type. It is, in the main, similar to FIGURE 27 or it may follow the building type and have two trees or in some other detail vary but usually it will be as pictured.

We may find the building much too large for the bowl as in FIGURE 28 where it appears absurd in its proportions. The door may have been made too low or the sill may be much too high, but like the rose it is still a school house and possibly the one in which they were taught, or possibly a sketch or picture was on the wall for them to copy.

FIGURE 29 is a Town House complete with trellis on each side which is a very unusual and difficult item to find. Although it is not one of the colorful type it is beautifully done and extremely interesting.

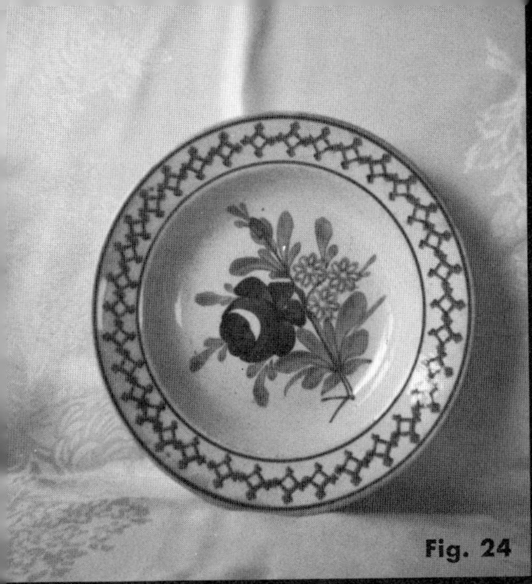

Fig. 24

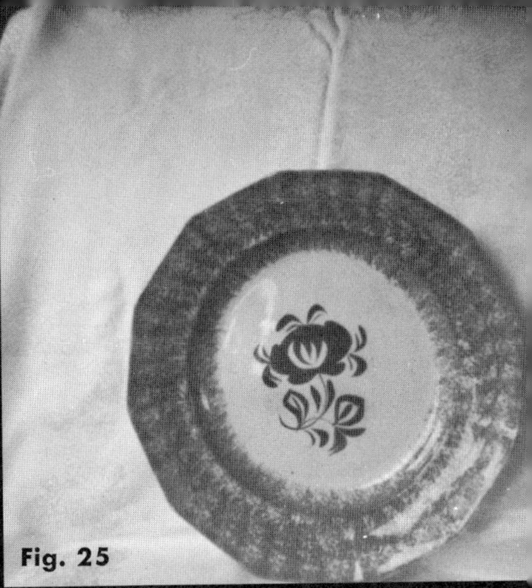

Fig. 25

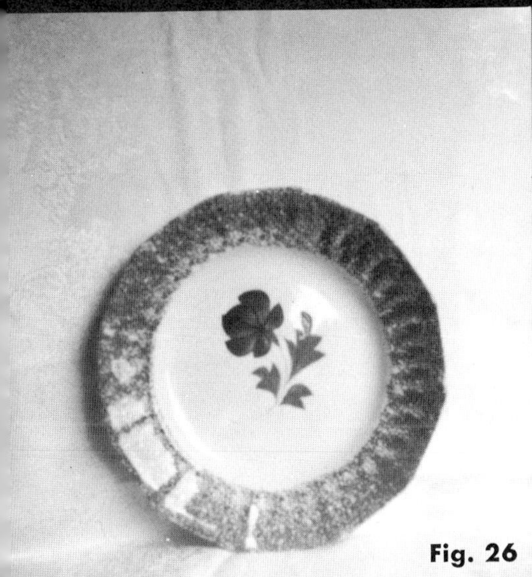

Fig. 26

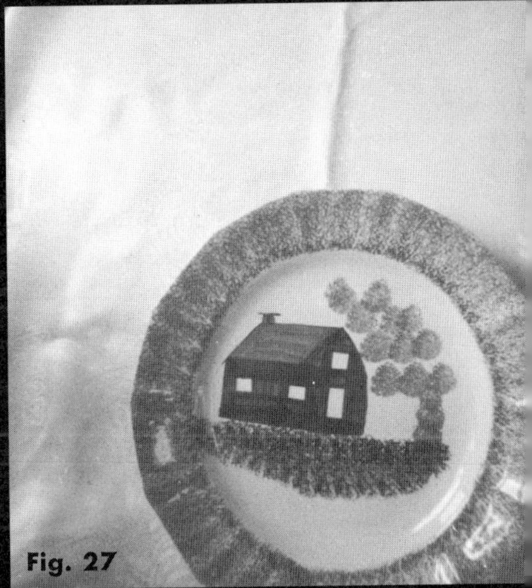

Fig. 27

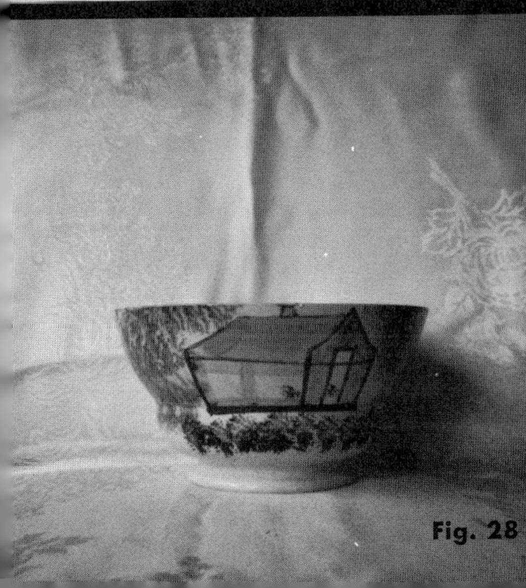

Fig. 28

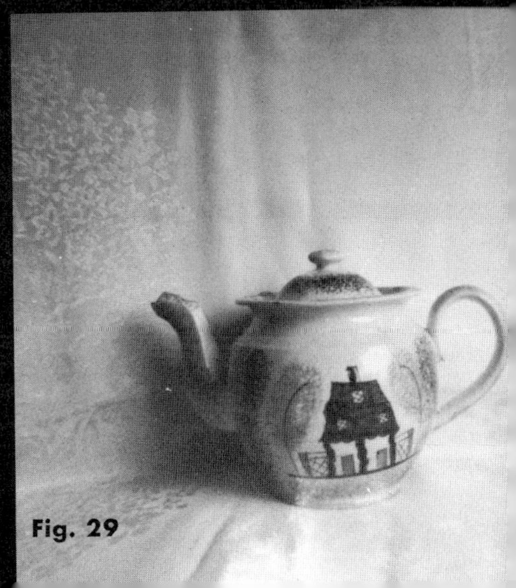

Fig. 29

In order to illustrate the intertwining of the designs and the closeness of the spatter and the design border periods we attach FIGURE 30 of a Primrose plate and FIGURE 31 and 32 also of Primrose plates and it can readily be determined that the central design has similar handling although the design on the borders vary and add a new depth and beauty to these ceramic objects.

FIGURE 33 is that of an Acorn plate which is available in light yellow and in dark brown acorn types. All, of course, in the usual variety and combinations of colored borders.

These students were given later and tougher assignments and the teachers having found a ready and free labor for the executing of their products were not in a hurry to release them to their future employers so that some of the later spatter products were quite well done for the customers who undoubtedly were becoming more demanding in their purchases.

FIGURE 34 is a cup and saucer in the Cherry pattern. It seems to have been enameled and has a peculiar glaze similar to a tin glaze. It is a very unusual and lovely pattern.

FIGURE 35 is the Pomegranite. This is one of the patterns usually referred to as definitely Pennsylvania Dutch and it may be possible to secure a fairly representative number of these patterns if desired. They are not too plentiful but keep turning up all over constantly and regularly.

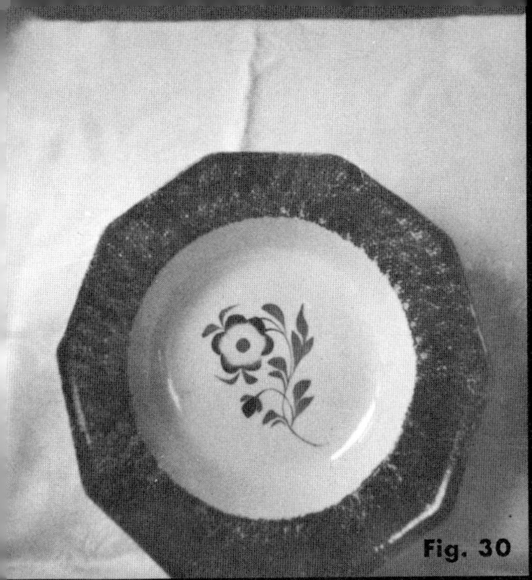
Fig. 30

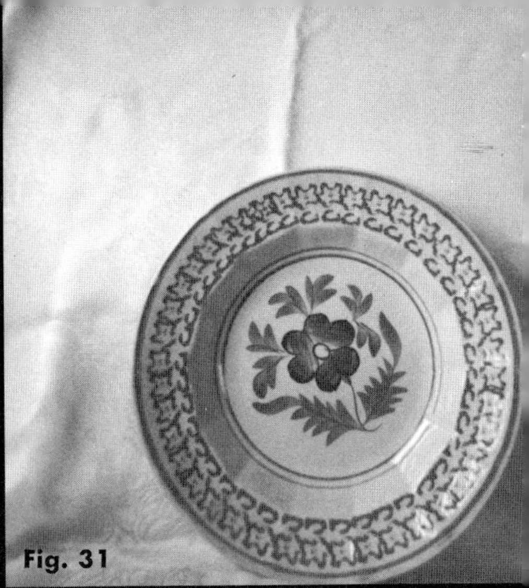
Fig. 31

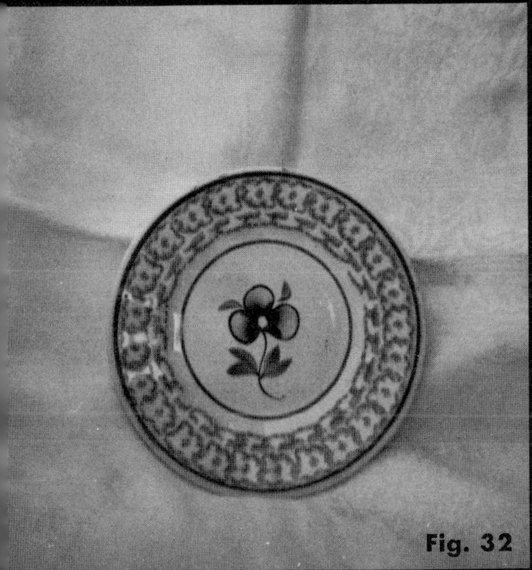
Fig. 32

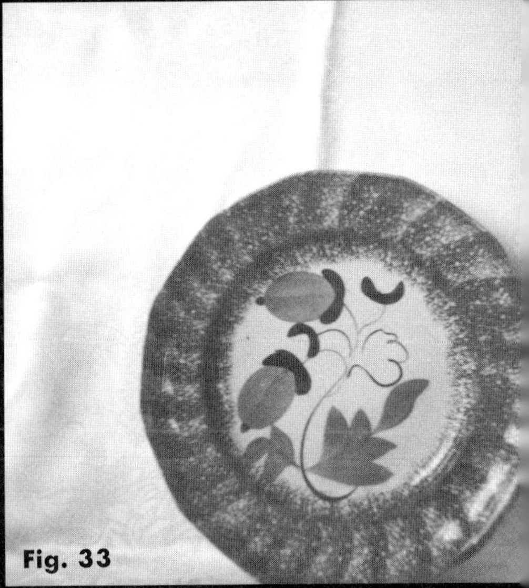
Fig. 33

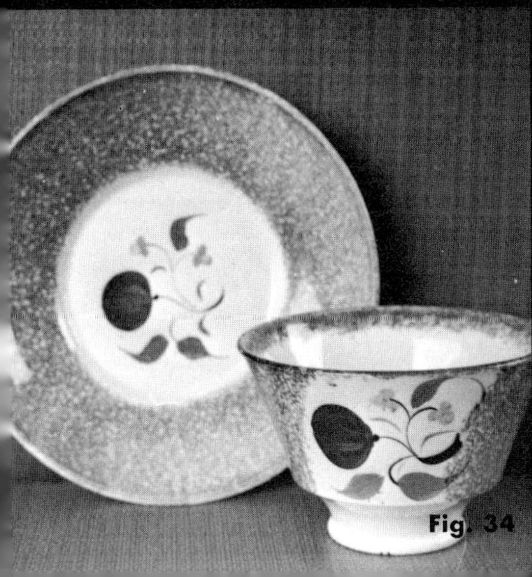
Fig. 34

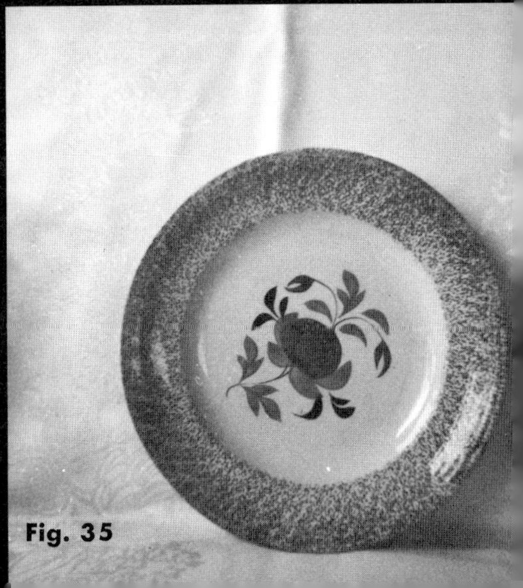
Fig. 35

FIGURE 36 is the Pineapple. We are happy to have the opportunity to picture one of this rare and unusual pattern which is seldom found. It is of Pearlware and seems from the crazing and bluish collection of glaze at the inner rim to be very early in the Regular paste era.

In the flowers we again run into a large number of varieties or patterns and FIGURE 37 is one of the unusual types and once more a fantastic rendition of the figment of a vivid imagination, but this Umbrella Flower is colorful and was, no doubt, at that time quite a conversation piece.

FIGURE 38 is the Daffodil pattern and it is surprising how the outline at back of flower gives so readily the desired effect.

FIGURE 39 is an 8 petal lavender flower and having a blue inner petal, name unknown.

FIGURE 40 is the conventional Dahlia pattern.

FIGURE 41 is the usual Tulip pattern in a cup and saucer.

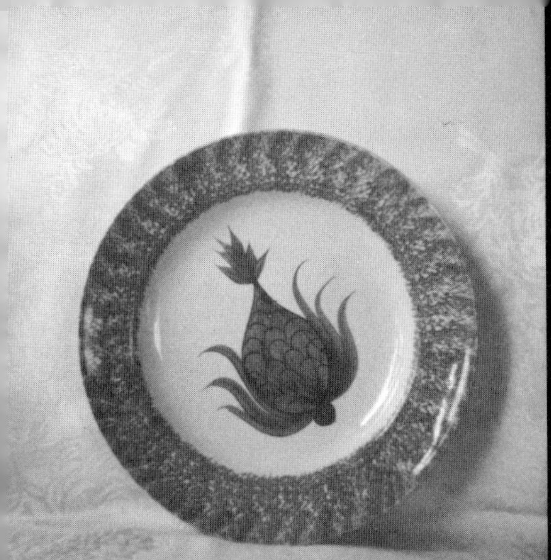
Fig. 36

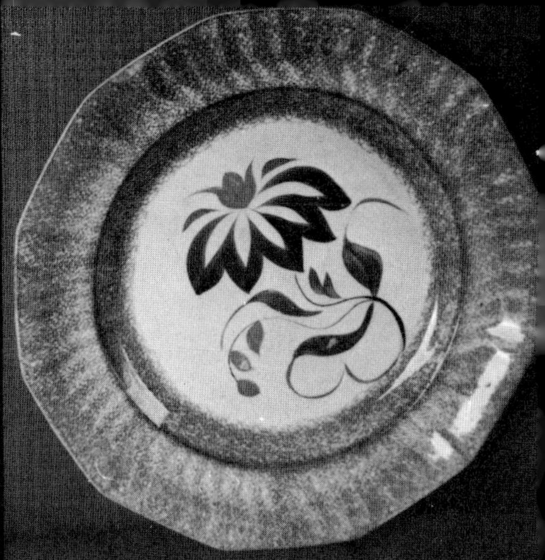
Fig. 37

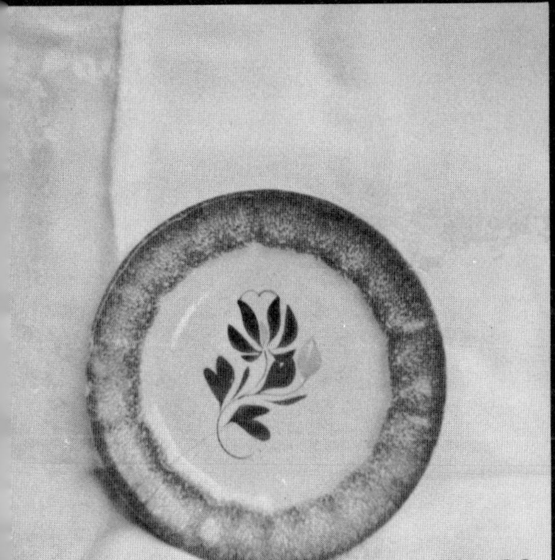
Fig. 38

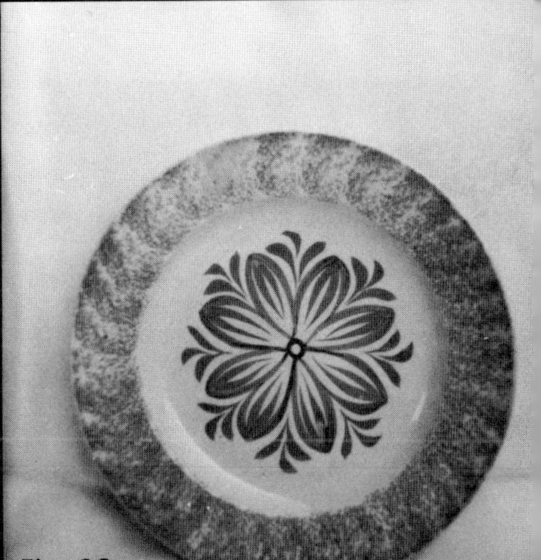
Fig. 39

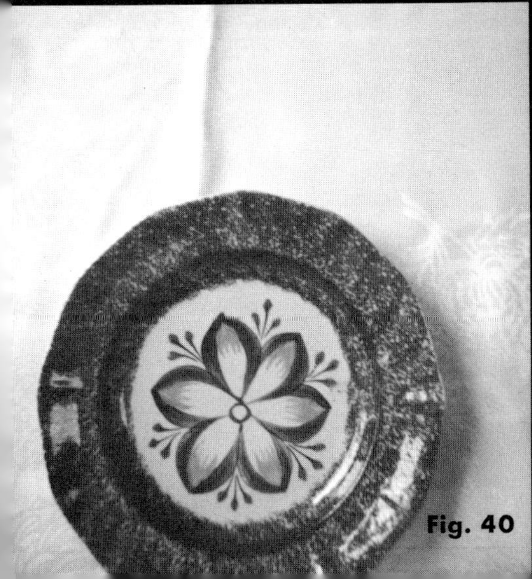
Fig. 40

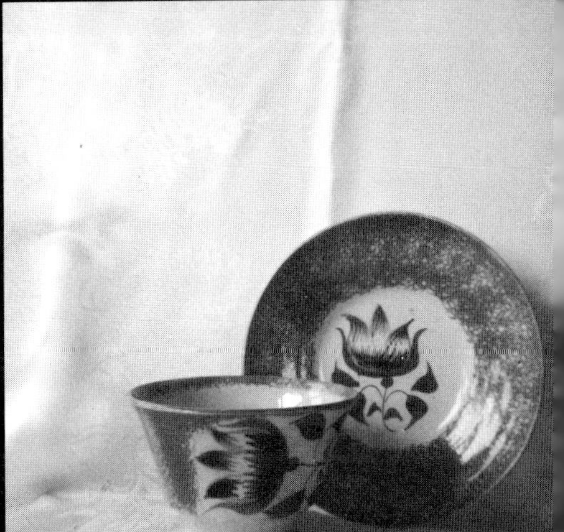
Fig. 41

FIGURE 42 is the Tulip pattern with practically no foliage but with four very large green buds in an extremely unusual handling of this subject.

FIGURE 43 illustrates the Memorial Tulip, an entirely different kind of flower.

FIGURE 44 is the Morning Glory pattern, a not too frequent find.

FIGURE 45 is a Blue flower, otherwise unnamed.

FIGURE 46 is the Lilly of the Valley pattern a delicate and unusual pattern.

FIGURE 47 is the Cockscomb and many times is confused by collectors with the Thistle, but a careful study will reveal the difference.

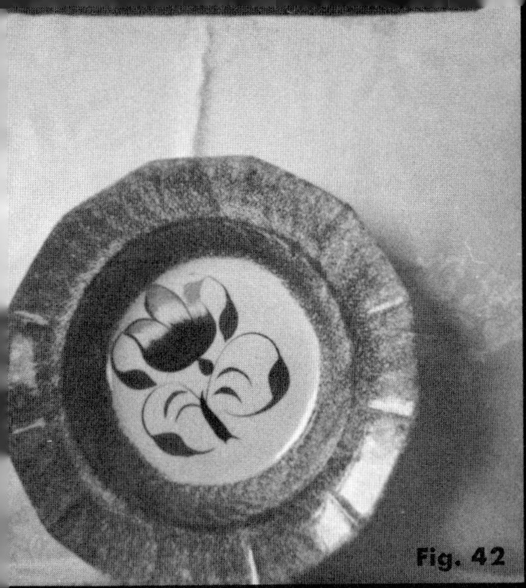

Fig. 42

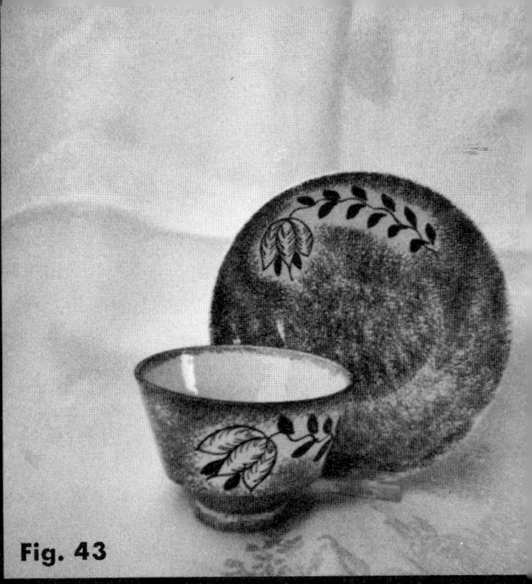

Fig. 43

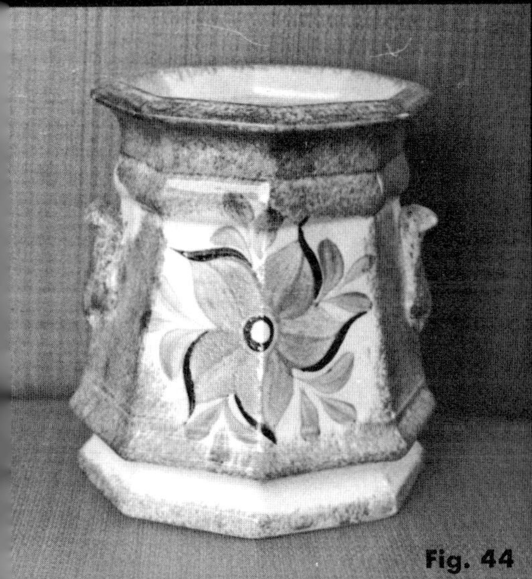

Fig. 44

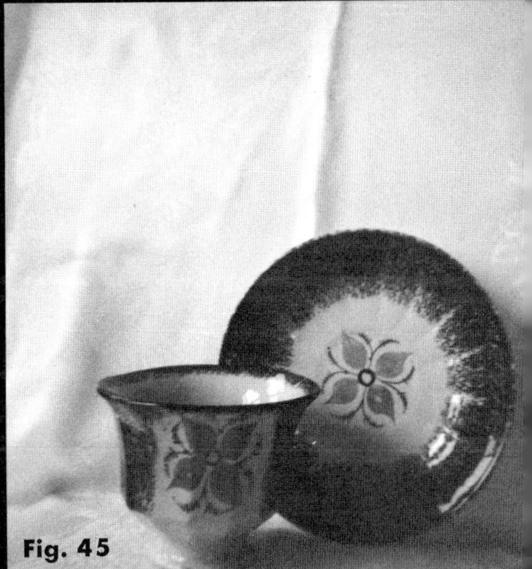

Fig. 45

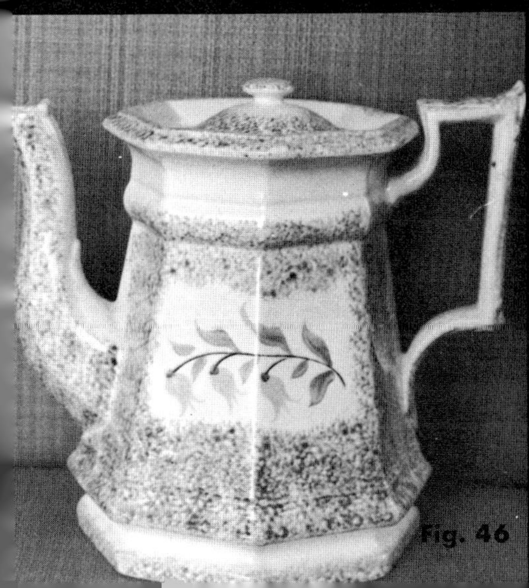

Fig. 46

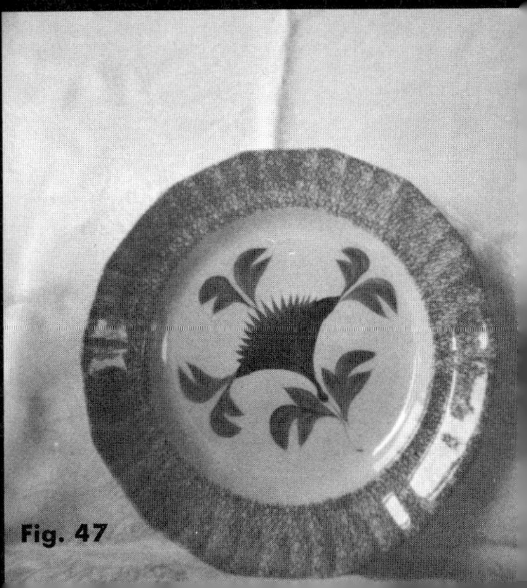

Fig. 47

FIGURE 48 is the 4 petal Blue Flower, otherwise unnamed.

FIGURE 49 is the Thistle with Cornflower pattern.

FIGURE 50 is the Tulip in a Design border pattern interpretation, a beautiful yellow and purple flower.

FIGURE 51 is the Columbine with Rose Bud and Thistle in the Design border series.

FIGURE 52 is the Thistle and Lilly of the Valley in a Design border series.

FIGURE 53 is the Red Clover pattern.

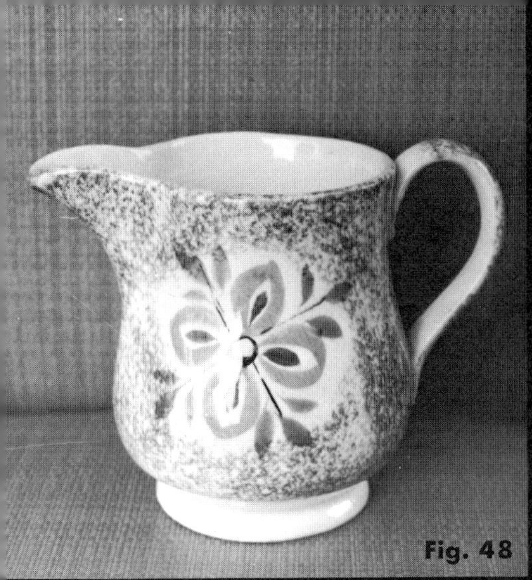
Fig. 48

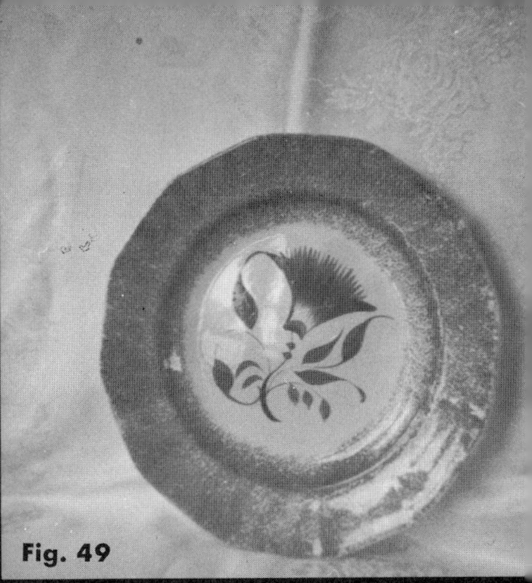
Fig. 49

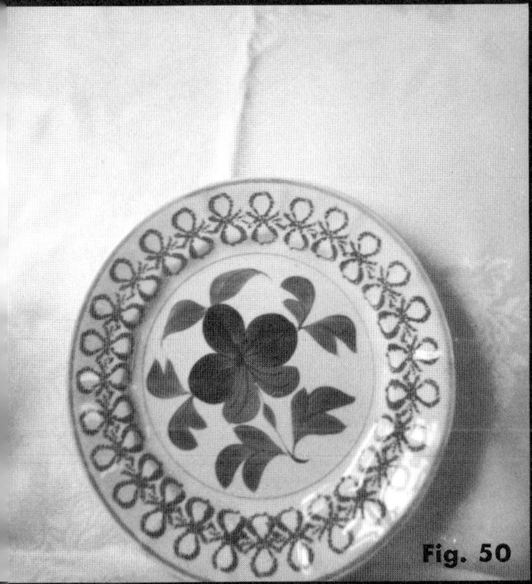
Fig. 50

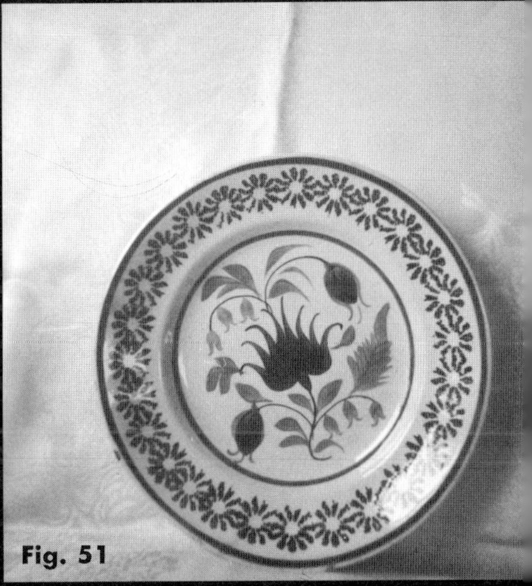
Fig. 51

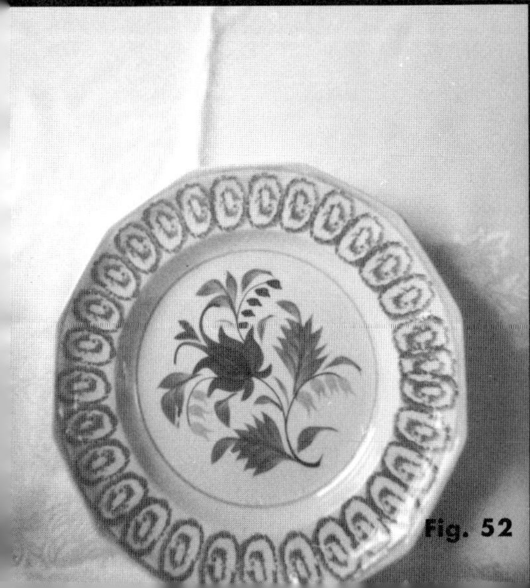
Fig. 52

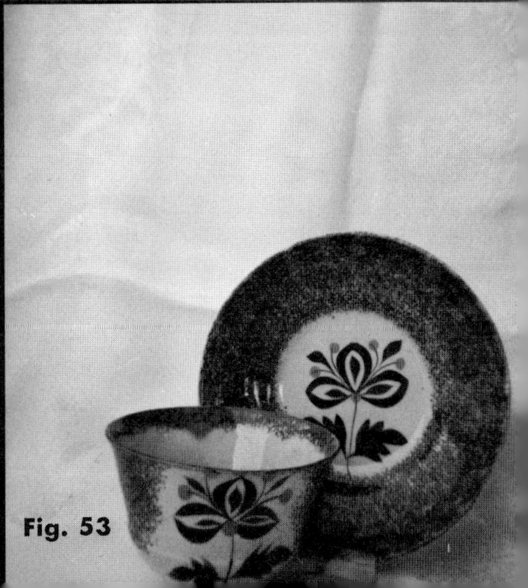
Fig. 53

FIGURE 54 is the Forget-me-not pattern in a very unusual outline Star Spatter border design. It seems to be of an enameled type of flower and has a type of tin Glaze effect. Very unusual, different and difficult to find.

FIGURE 55 is the Cluster of Buds pattern with the four cluster arrangement both on the inside and the outside.

FIGURE 56 is the same Cluster of Buds, but this time with a four bud cluster on the saucer and a three bud cluster on the inside of the cup. This has been taken for a different flower and we feel that it should be separately shown.

FIGURE 57 illustrates a Small Spatter Dot center.

FIGURE 58 illustrates a large Spatter dot.

FIGURE 59 illustrates a Spatter Criss Cross pattern.

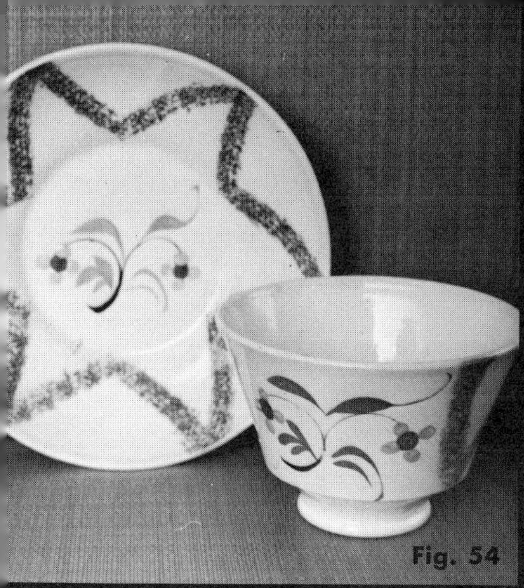

Fig. 54

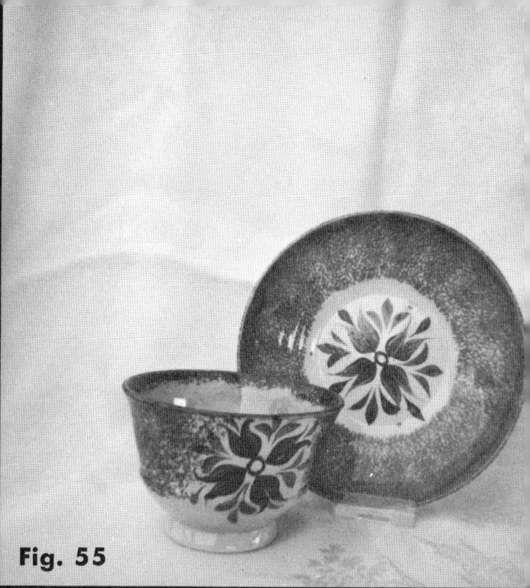

Fig. 55

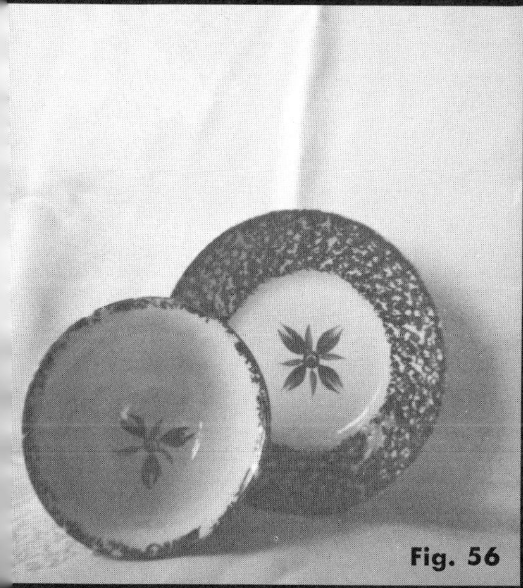

Fig. 56

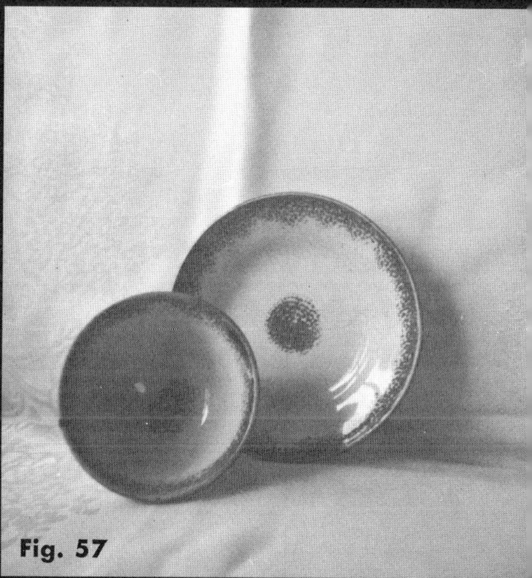

Fig. 57

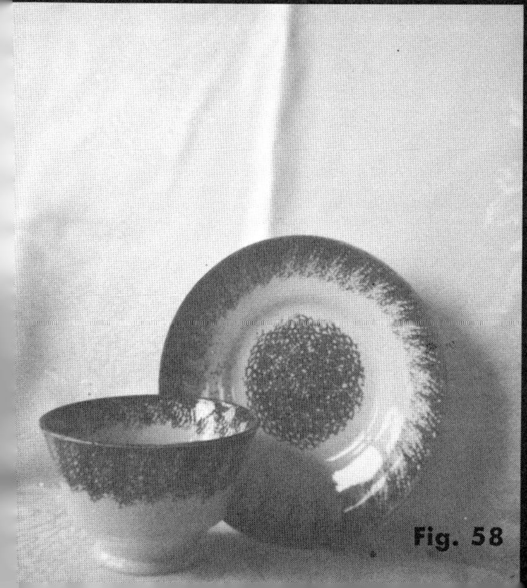

Fig. 58

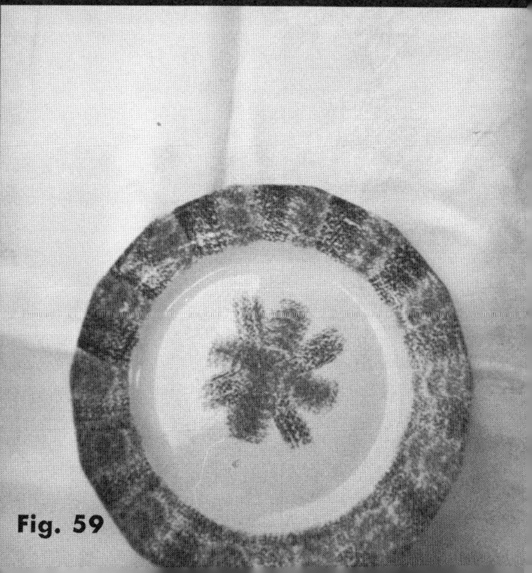

Fig. 59

FIGURE 60 is a plain center with a Spatter and Leaf border.

FIGURE 61 contains a marbelized all over Spatter effect.

FIGURE 62 features a Bull's Eye plate, a two color Rainbow plate with alternating stripes and a similar circular central design which gives the effect of a Bull's Eye.

This effect is, like all the rest, available in the usual number of colors and some of the effects are quite weird.

FIGURE 63 is the three color Rainbow pattern and it is peculiar to this type that the three colors usually run around the rim instead of across it as in the above. The outer color band is usually red, blue in the center, and green on the inner edge, and as seen in FIGURE 19, this pattern besides being used by itself also sometimes serves as the rim of a plate having another decorative motif in the center.

FIGURE 64 gives the same effect with the spatter work done in a design spatter effect with a center small dot and you can see the effect is very similar. This is on a miniature.

FIGURE 65 is a three color Rainbow pattern in a radial spatter border in which the stripes cross the border but in three colors, Blue, Red and Yellow.

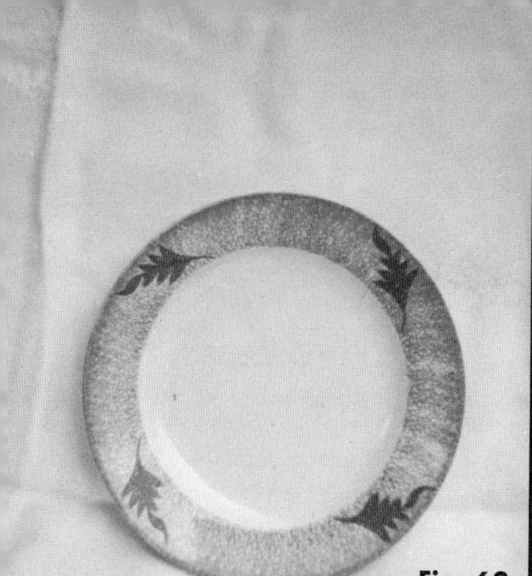

Fig. 60

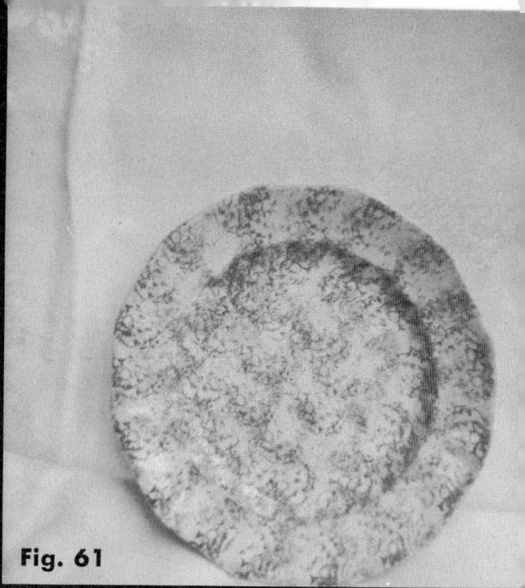

Fig. 61

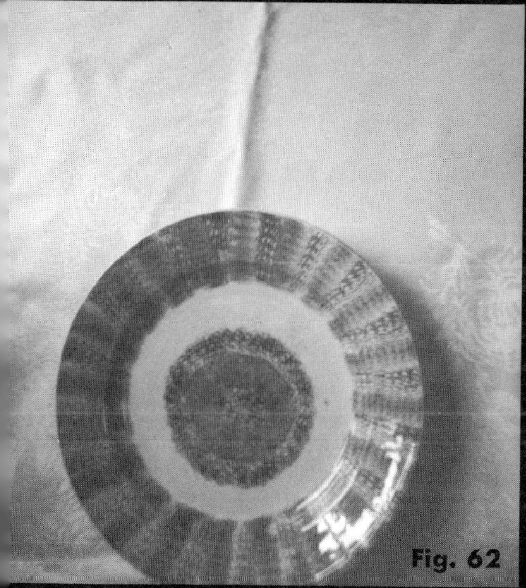

Fig. 62

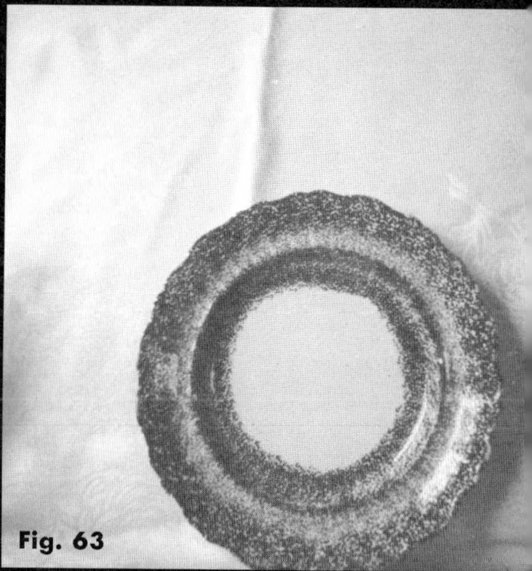

Fig. 63

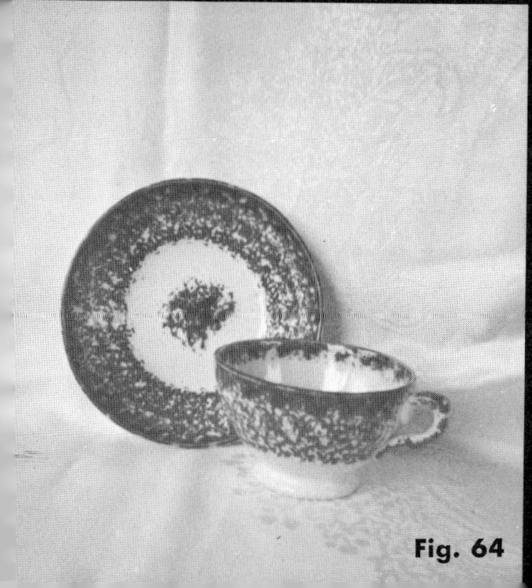

Fig. 64

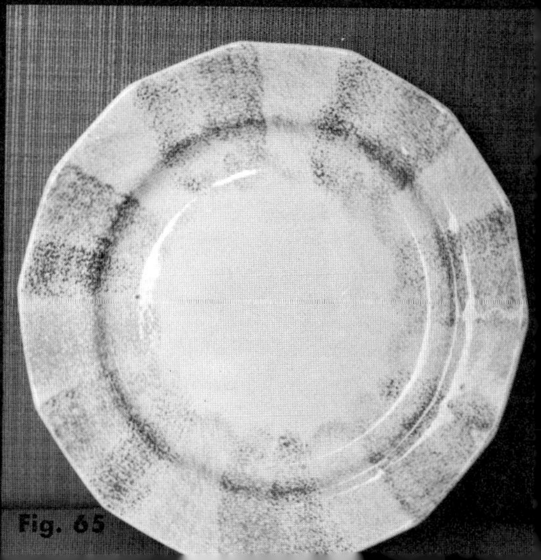

Fig. 65

FIGURE 66 is a Three color Rainbow Loop pattern, very different and effective.

FIGURE 67 is a three color Rainbow Festoon design.

FIGURE 68 is a three color Rainbow Half Moon and Star pattern.

FIGURE 69 is the two color Rainbow Drape design.

FIGURE 70 is the three color Strawberry or Thumbprint Design.

FIGURE 71 is the five color Rainbow pattern with green, yellow, black, blue and red stripes repeated about the entire pitcher.

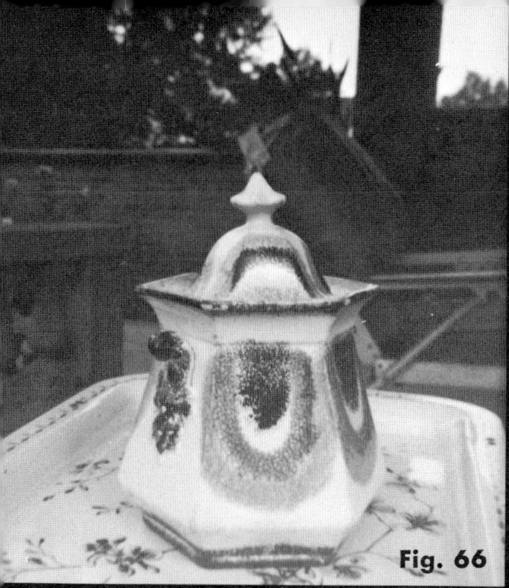

Fig. 66

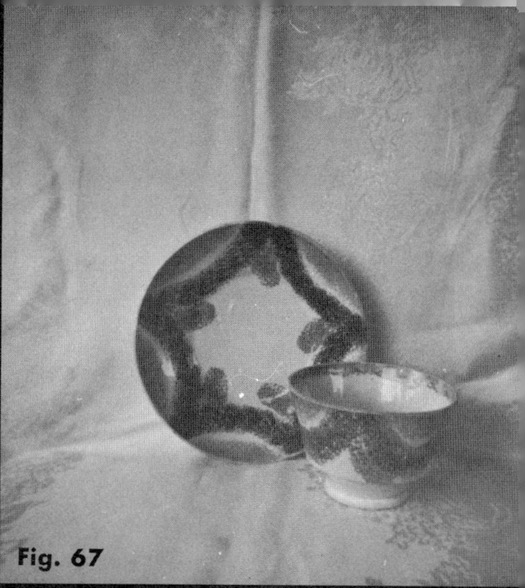

Fig. 67

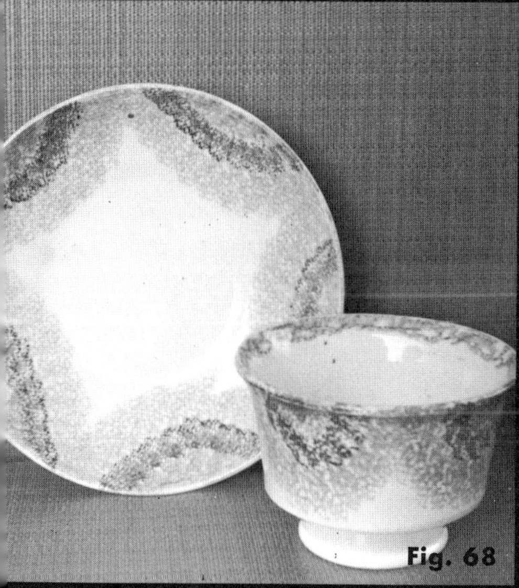

Fig. 68

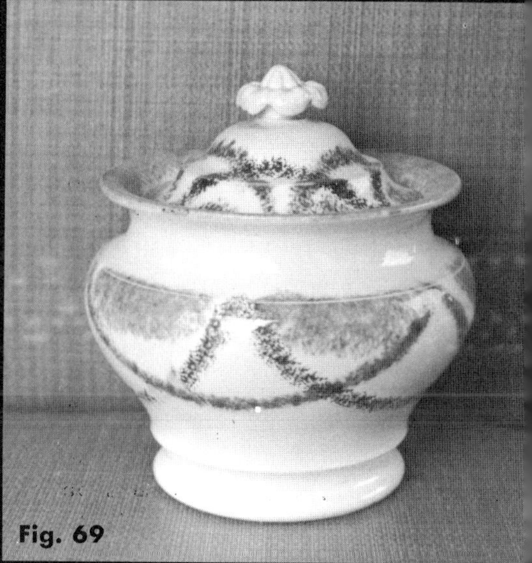

Fig. 69

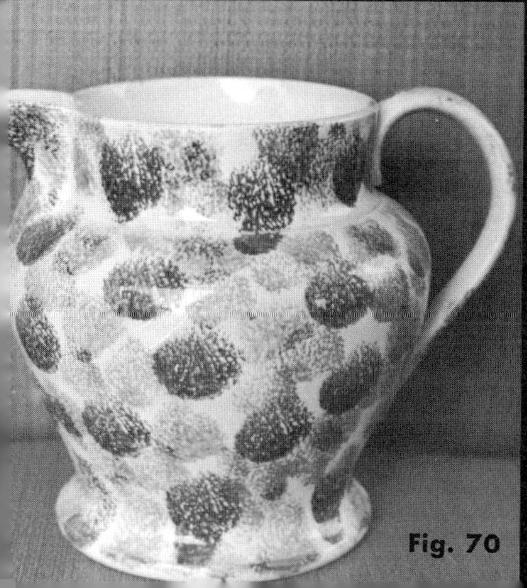

Fig. 70

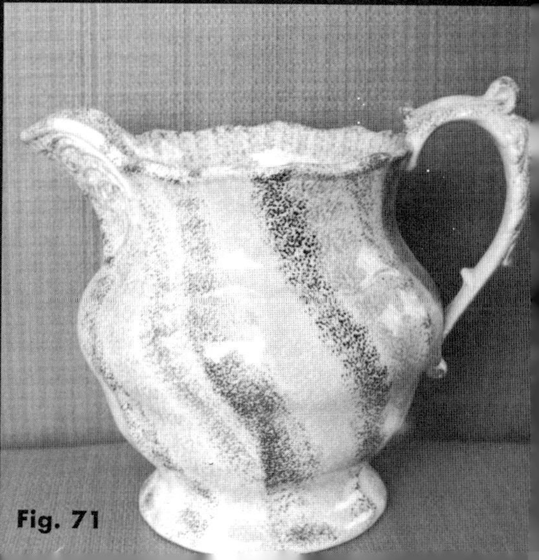

Fig. 71

FIGURE 72 is a two color red and blue stripe Rainbow coffee pot which you should observe carefully because the one side is red and blue and the other side has red and white stripes, the blue stripe was forgotten by these children and since they had apparently no checking system this was overlooked. If there are any doubts as to who performed these masterpieces this one will, we believe, convince one of the correctness of this estimate. This piece is not the same in back as it is in front. "Des iss net hinna wie fonna".

FIGURE 73 is the Clover flower pattern, a two tone Rainbow type with spatter dots resembling clover flowers.

FIGURE 74 is the Beehive and Strawberry in a Leeds type.

FIGURE 75 is the two color Festoon pattern.

FIGURE 76 is the Holly Berry pattern.

FIGURE 77 is the Castle or Fort design.

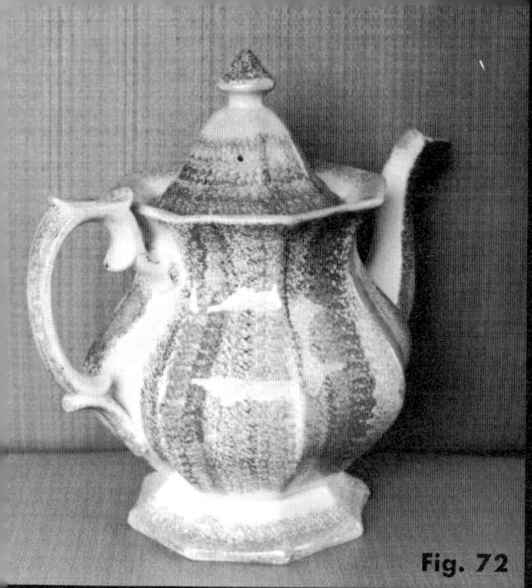
Fig. 72

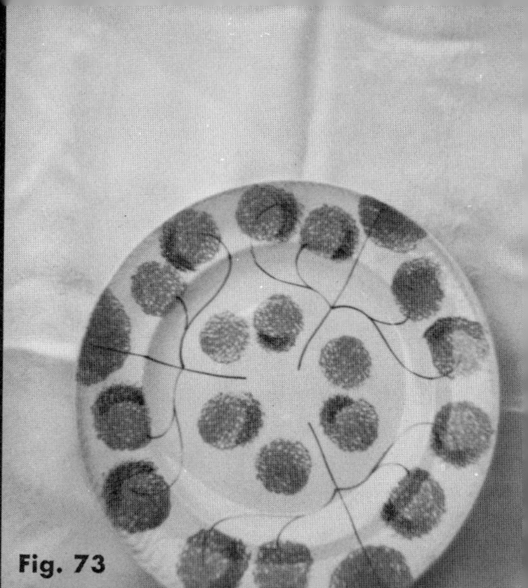
Fig. 73

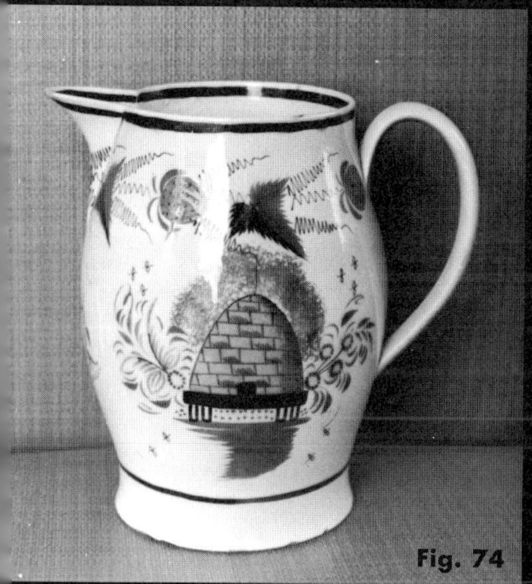
Fig. 74

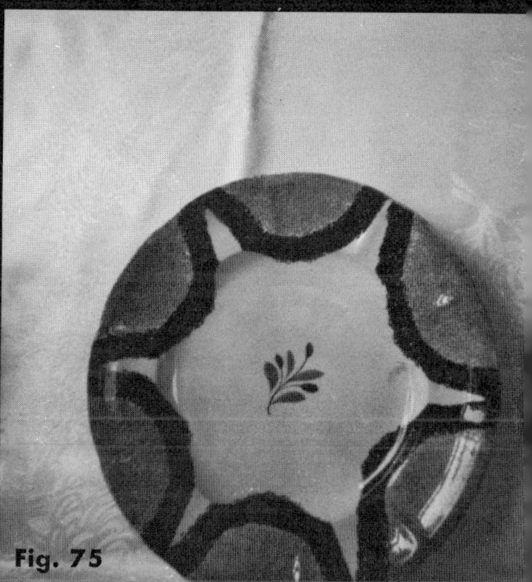
Fig. 75

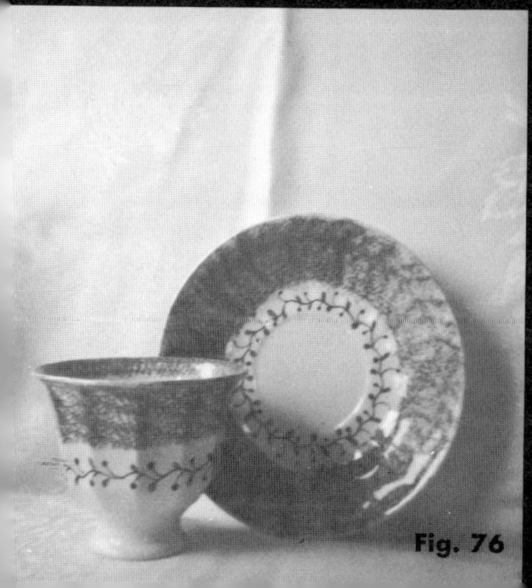
Fig. 76

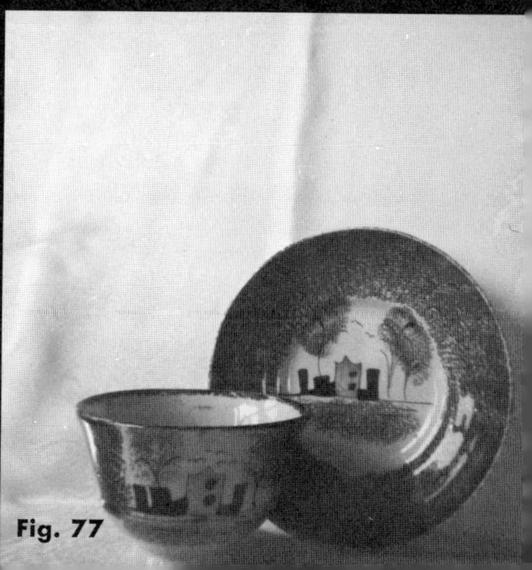
Fig. 77

FIGURE 78 is the Castle design and is made in the blue and in Brown colors to the best of our knowledge although some additional colors may be available, one can never be too sure with this line of ceramics, but these two we have.

FIGURE 79 is the tree pattern, and lately when talking to a dealer he told us that he had last week had one with an Apple Tree on it, and he repeated his statement—This being a new item to us we made inquiries and found that this is indeed correct—there is one with an Apple tree on it, however, our new inquiry brought out the fact that they thought it was a Cherry Tree—so Apple, Cherry Tree—"Wass machts ess ous"—What difference does it make—"Ess hut doch eppes draw khot"—It had something on it—We now know of a new and previously unknown pattern, a new challenge, but also an indication that as long as you keep looking or keep asking new patterns will be over the horizon, beckoning you on in this never ending, absolutely endless chase of patterns of what we sincerely believe will prove to be one of the most important ceramics that has ever come to the attention of collectors of antiquity and will unlock the door to further research among other related items.

FIGURE 80 is the Deer pattern where the Deer is on the saucer only and the cup is plain spatter outside and completely plain inside.

FIGURE 81 is the Windmill pattern.

FIGURE 82 is the Christmas Balls pattern, again a three color design.

FIGURE 83 is the Vine and Berry pattern.

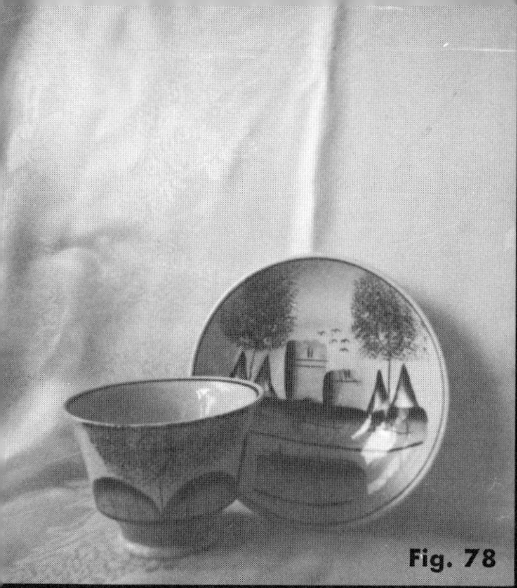

Fig. 78

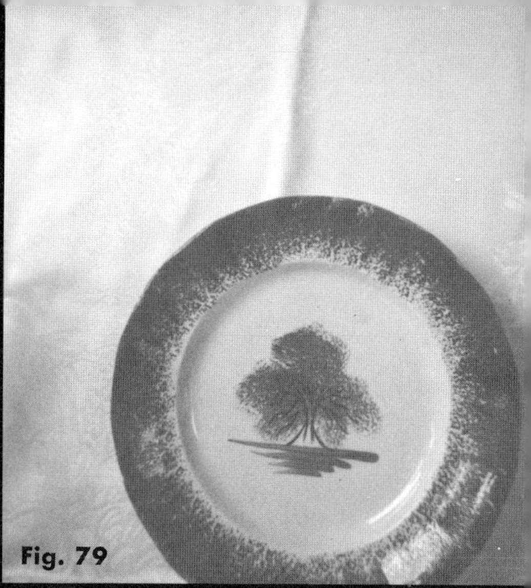

Fig. 79

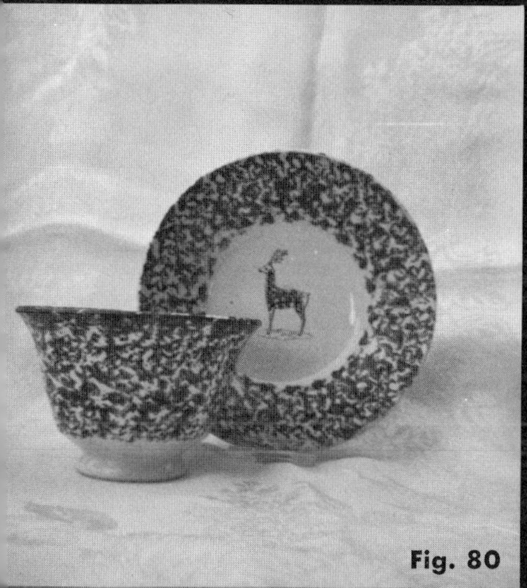

Fig. 80

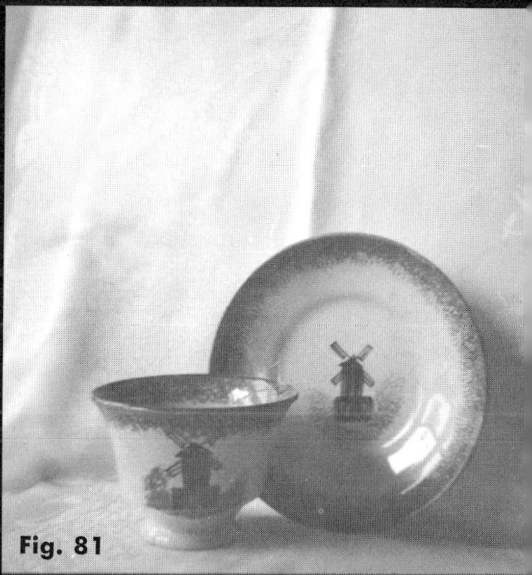

Fig. 81

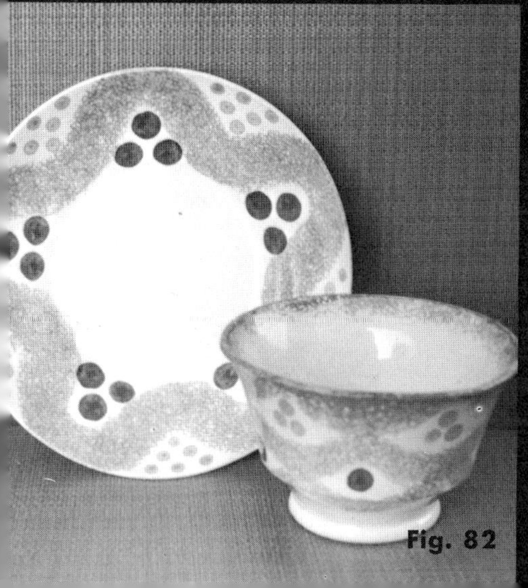

Fig. 82

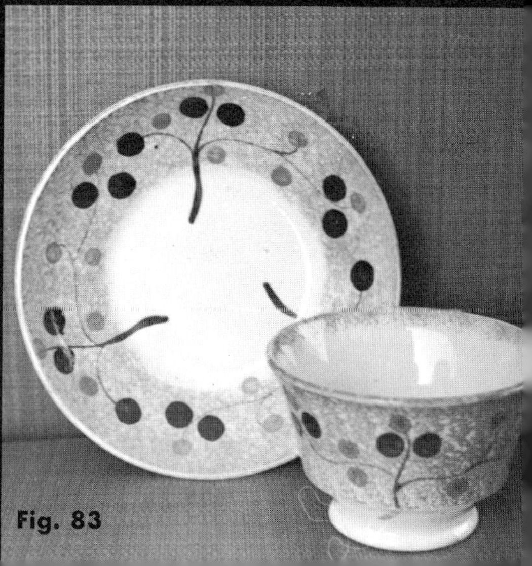

Fig. 83

FIGURE 84 is the Pinwheel design with an irregular star shaped spatter border.

FIGURE 85 is the Red and Green Star design spatter cup and saucer, an exceptionally colorful stunning and clean looking pattern—beautiful.

FIGURE 86 is the 26 Dot pattern.

FIGURE 87 is the Star pattern in a plain spatter border.

FIGURE 88 is the Star pattern but this time in a Sunburst spatter border.

FIGURE 89 is Two Men on a Raft design, very similar to the work of Edkins and Bowen illustrated by Major R G Mundy, in English Delft Pottery.

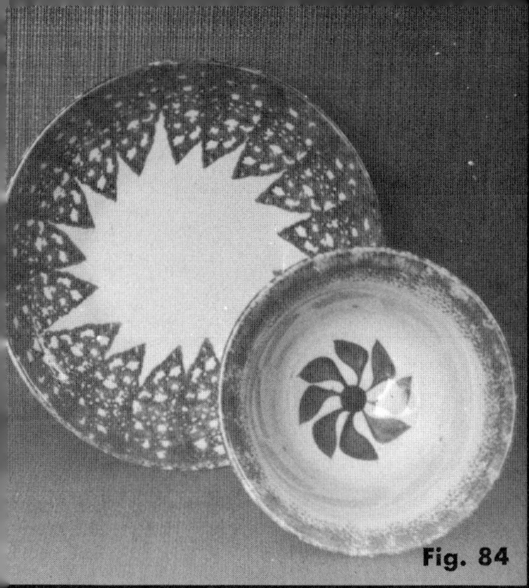
Fig. 84

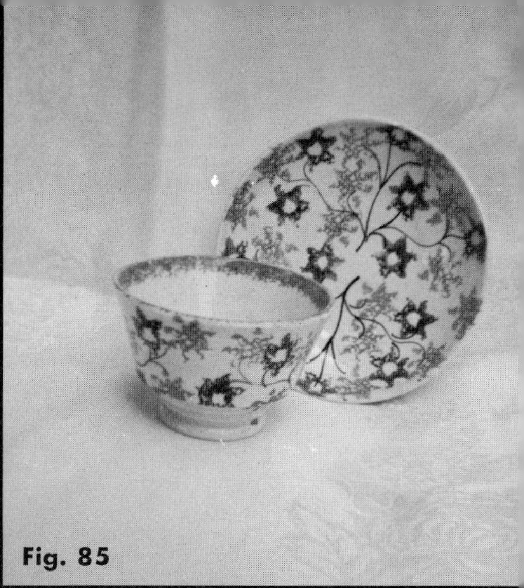
Fig. 85

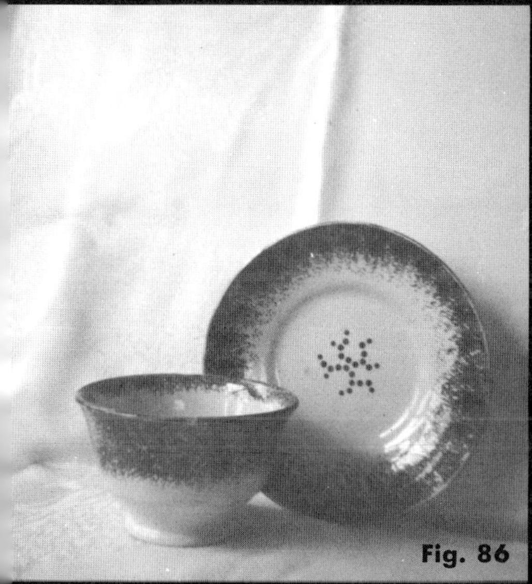
Fig. 86

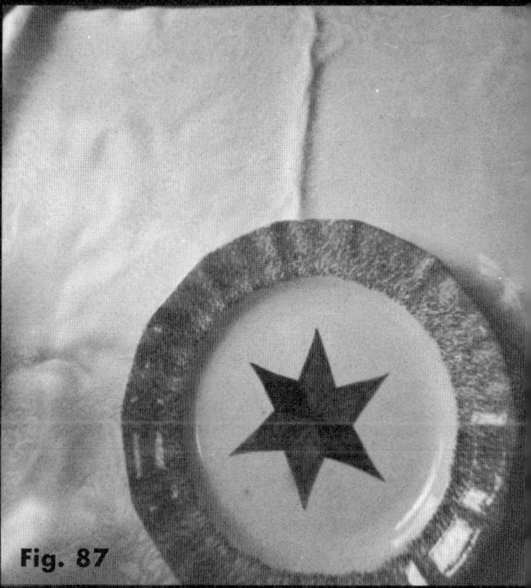
Fig. 87

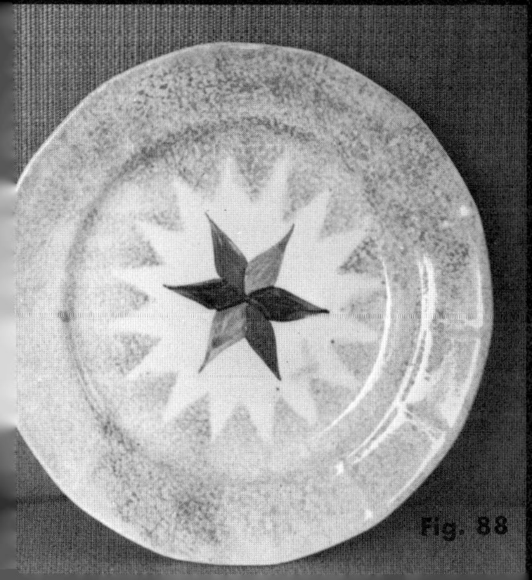
Fig. 88

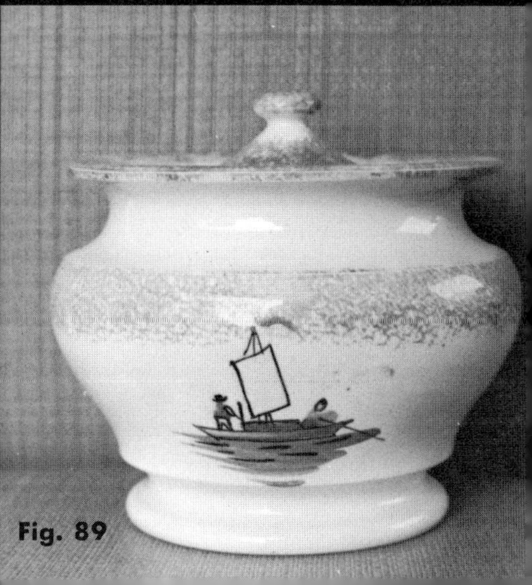
Fig. 89

FIGURE 90 is the Sailboat or Clipper Ship pattern.

FIGURE 91 is the Chinese celebration pattern, a transfer design.

FIGURE 92 is Children at Play pattern.

FIGURE 93 is the Wild Horses pattern.

FIGURE 94 is the Eagle and Shield pattern.

FIGURE 95 is the Flying Eagle pattern.

This plate is marked T Walker—who we believe operated the Lion Works, Tunstall—1845-1851. The shape, the glaze and the body of our other Flying Eagle transfer patterns indicate a similar Staffordshire origin. The Eagle and the Eagle and Shield transfers are so similarly executed as to indicate that they are the product of the same engraver.

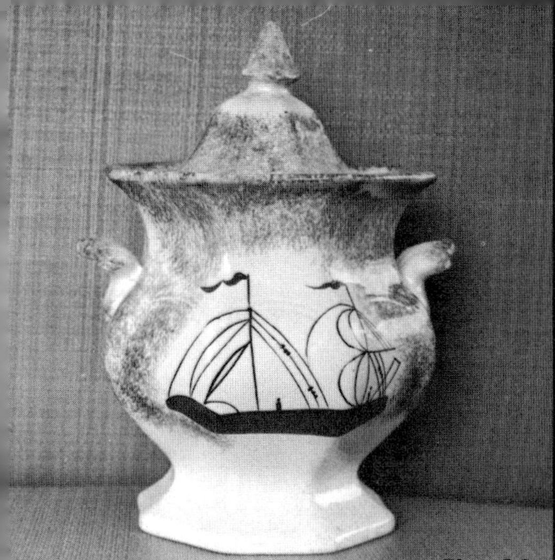

Fig. 90

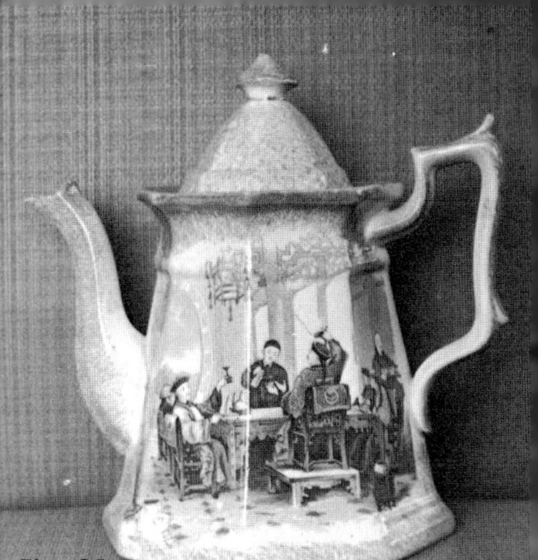

Fig. 91

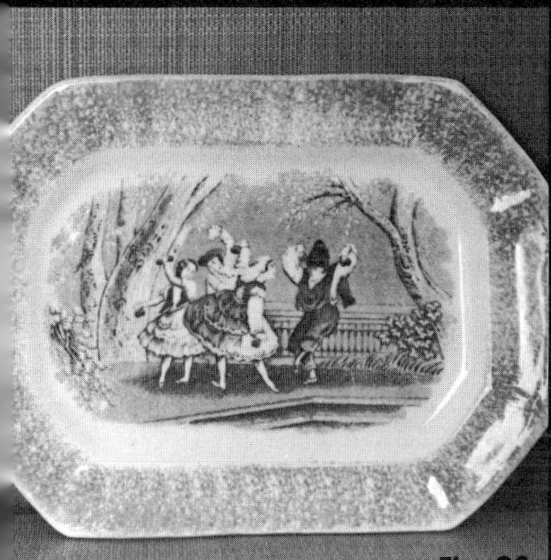

Fig. 92

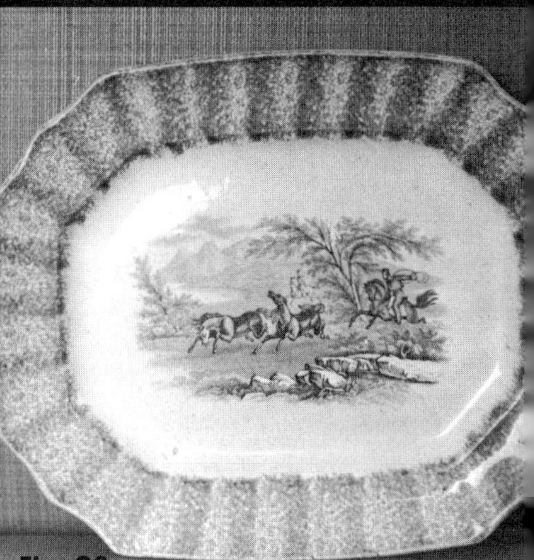

Fig. 93

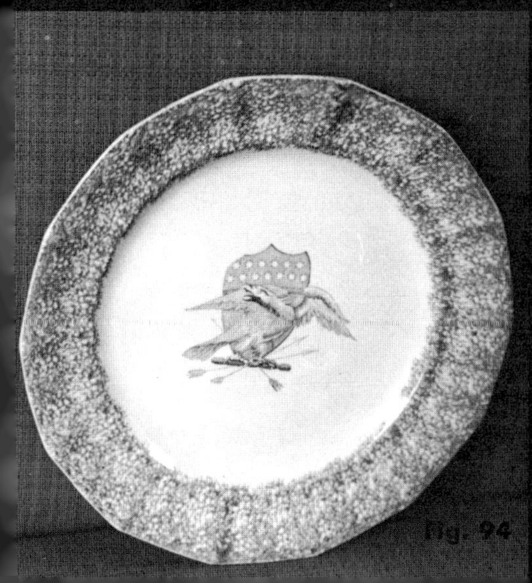

Fig. 94

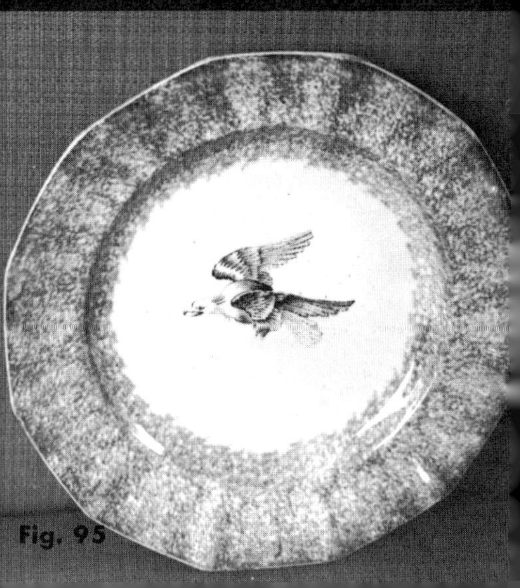

Fig. 95

FIGURE 96 is the design spatter Roseace and Diamond type—If one can conceive of the large, the center and the small circles in a medium blue, the outer decorative design in red and the inner design in yellow—It is colorful and will add beauty and life to any corner and enliven the whole room, it is very lovely.

FIGURE 97 is a cup and saucer—the Roseate in red and the diamonds in black—but we are certain that you can find it in practically any color that will fit in with your decorative effect.

FIGURE 98 is a Star and Festoon with a green Star, a Red festoon and a blue top border.

FIGURE 99 is a Roseate plate—Red rays or petals on a green center.

FIGURE 100 is a green spatter background with a number of design spatter type figures scattered over the background in red, yellow and black.

FIGURE 101 is a Spray and Spatter border on a plain background.

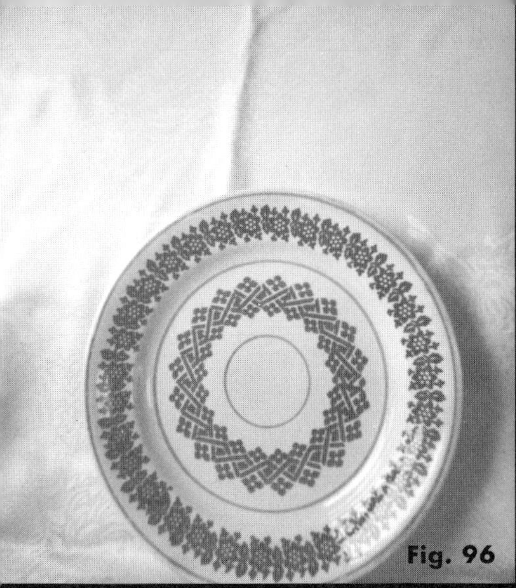
Fig. 96

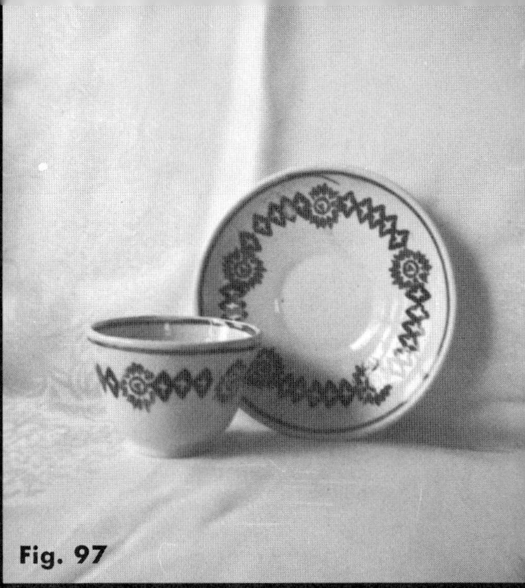
Fig. 97

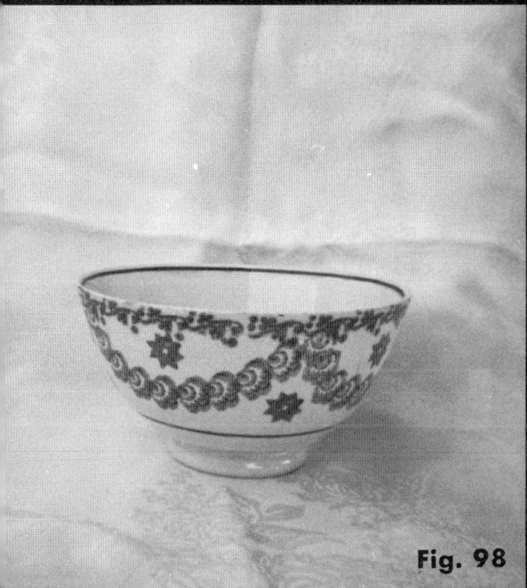
Fig. 98

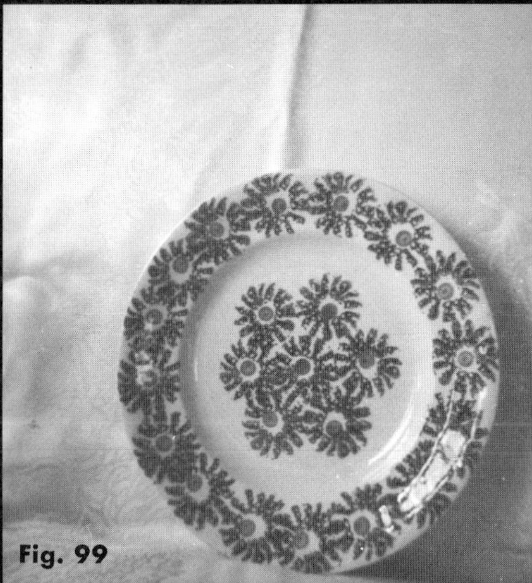
Fig. 99

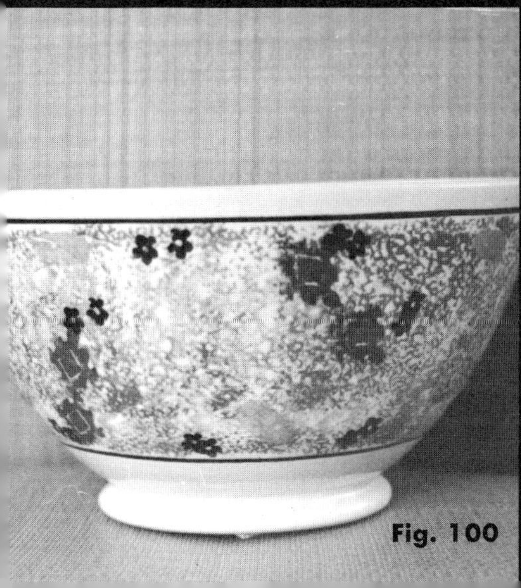
Fig. 100

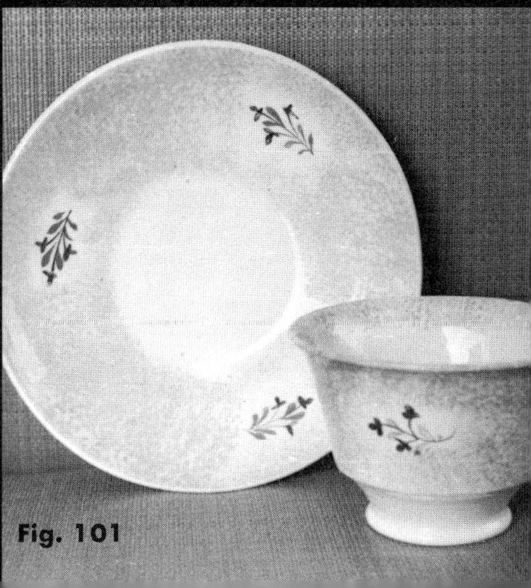
Fig. 101

FIGURE 102 is the Spray cup and saucer in a miniature size.

FIGURE 103 is a plain overall Spatter cup and saucer in a miniature size.

FIGURE 104 is an odd light and dark blue flower with a similar colored spatter border marked Flora and T Walker.

FIGURE 105 is a Dot and Swirl pattern with white and blue stripes, a very effective design for a platter.

FIGURE 106 is the Thistle pattern.

FIGURE 107 is an Eagle pattern in design spatter.

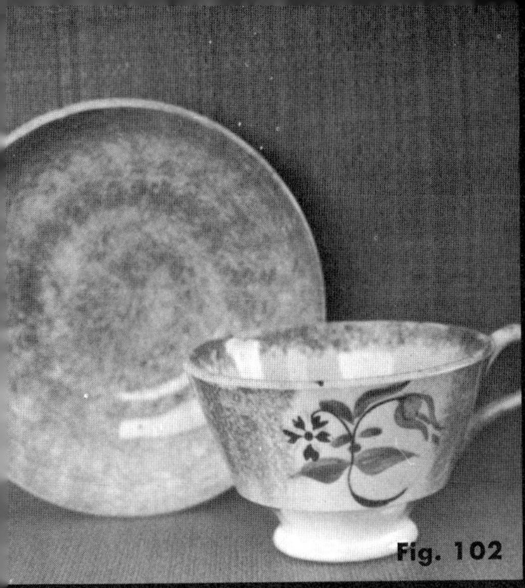

Fig. 102

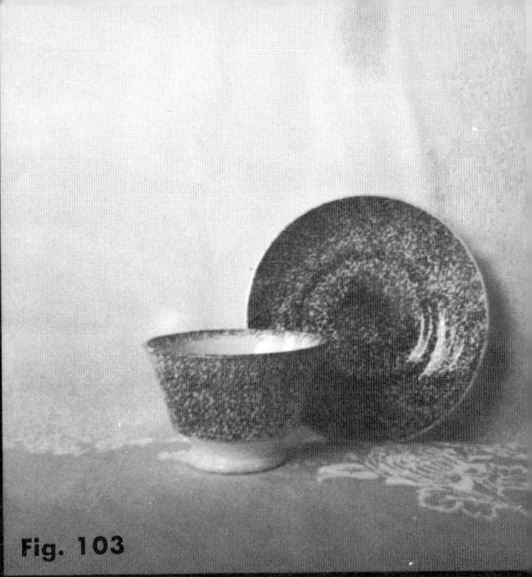

Fig. 103

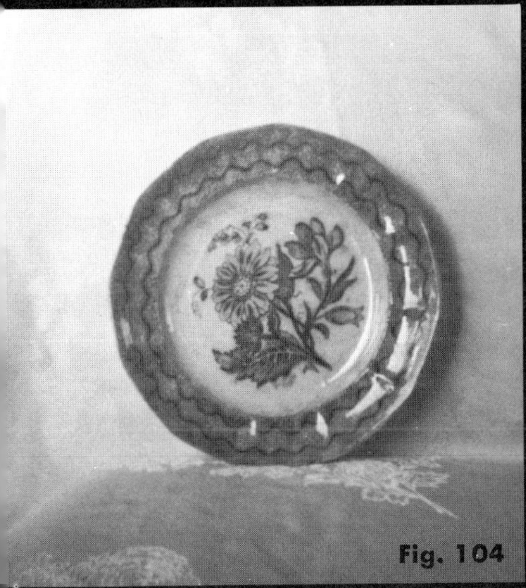

Fig. 104

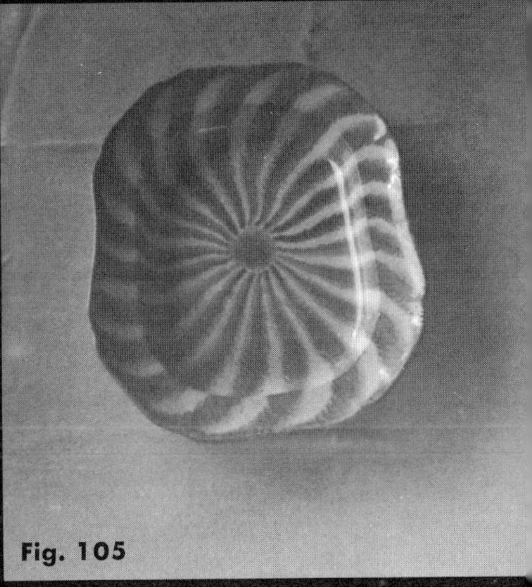

Fig. 105

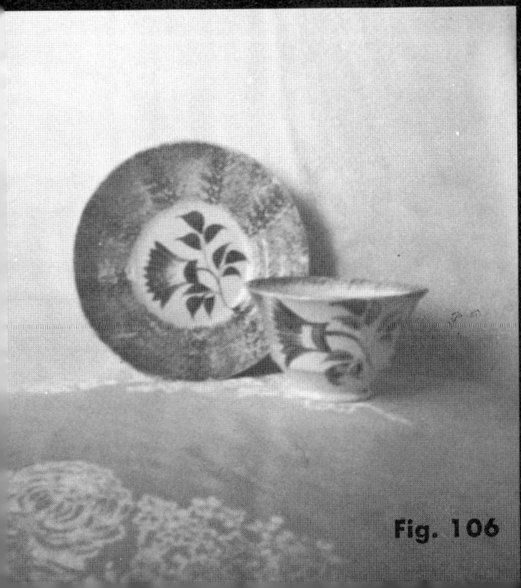

Fig. 106

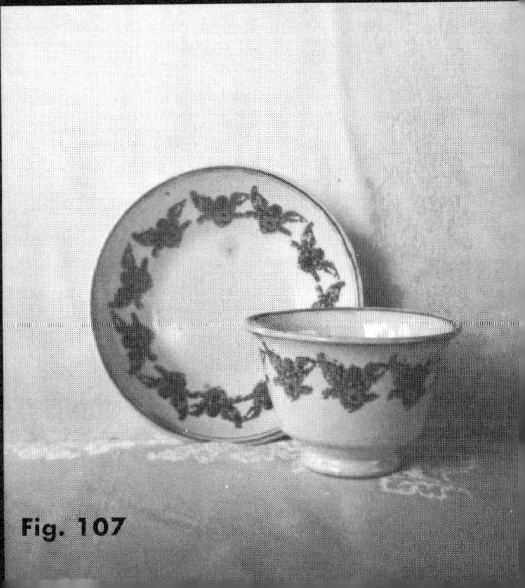

Fig. 107

FIGURE 108 is a Star design spatter border.

FIGURE 109 is a $6\frac{1}{2}$-inch plate design spatter type—the tree effects are blue—the circles and the roses are red, and the leaves are green.

We do not, for obvious reasons, illustrate a cow, or a painted (not transfer) Eagle, a raised floral border plate (similar to Pratt Ware) with two colors (Red and Green) rainbow Bull's Eye type center, a Bird of Paradise, the Cannon, Bird on a Fence (not Peafowl), Fighting Cocks, Reclining Deer, Plough and Hay Rack, Sheaf of Wheat, or Schoolhouse with 2 boys, 1 girl and a dog romping in front of it—While we have just missed several and they seem to be in fair supply they have to date been somewhat elusive, but we did want to list them to keep the record straight for those that may desire to know what additional pieces may still be available to our knowledge.

While it is not our practice to select cups without saucers we did select several just to illustrate as many as we were able to do and therefore we list:

FIGURE 110 the Bleeding Heart pattern.

FIGURE 111 the Red Bird pattern in miniature.

FIGURE 112 the Public Outhouse pattern. Probably the one behind the Schoolhouse. The roof is black, the facing board at the edge of the roof is white, the front of the building is black and the barricade surrounding the structure is red. There seems to be additionally a white window in the barricade but this probably, like the chimney may have been wishful thinking on the part of the student. There are semi-circular cut-outs at the bottom and the doors are white, both the his and the hers doors. A very novel and interesting piece.

FIGURE 113 illustrates a Cacti plate in Creamware—Circa 1785-1790.

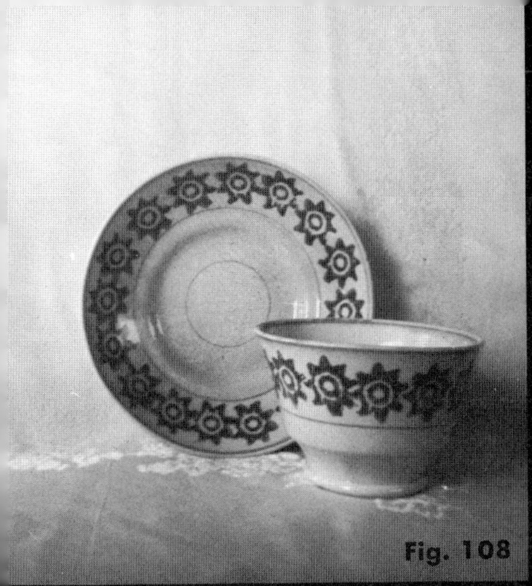

Fig. 108

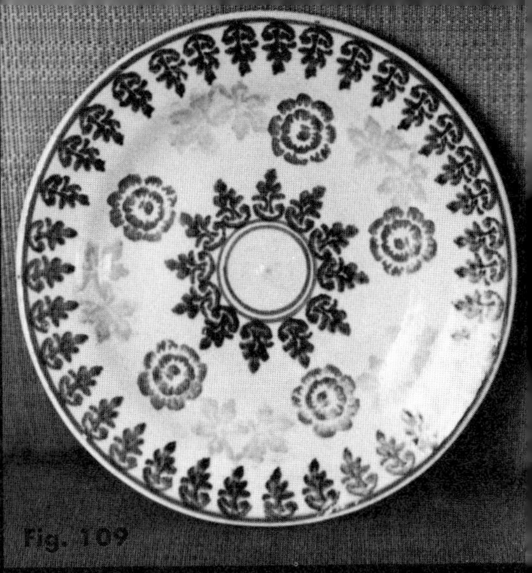

Fig. 109

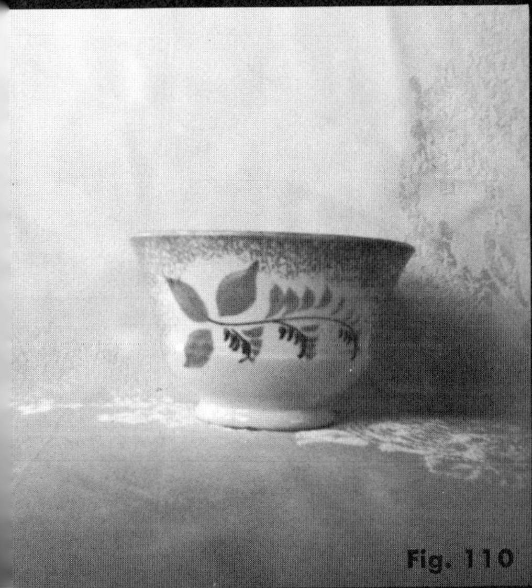

Fig. 110

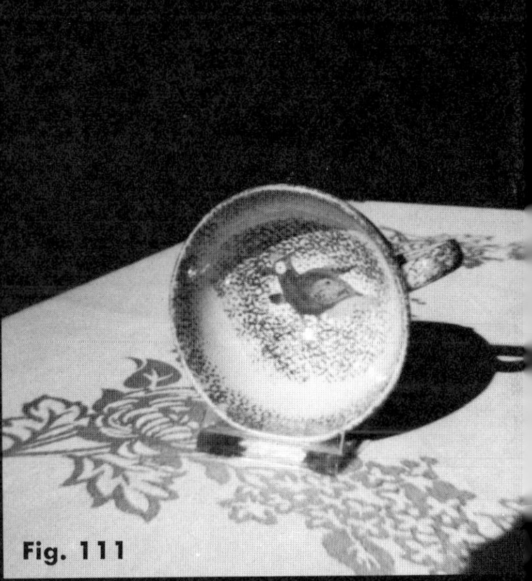

Fig. 111

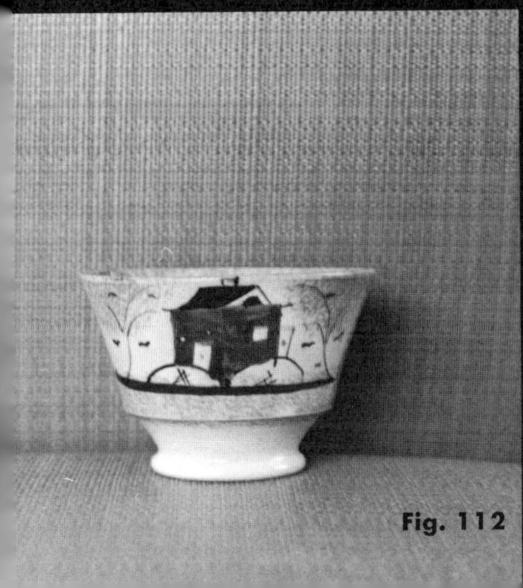

Fig. 112

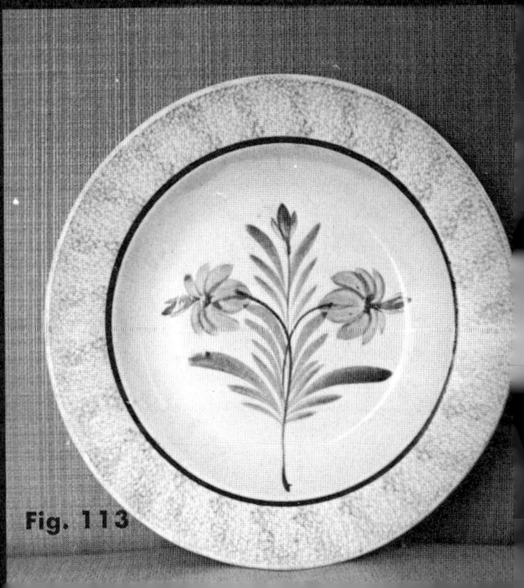

Fig. 113

FIGURE 114 illustrates a Cacti and Tulip plate on Creamware 1785-1790 potting.

FIGURE 115 illustrates a Tulip and six Brown Buds, also on Creamware as above.

FIGURE 116 illustrates a Yellow Bird in a Tree, another Creamware plate 1785-1790 vintage and we believe a rare example seemingly inspired by the Bowl in the People's Palace Museum, Glasgow, Scotland—Figure S A.

FIGURE 117 is the Apple Tree above referred to and of which we have been able to secure a cup only but it will again illustrate an example of a new and different type, En Epple Baum.

FIGURE 118 a personalized cup marked Jane—an unusual custom in Spatterware.

FIGURE 119 is the Earthworm Spatter version.

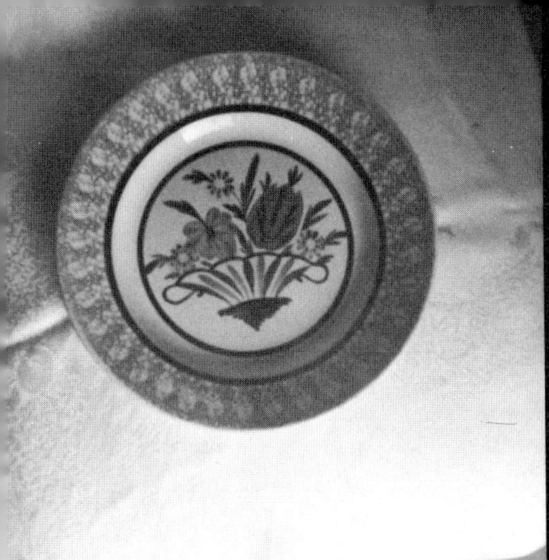

Fig. 114

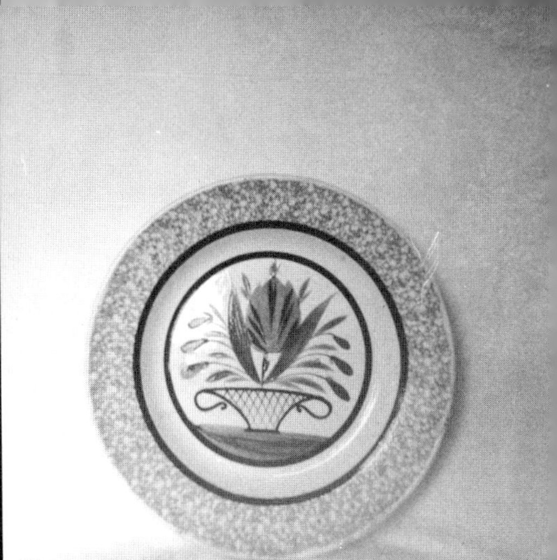

Fig. 115

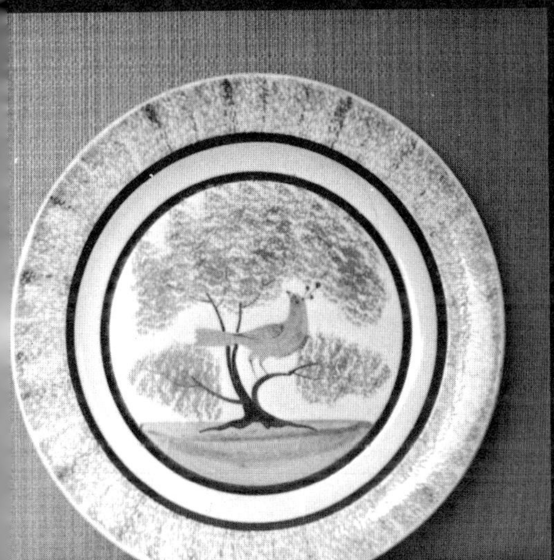

Fig. 116

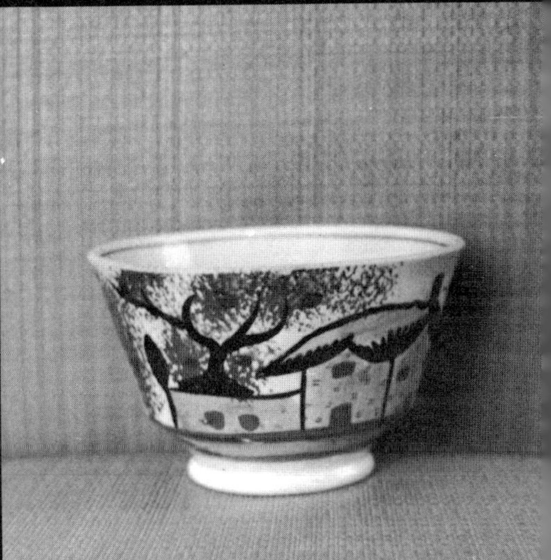

Fig. 117

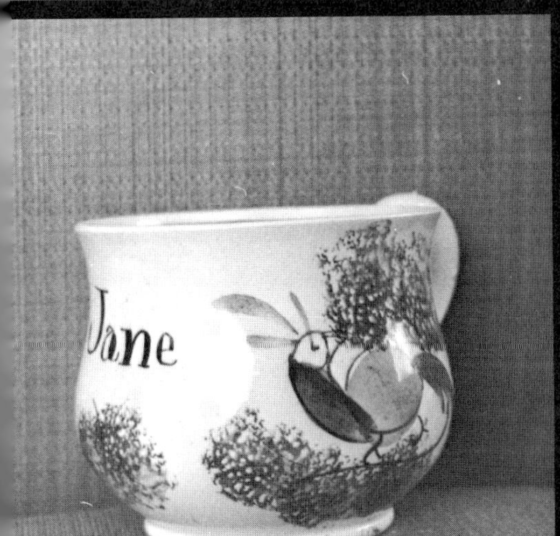


Fig. 118

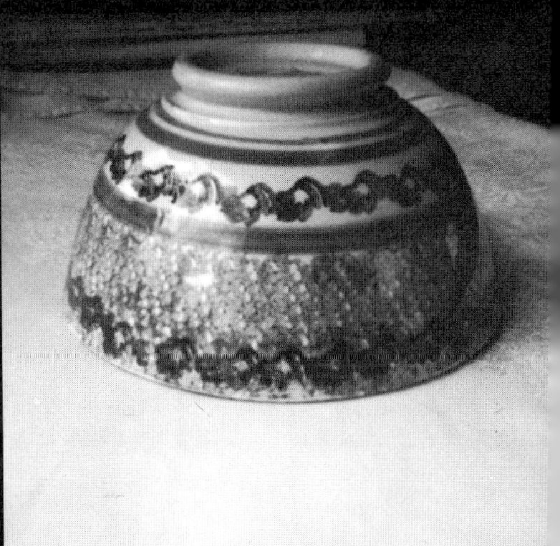

Fig. 119

FIGURE 120 is Iris with 5-7 petal Blue flowers.

FIGURE 121 is a Red Bird on a Leed's type saucer.

FIGURE 122 is another type Red Bird on a Leed's type saucer.

FIGURE 123 is a Rooster Design in the conventional spotted or bemeasled Spatterware.

FIGURE 124 is Thatched Roof House and Tree, a monochrome design all in Blue. This is what might be known as a commercial match to number 117—The Apple Tree—The roof is not quite the same shape but the thatching and the general contour is similar—The Apple Tree has a blue house, fence and roof—mustard shade doors, chimney and windows—green foliage in a spattered effect and red apples whereas the FIGURE 124 here illustrated is all blue. With no fruit showing it can be presumed to also be an Apple Tree (Mit Ken Epple) since the shape is similar. Additionally it is of an earlier lighter paste body usually referred to by our dealers as soft paste.

FIGURE 124-A is top view of 124 to more clearly show rim shape, decorative treatment of handle and spout as well as the Beehive shape of the finial on lid.

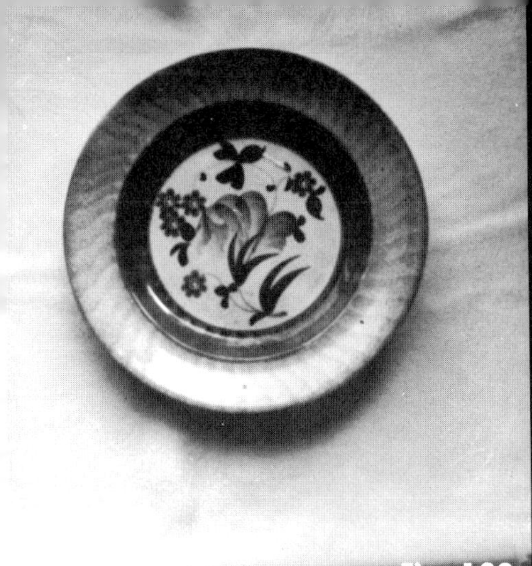

Fig. 120

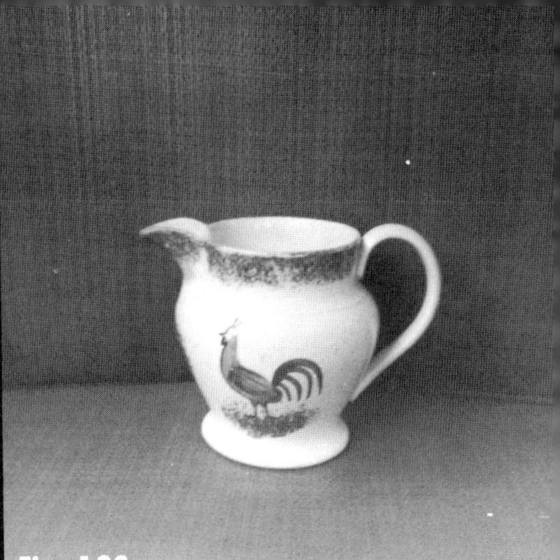

Fig. 123

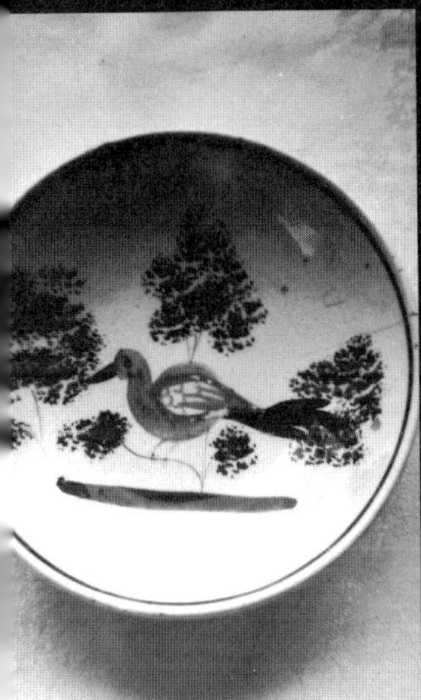

Fig. 121

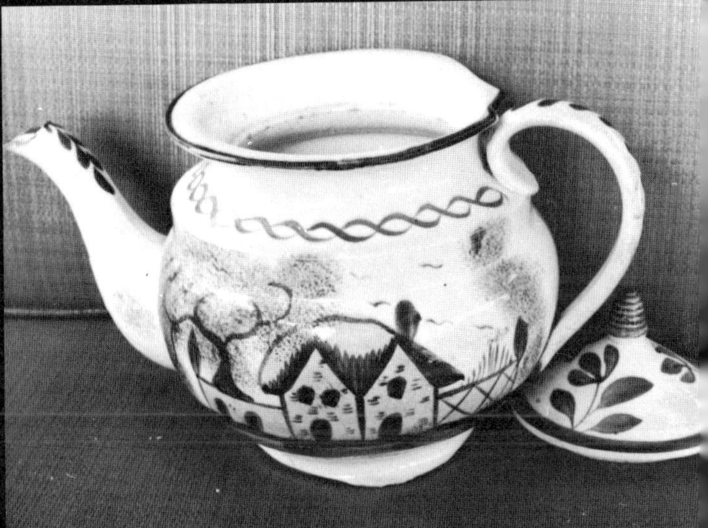

Fig. 124

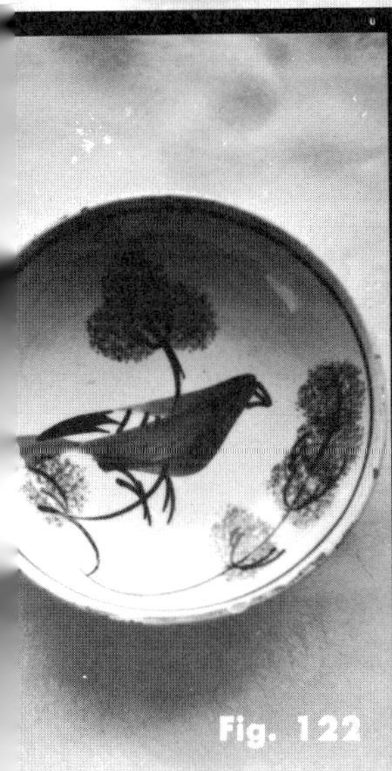

Fig. 122

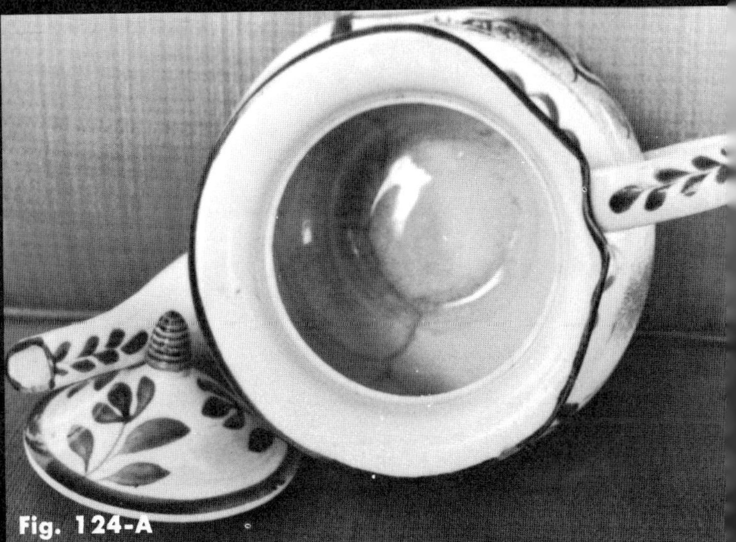

Fig. 124-A

FIGURE 125 is a Peafowl (Leed's type) with a raised decorative effect on the uncolored 12 sided border.

FIGURE 126 is a Tulip, but done so delicately in an outlined type of design that we felt that it should be illustrated.

FIGURE 127 is the conventional type Tulip but it is illustrated to indicate how deeply the Spatter border is often carried and to illustrate that the border was applied first and the center design last, since the Spatter dots show through where the leaves cover them.

FIGURE 128 is the same conventional Tulip but this time with four buds and with the use of an unusually coarse effect for the Red and Blue Spattered or better *mottled* border.

FIGURE 129 is a two Rose and Blue Flower plate with a blue Spatter border.

FIGURE 130 is a Peafowl with three color (Red, Blue and Green) Spattered clusters of spots over the entire background in a rainbow type effect. An unusual and beautiful effect.

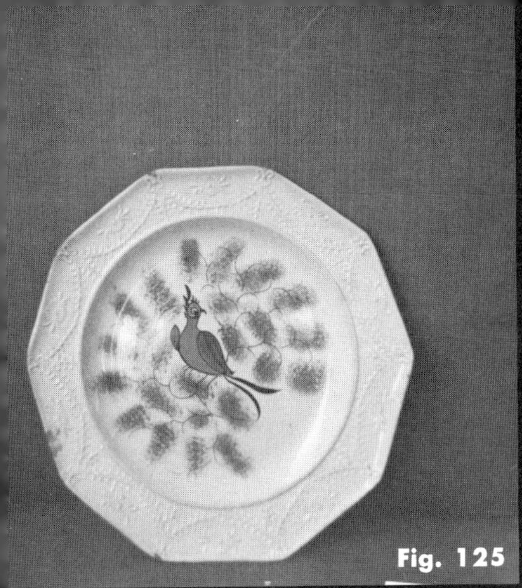
Fig. 125

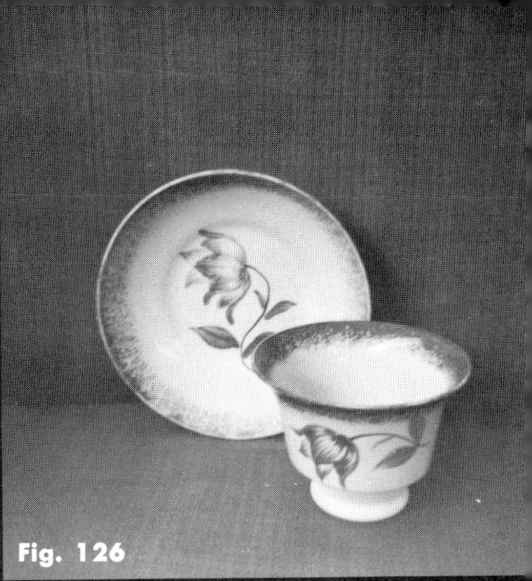
Fig. 126

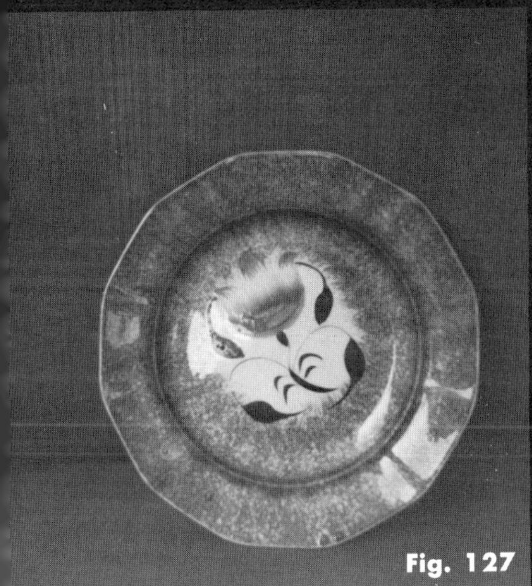
Fig. 127

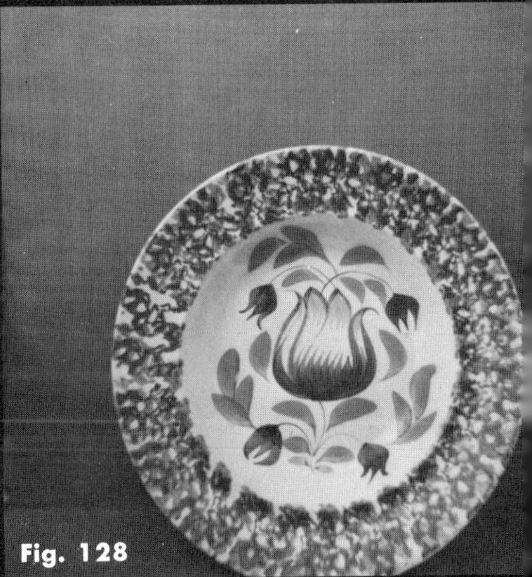
Fig. 128

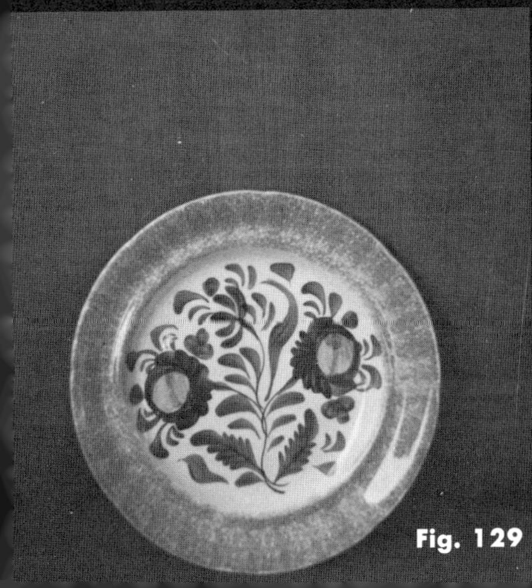
Fig. 129

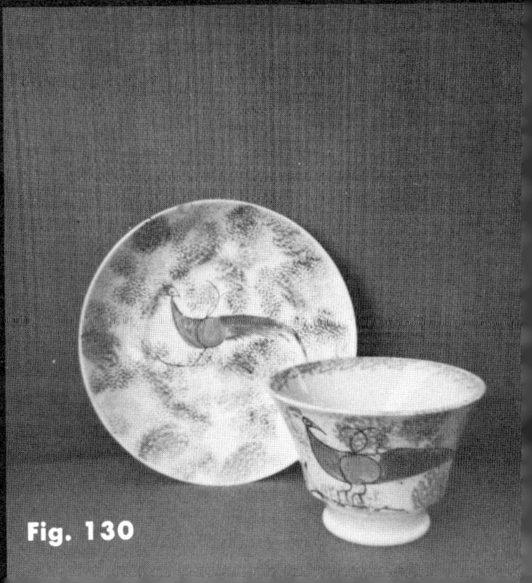
Fig. 130

FIGURE 131 is a Star Pattern in a Sunburst coarse type Spatter border and sufficiently different from FIGURE 88 to deserve separate listing. In this example the decoration is over-glaze and of a rough and grainy texture, indicating the sprinkling of a powdered englobe or substance on a design coated, film of oil or mucilagenous surface.

FIGURE 132 is a Rosebud and eleven Blueberries pattern on a Blue Spatter background.

FIGURE 133 is a Red Rose (design type) over Yellow Spatter Bowl.

FIGURE 134 illustrates a double Chain-design Spatter type Sugar Bowl.

FIGURE 135 is the Beehive—Regular Spatter type.

FIGURE 136 is a 12 sided Blue, Green and Red, extremely coarse Spattered Mug. Unusual pattern is uniformly applied.

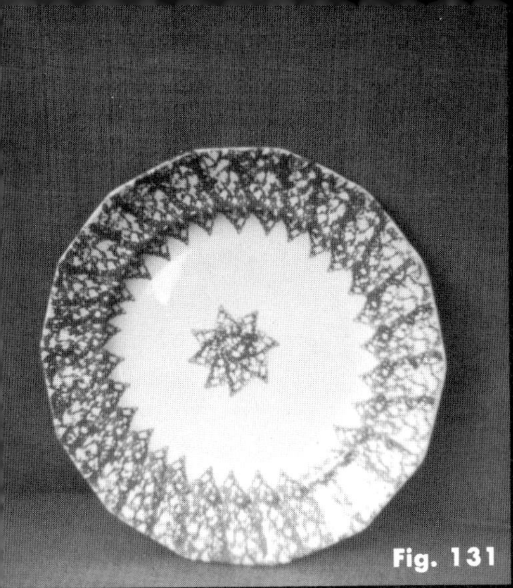
Fig. 131

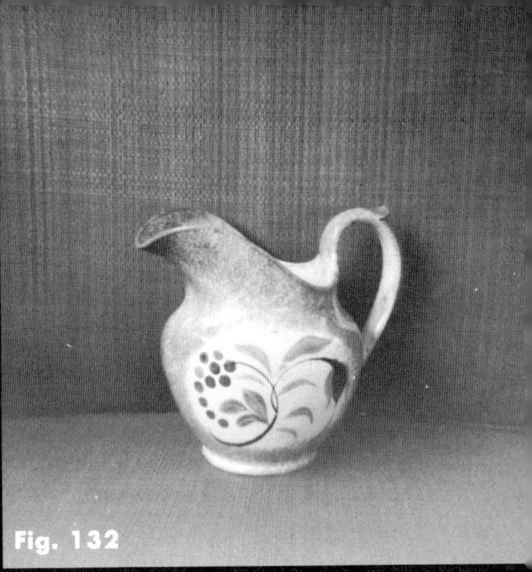
Fig. 132

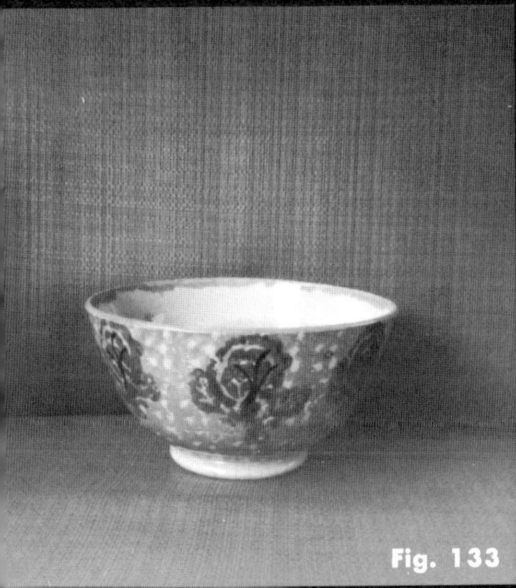
Fig. 133

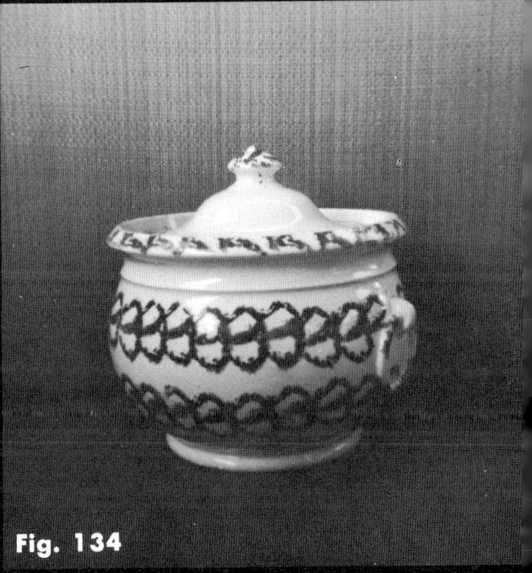
Fig. 134

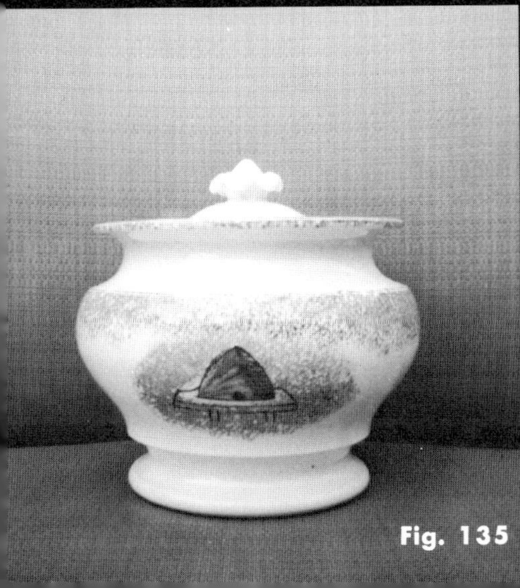
Fig. 135

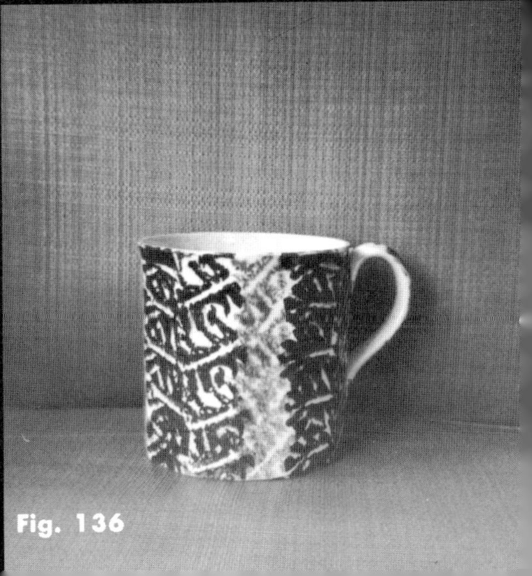
Fig. 136

FIGUER 137 is a platter with a garland of Blue and Green leaves inside of a Red Spatter border.

FIGURE 138 is a four Rose Bud design cup and saucer with a design Spatter border.

FIGURE 139 is a two color Rainbow Creamer with a Green Spatter stripe and a Red design Spatter stripe alternating around the body, an extremely unusual combination.

FIGURE 140 is a Red Spatter border with 4 clusters of 4 blackberries and 4 leaves each.

FIGURE 141 is a plate with Green and Purple leaves in a design Spatter type with Blue circles.

FIGURE 142 is a Red and Green Rainbow plate—Red and Green alternating stripes on the border and a Red Spatter circular band inside of border with a Green Spatter band inside of the Red band—a very colorful plate.

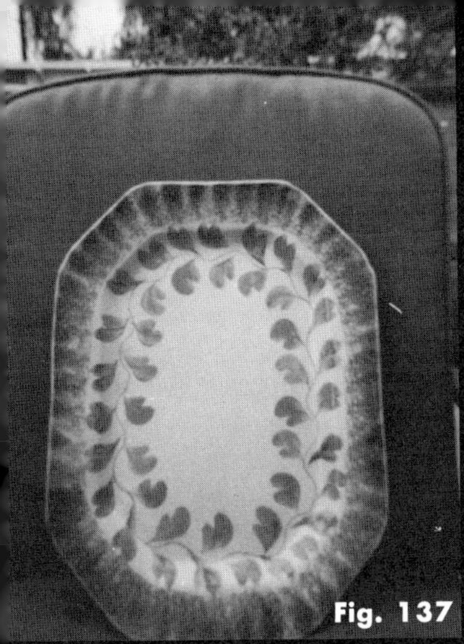

Fig. 137

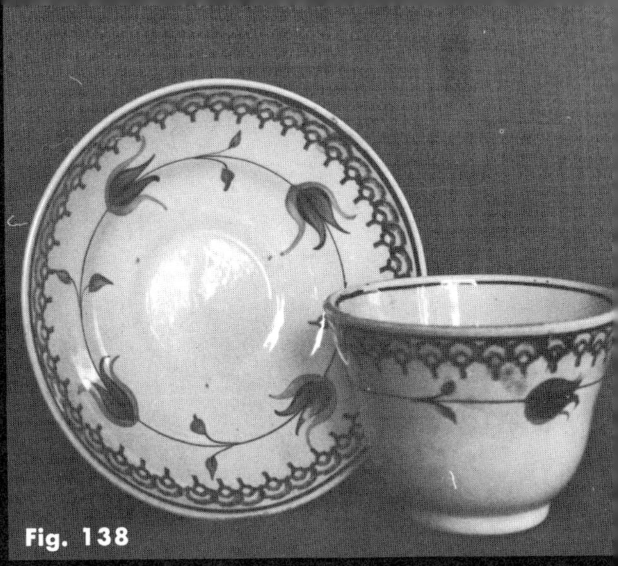

Fig. 138

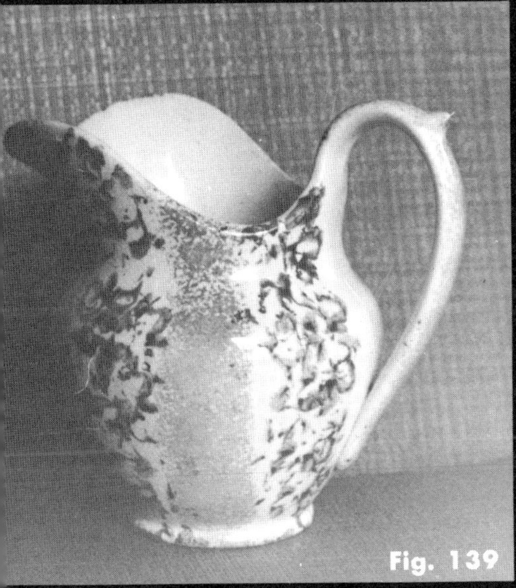

Fig. 139

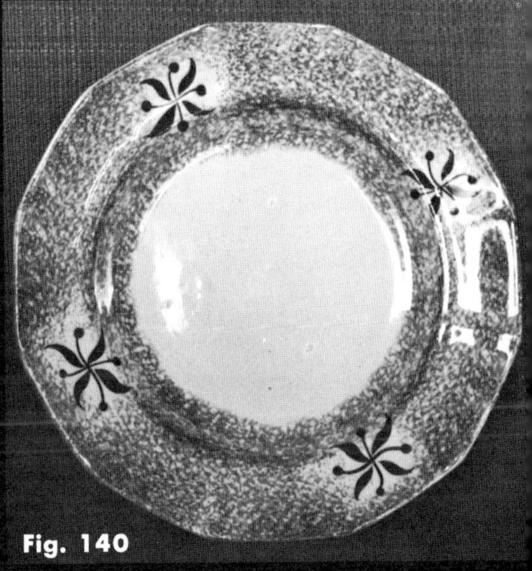

Fig. 140

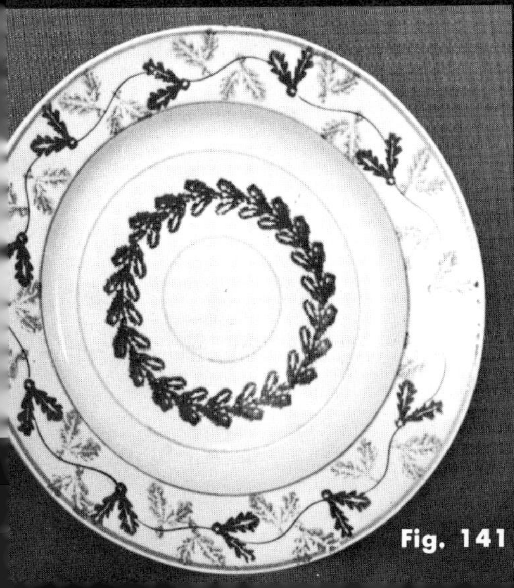

Fig. 141

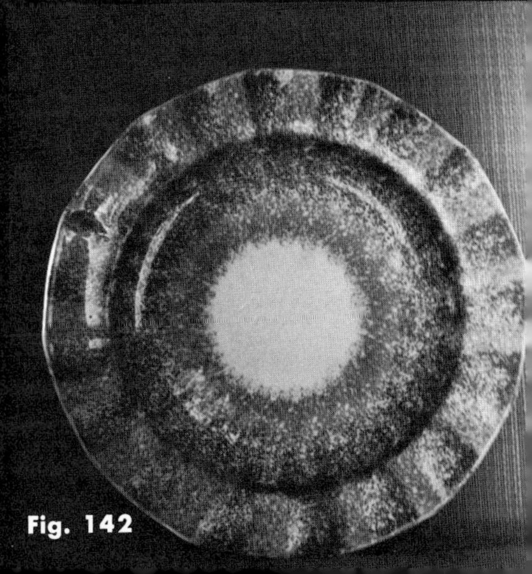

Fig. 142

FIGURE 143 is a 3-color Rainbow Sugar Bowl—The top stripe and the festoons are Green Spatter—The spaces inside this area are filled in in yellow and the darker mark at the bottom is Red.

FIGURE 144 is a 4-color Shield shape Rainbow Spatter Sugar Bowl—Right-hand side of shield is Red—Left-hand side is Yellow—Second from left is Green Spatter and center or largest area is Blue Spatter.

FIGURE 145 is a Red Design Spatter border with Blue flowers having yellow centers and with Green and Blue leaves.

FIGURE 146 is a Three Rose pattern with a Design Spatter border. It is, however, one of the finest decorated plates, of this type, that we have ever seen and indicates the hand of a skilled artist.

FIGURE 147 is a single Rose pattern very similar to 146 but with a Star Design border. Very artistically done also.

FIGURE 148 is a somewhat similar single Rose pattern with an extremely coarse Blue and Red mottled border.

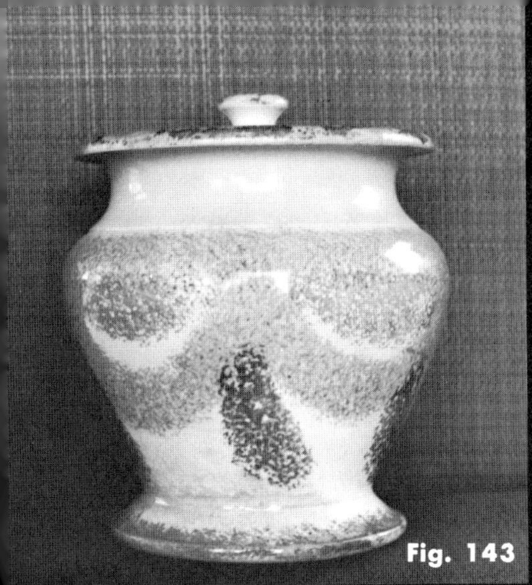
Fig. 143

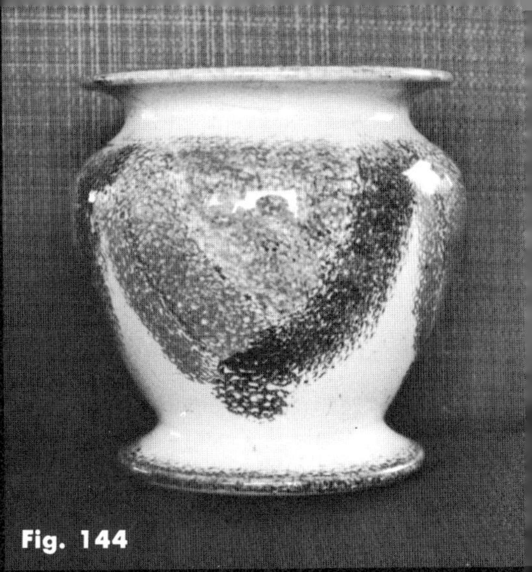
Fig. 144

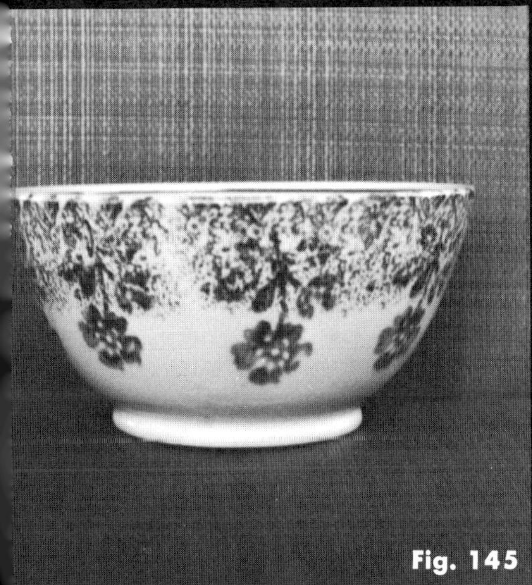
Fig. 145

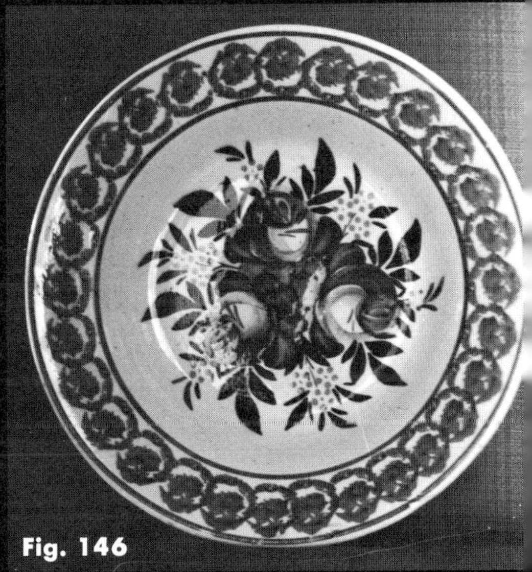
Fig. 146

Fig. 147

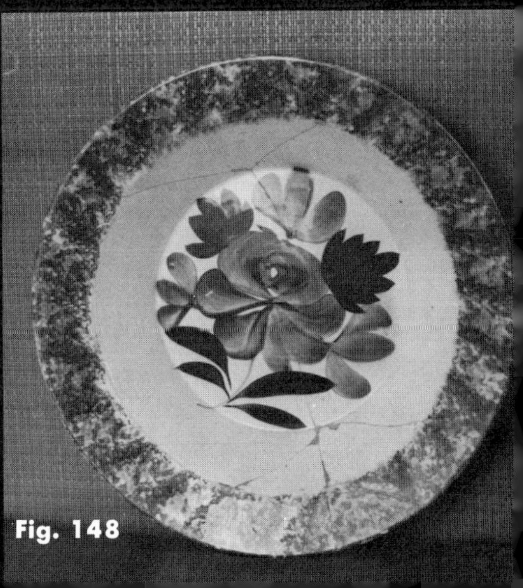
Fig. 148

FIGURE 149 illustrates a coarse purple lustre spongeware cup and saucer.

FIGURE 150 is a Sugar Bowl in Blue Spatterware with a pink transfer design of two prospectors and three loaded mules which would, we believe, be appropriately termed "Mule Train" or "Gold Rush."

FIGURE 151 is an early soft paste, lead glazed Staffordshire Mask Cup or Jug in the early speckled, bemeasled, Spatterware type.

FIGURE 152 is a Parrott Sugar Bowl done by means of sponges and indicating more graphically than FIGURE 9 the Flowing Spatter associated with the use of a sponge.

FIGURE 153 is a 3-color Rainbow plate with the vertical stripes going clear across the plate. The Green and Red stripes are single width but the Blue stripes are double width and we suggest that the center Blue stripe be studied very carefully. While all of the stripes indicate one unbroken, continuous spatter effort clear across the plate, this center Blue stripe is the only one which seems to have had paper protection on both sides to secure some semblance of a straight edge to the stripe and an evenness of overlap where the two spatterings side by side overlapped.

FIGURE 154 is a bold 2-color Rainbow Sugar Bowl, Red and Green Spatter with a Rose. The Spatterwork is of a finer type with extremely small dots.

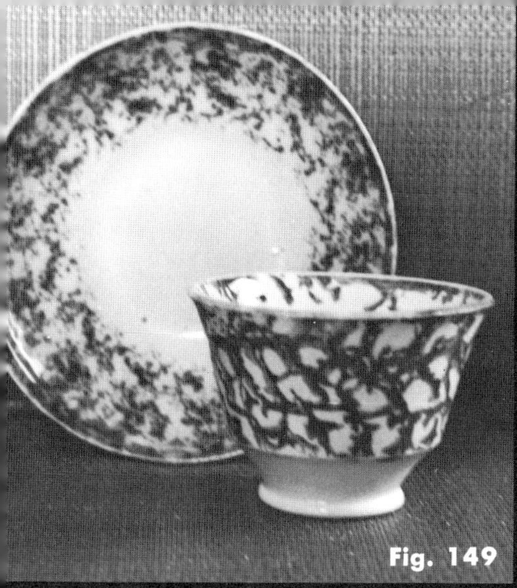
Fig. 149

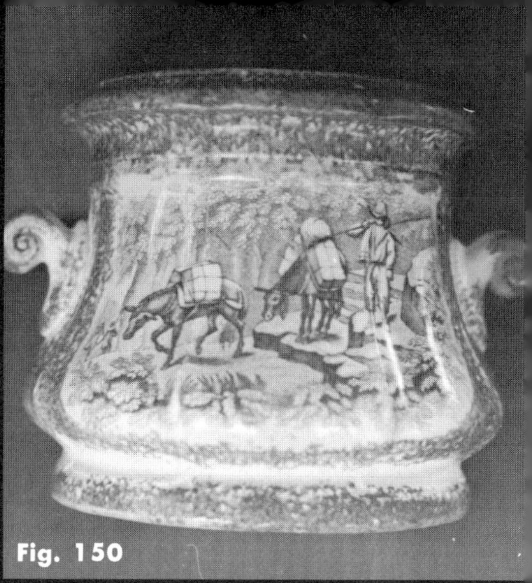
Fig. 150

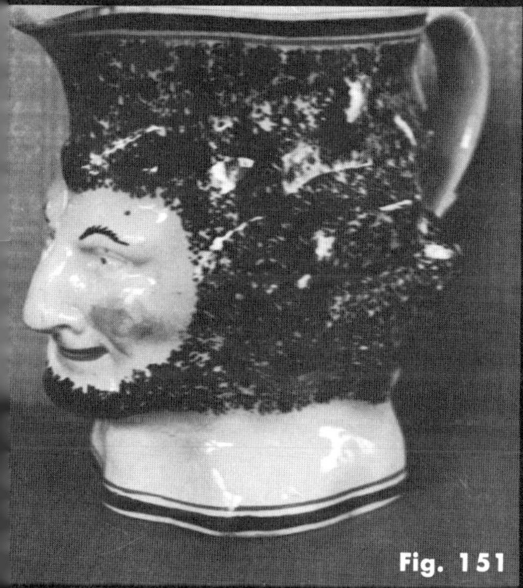
Fig. 151

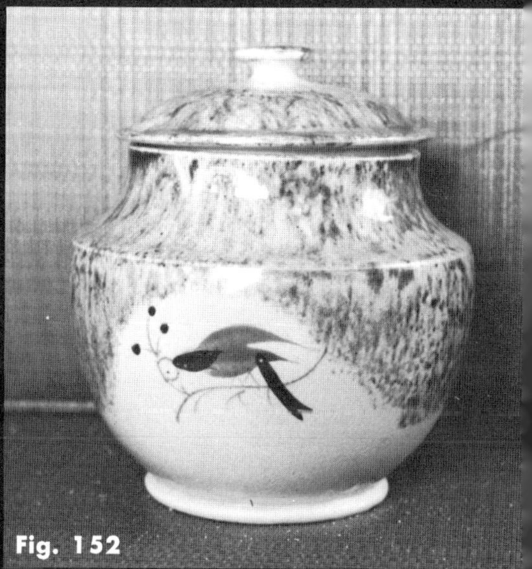
Fig. 152

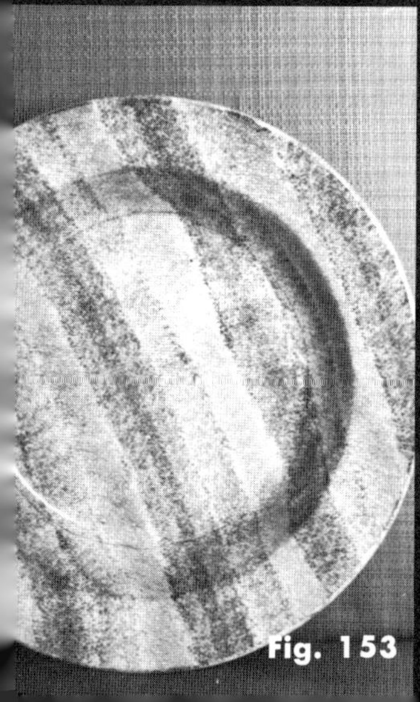
Fig. 153

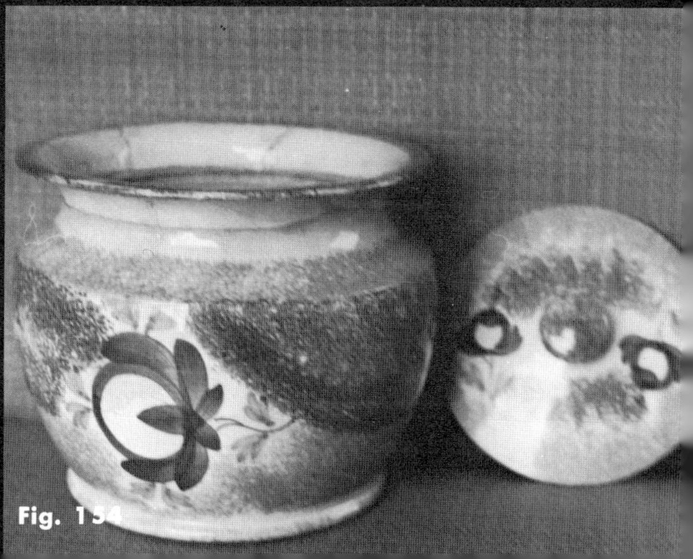
Fig. 154

FIGURE 155 is a 3-color Sugar Bowl with Blue stripes around the body at top and bottom, Red stripes running top to bottom and Green stripes around center.

FIGURE 156 is a 4-color Rainbow Pinwheel design—Black, Yellow, Red and Green.

FIGURE 157 is an odd shaped Peafowl plate with a design Spatter border marked Cotton & Barlow.

FIGURE 158 is an overall Blue Spattered Tea Pot with a decorative arch on the body, raised in a self design.

FIGURE 159 is a design Spatter Sugar Bowl—The daisy type design is in Green and the bow or double loops are in Brown.

FIGURE 160 is a tea pot with identical design and colors to FIGURE 159 above.

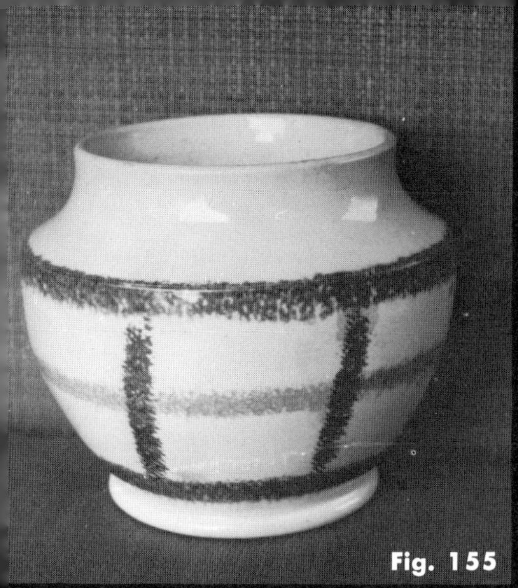
Fig. 155

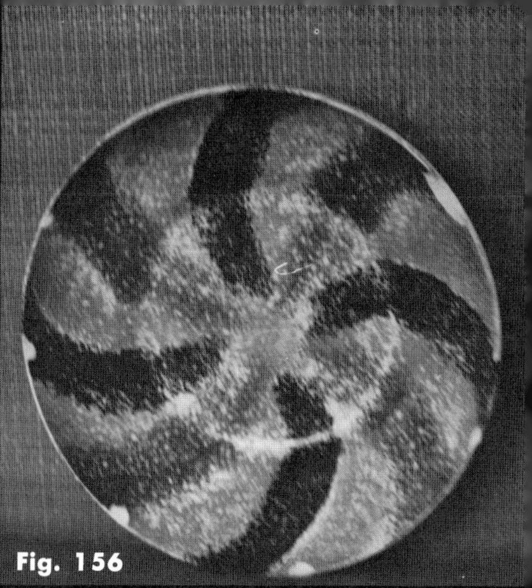
Fig. 156

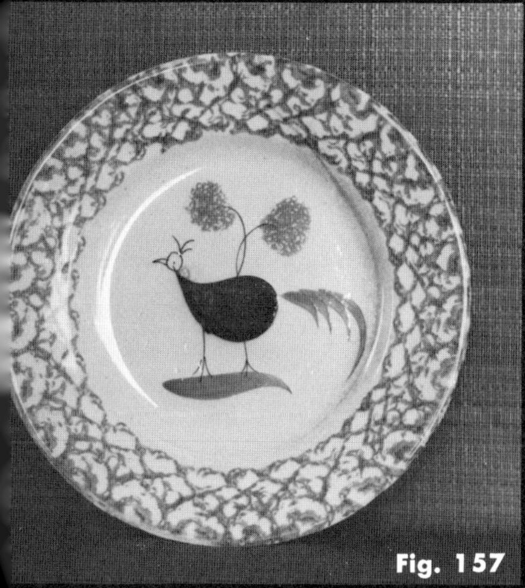
Fig. 157

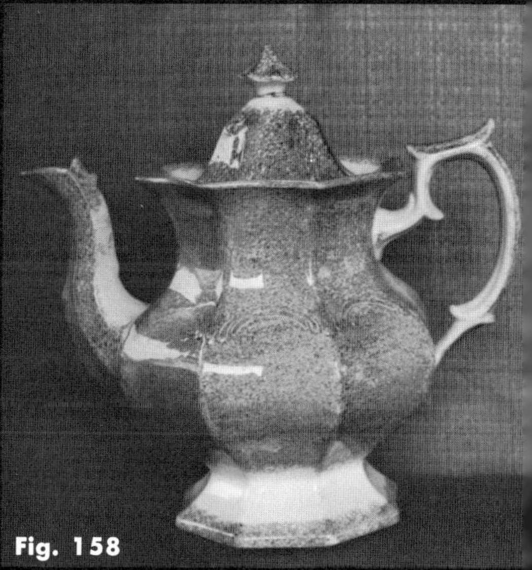
Fig. 158

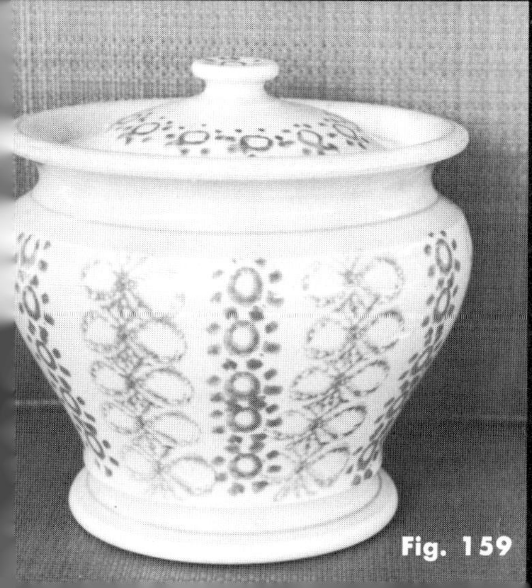
Fig. 159

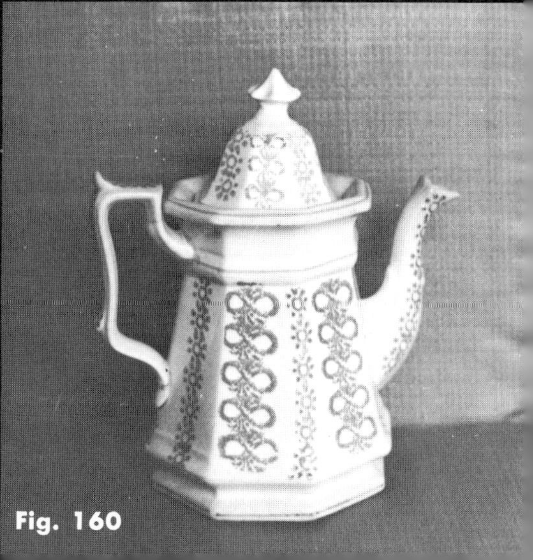
Fig. 160

FIGURE 161 is a Yellow Castle on a seemingly early type soup plate body —Blue Spatter border with Red ovals over the Blue Spatter at intervals of about 2½ inches apart, Made in France, marked "St. Clement." circa 1819.

FIGURE 162 is a Brown Spatter Salt Shaker with two Green stripes, one on each side running the heighth of the shaker.

FIGURE 163 is a Spongeware cup and saucer in Blue of really gigantic size. The saucer is 8½-inches in diameter and the cup is 5¼-inches in diameter—a mush cup we are told.

FIGURE 164 is an unnamed specimen of the many varietied Rainbow family—The semi-circle is in Yellow—the inside color is Red—The leaves and stem are Green and the Cornflower is Blue.

FIGURE 165 is one that was represented to us as a pansy—another fantasy of a vivid imagination—the Spattered border is Blue—The flower is composed of 5 petals as shown, the top 2 petals are Red and the bottom 3 petals have a somewhat Cornflower shape but more opened and a much deeper color of Blue—the leaves are of course Green and there are two Buds that are a Blue color.

FIGURE 166 indicates that Spatterware was made in France as well as in England. This example is marked Sarreguemines.

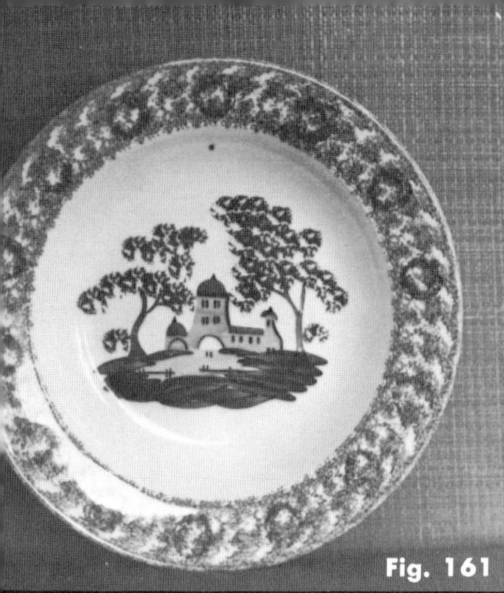
Fig. 161

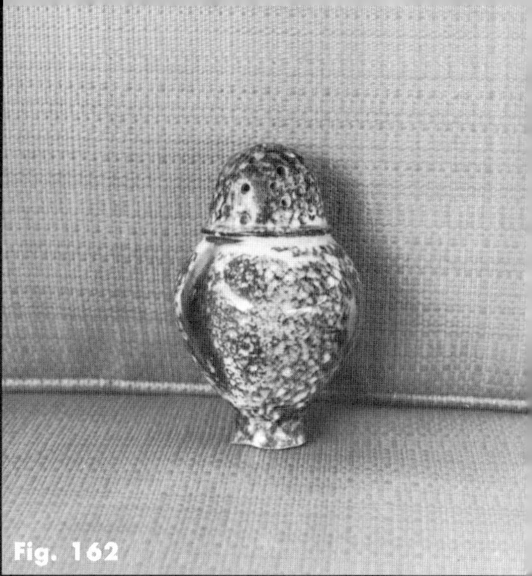
Fig. 162

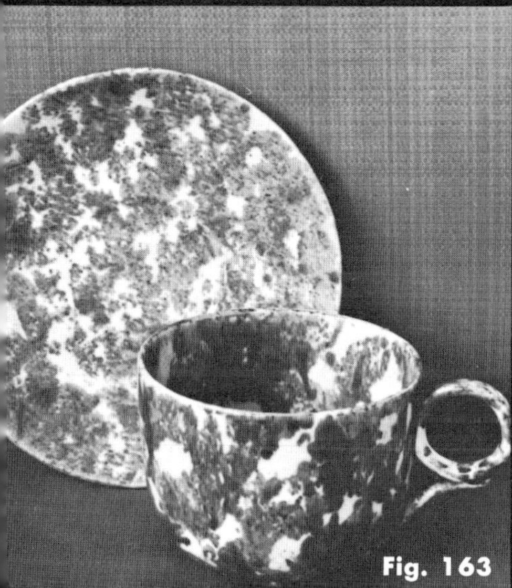
Fig. 163

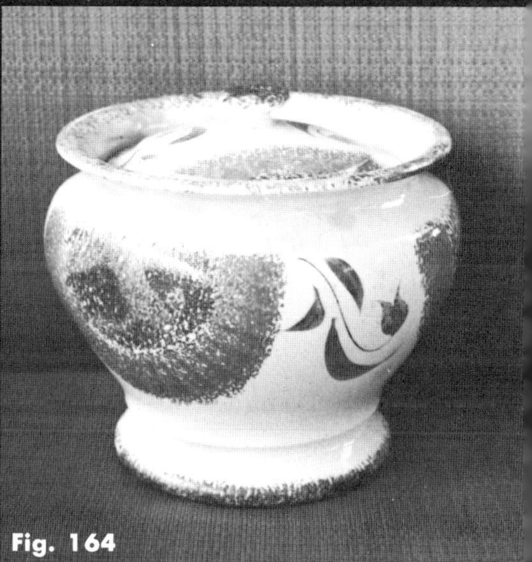
Fig. 164

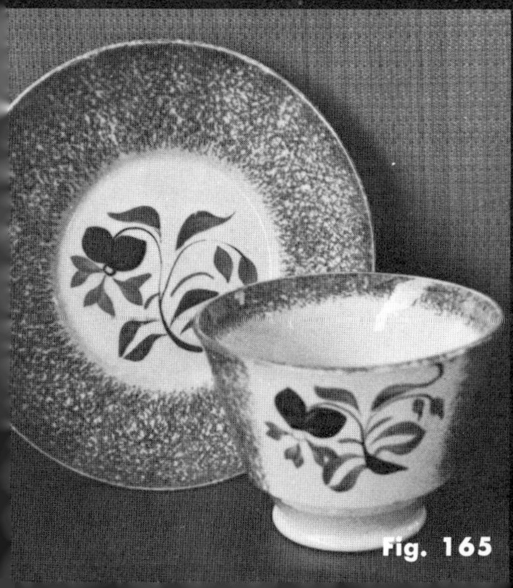
Fig. 165

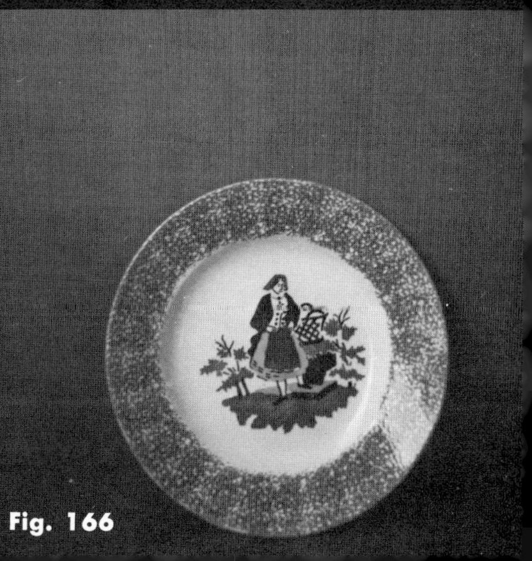
Fig. 166

FIGURE 166-A is the back of plate bearing the mark for your reference. This example assists in establishing rather definitely that the preceding examples were with practically no exception made in England. The design and the workmanship, as well as the body, tell their own story.

FIGURE 167 is a purple lustre spattered pitcher with Masonic Printed transfer and verse.

FIGURE 167-A reverse side of above showing verse.

FIGURE 168 is an 8¾-inch plate, Red and Green Holly Leaf pattern design Spatter, impressed Elsmore & Foster, a potter sometimes included on lists as a manufacturer of Spatterware—Pale Grey Blue circles.

FIGURE 169 is an 8-inch plate—Green 6 point stars and Red dotted circle design Spatter—Brown circles—design Spatter usually has 8 pointed stars.

FIGURE 170 is a 9-inch plate, Red Design Spatter flowered border and three Red Design Spattered flowers in center, the leaves are two shades of green.

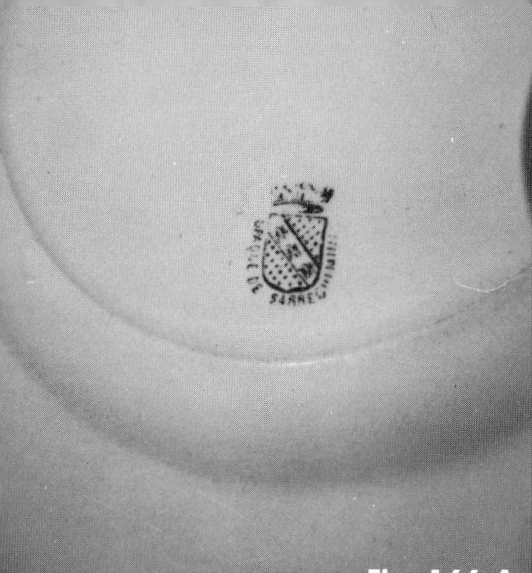

Fig. 166-A

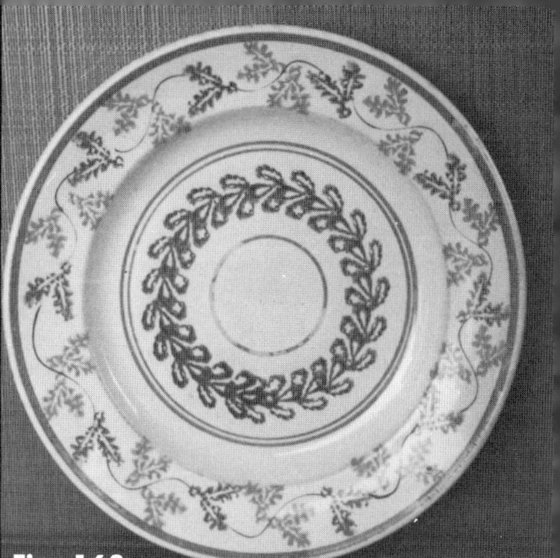

Fig. 168

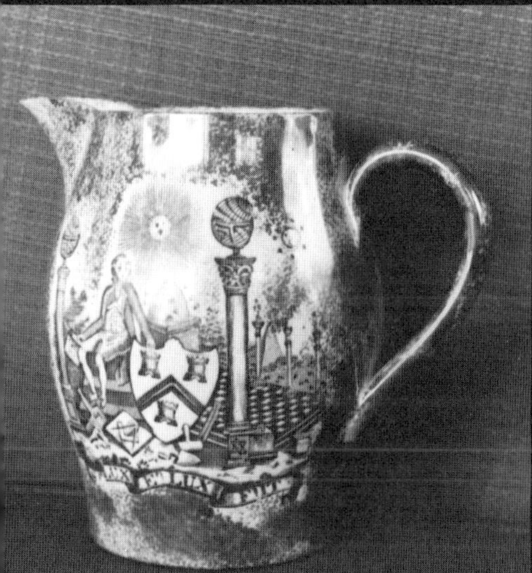

Fig. 167

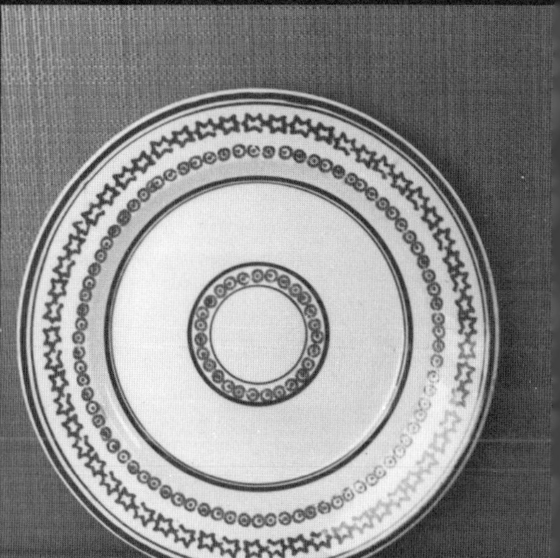

Fig. 169

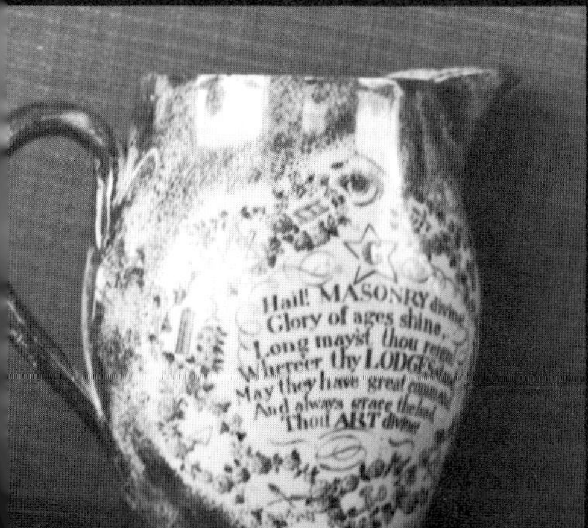


Fig. 167-A

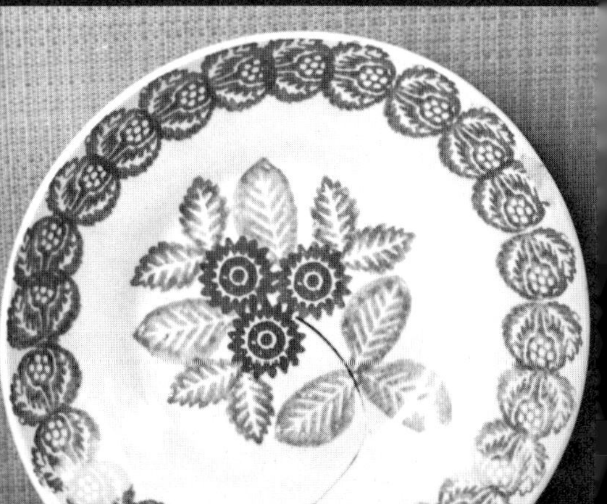

Fig. 170

FIGURE 171 cup with a Black Fish with Red Fins on a Green Background —otherwise Blue Spattered. The Fish is very similar to that pictured in bowl—Figure S A.

FIGURE 172 Open Salt-Blue Spattered.

FIGURE 173 Eagle and Shield Pitcher with a space beside the Shield left open to receive the Spatter initials — J K — presumably those of the decorator.

FIGURE 174 cup plate in an early soft paste with green Spattered border and Boy playing Leapfrog over a Sawbuck.

FIGURE 175 cup plate in early soft paste with a green Spattered border and a Boy doing a high Jump with a girl watching.—Transfer.

FIGURE 176 Toddy plate in early soft paste—Farm Scene in transfer.

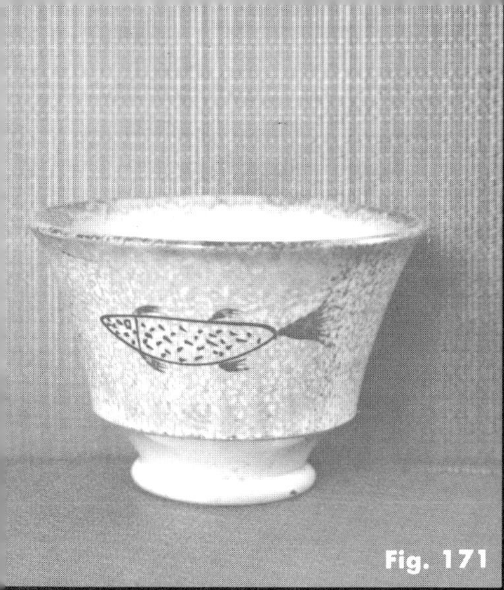

Fig. 171

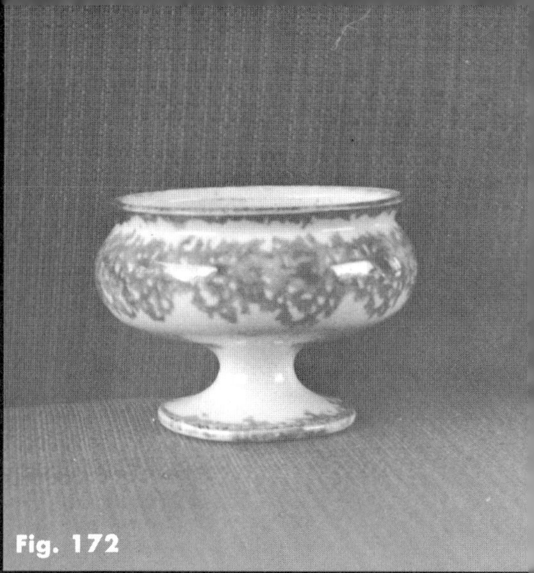

Fig. 172

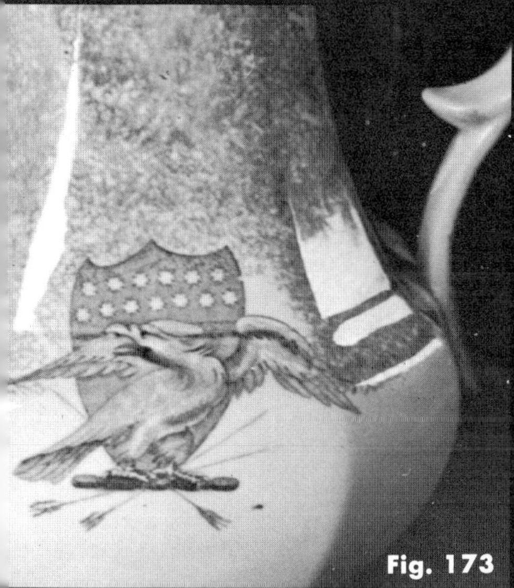

Fig. 173

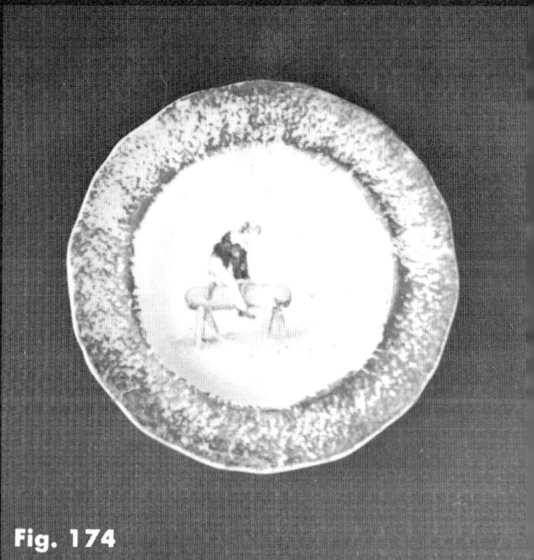

Fig. 174

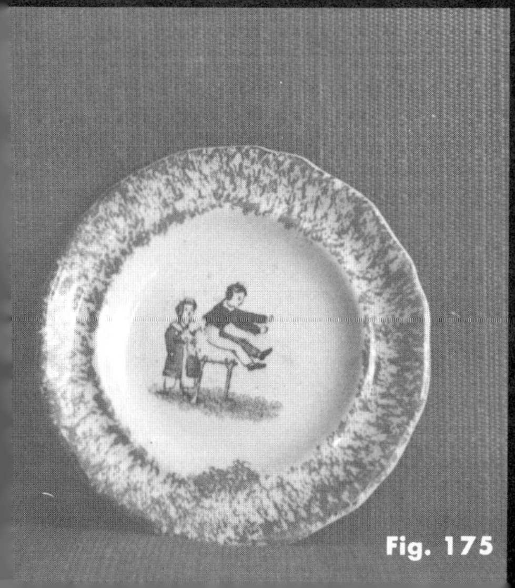

Fig. 175

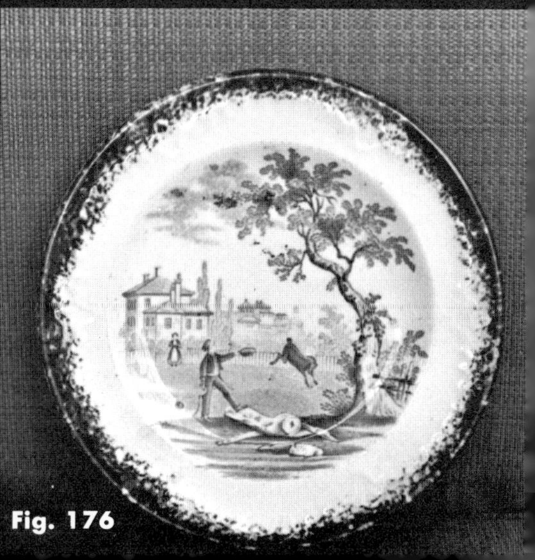

Fig. 176

FIGURE 177 unusual Rainbow Miniature cup and saucer — The center circle and the three elongated border outlines are in Purple Spatter, the space between is a green Spatter and the center of Circle and the inside of elongated outlines are in yellow with two dots in this yellow space in black —extremely difficult to describe.

FIGURE 178 a Blue Spattered Schoolhouse Honey Jar—The Schoolhouse is Red with a Yellow Roof—The space at right of building is green and the ground is brown.

FIGURE 179 Red Spattered Creamer customarily referred to as "Hex Sign".

FIGURE 180 unusual Deer cup 3-inch diameter by 3 inches high—Soft paste—very early—Cut sponge design in brown-yellow ground—green dashes with brown spots to resemble flowers and sod.

FIGURE 181 mug with Spattered X—Spattered top and bottom edge and with a Strawberry or Thumbprint design.

FIGURE 182 Rose design similar to Figure 21 except in two shades of Blue.

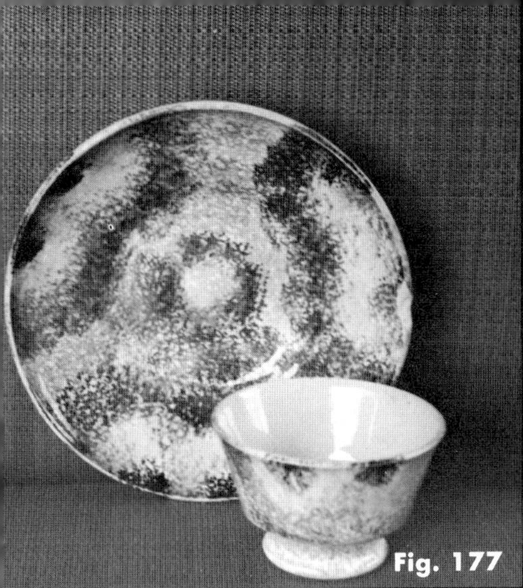
Fig. 177

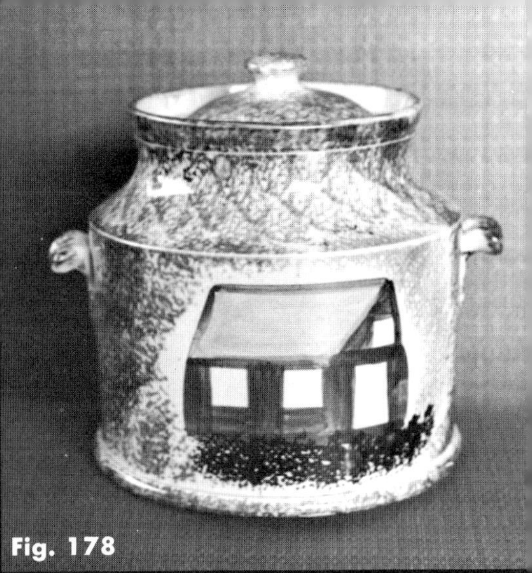
Fig. 178

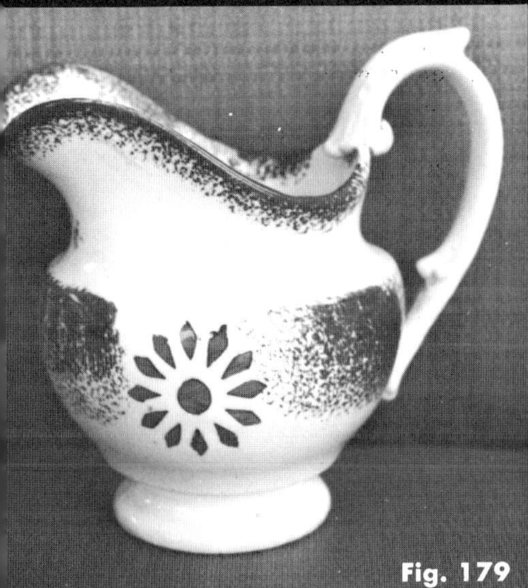
Fig. 179

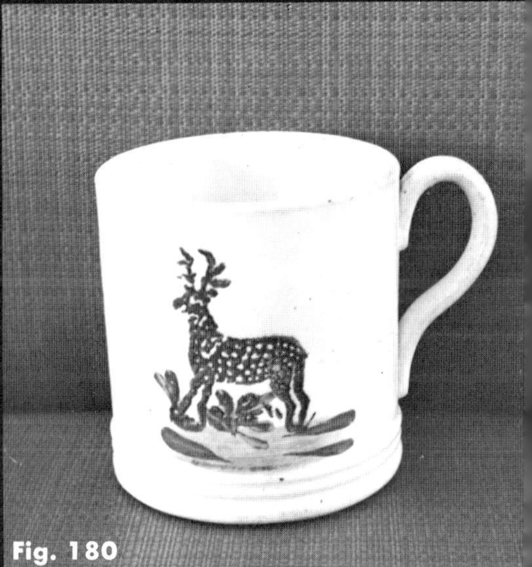
Fig. 180

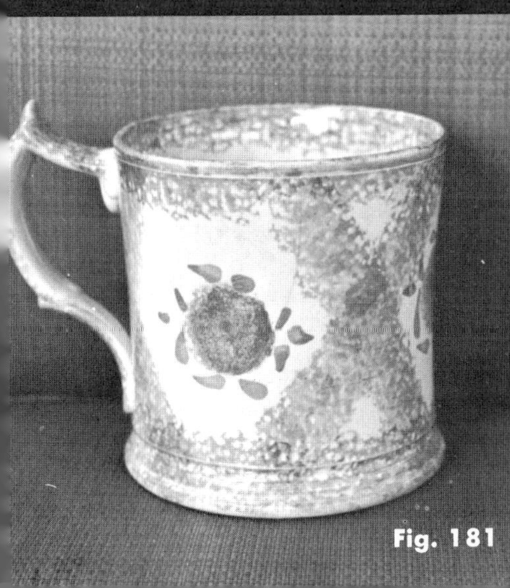
Fig. 181

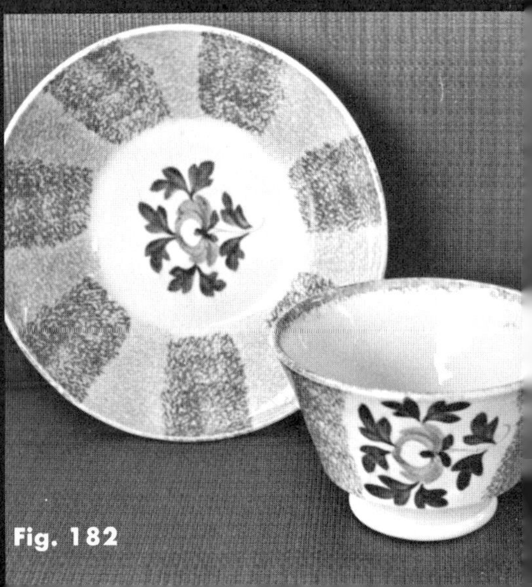
Fig. 182

FIGURE 183 Large Spattered Dot like #58 except the border here is Red and the center Dot is Yellow instead of matching border.

FIGURE 184 Six Petal Red Flower—the center is a similar shade of Red—the small marks between the petals and the buds are a dark blue and the leaves are green.

FIGURE 185 Primrose creamer—the top edge and the bottom are Green Spattered and the portion from the flower to the white section above it is Blue Spattered. The flower is an off shade of Red—more like Rust.

FIGURE 186 Rose bud but the Rose is Red and the foliage immediately behind the Rose as well as the Bud is a dark Blue.

FIGURE 187 Chinaman in a Garden—Creamware-1790 potting-Wedgwood shape.

FIGURE 188 Windmill with ladder—inspired by Edward Ward, Senior, Brislington, 1680—The Windmill is elevated with no visible means of support, the ladder seems to go to the water level, but it supports the weight of the man who is descending it with an object on his head which he is holding, there are two types of boats navigating the stream and the apple tree beyond the fence line is heavily laden with fruit—see FIGURE V.

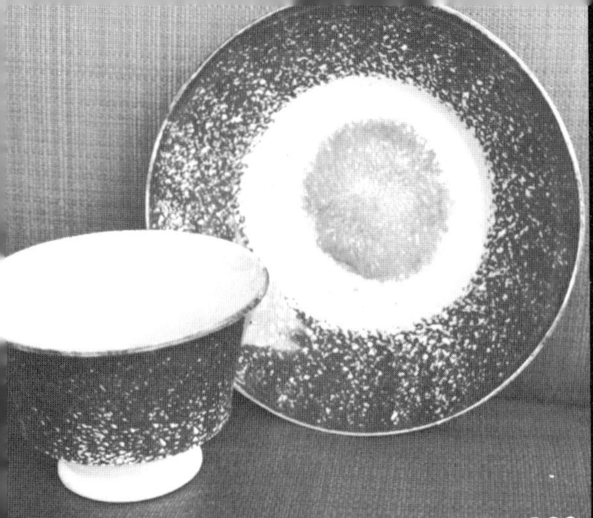
Fig. 183

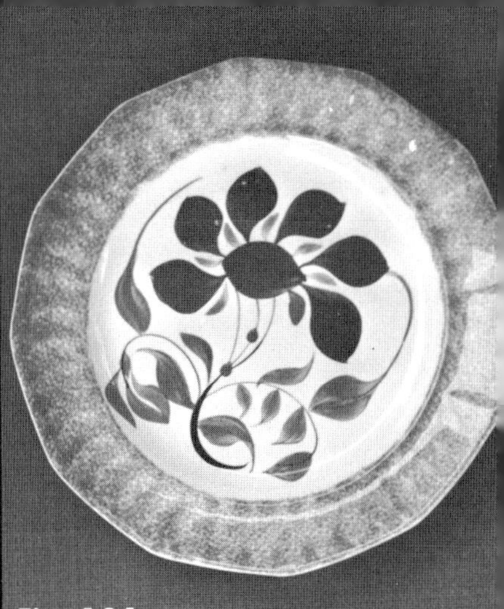
Fig. 184

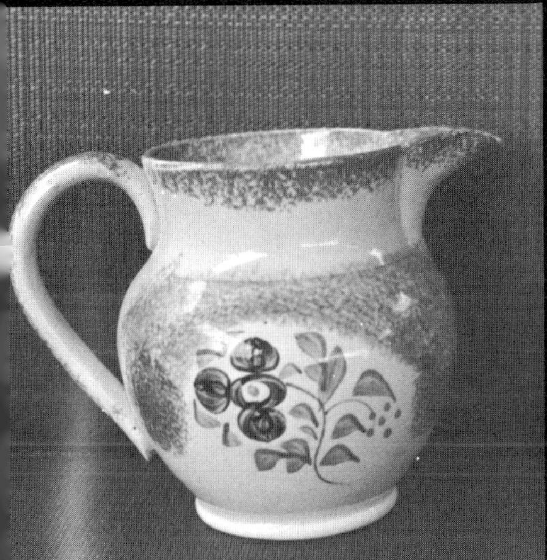
Fig. 185

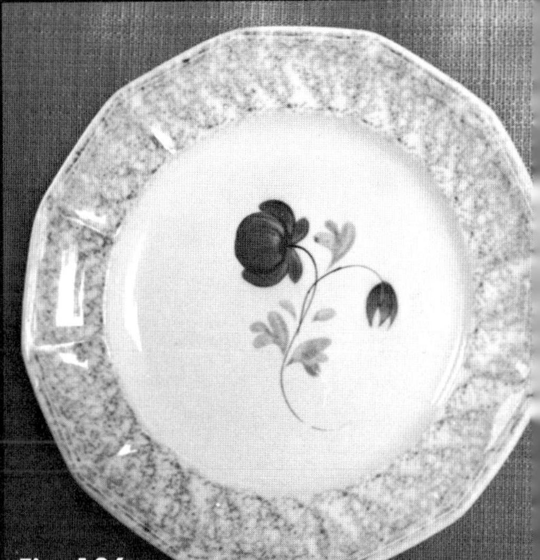
Fig. 186

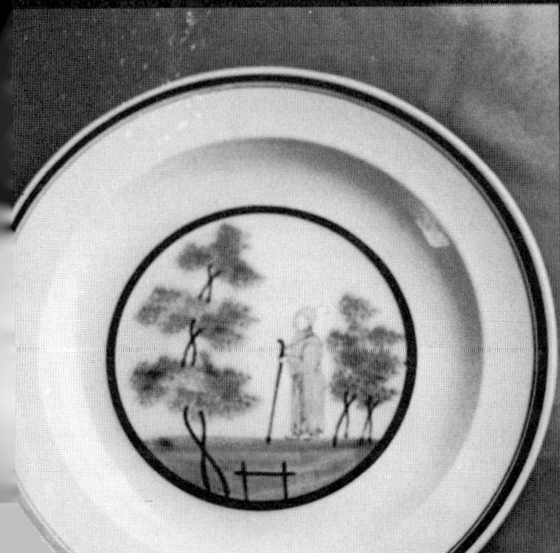
Fig. 187

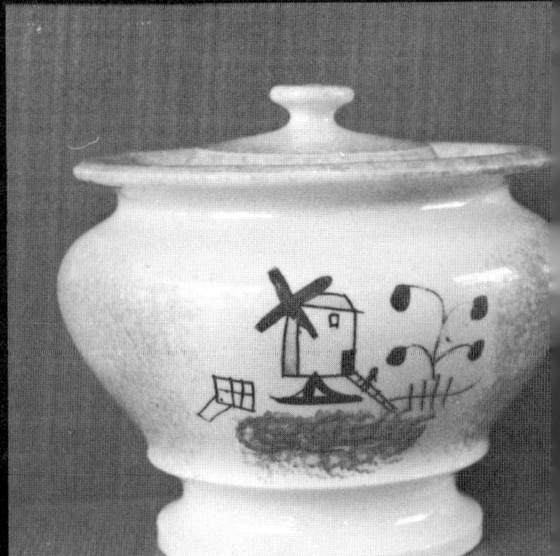
Fig. 188

FIGURE 189 Deer Trade Mark of Adams used 1804 to 1904—as per William Turner-William Adams—"An Old English Potter"—page 128.

FIGURE 190 Eagle and Shield Trade Mark combined with Registry mark of Adam's used 1840 to 1904 as per William Turner—see above—This mark was used by Adam's Pottery on their Graniteware, and does not cover the design.

FIGURE 191 Adam's Design Spatterware produced by means of cut sponges as described by William Turner and using Trade Mark as FIGURE 190 above.

FIGURE 192 as above (an open vegetable dish—not pictured—bears the Deer Trade Mark as FIGURE 189 above).

FIGURE 193 Adam's Design Spatterware bearing mark as FIGURE 190 also.

FIGURE 194 Adam's Design Spatterware covered vegetable dish marked as FIGURE 190 above.

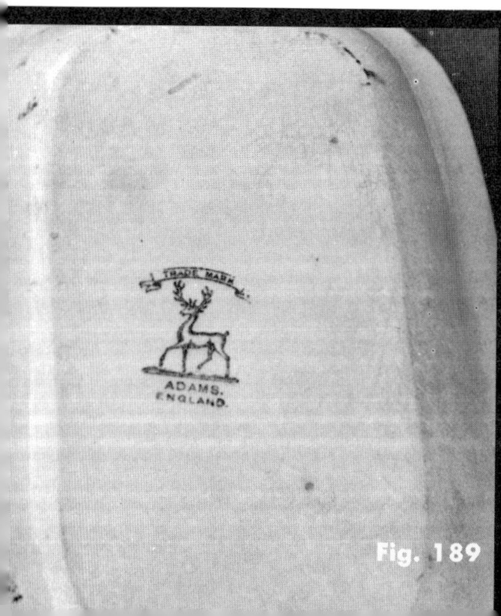

Fig. 189

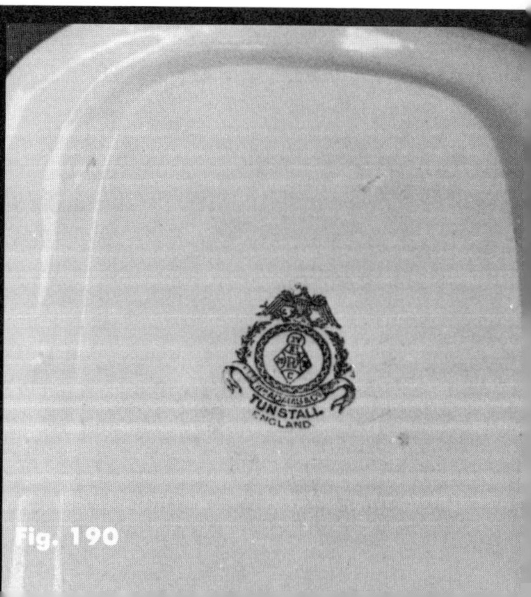

Fig. 190

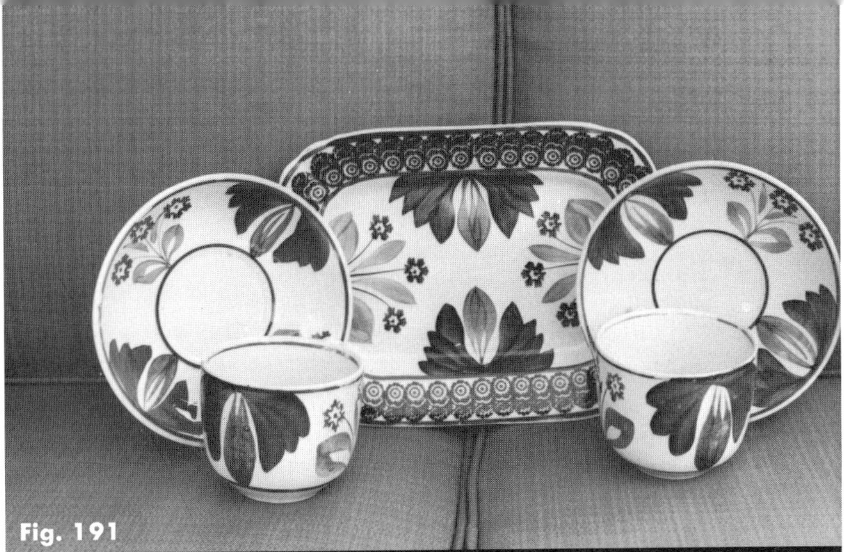

Fig. 191

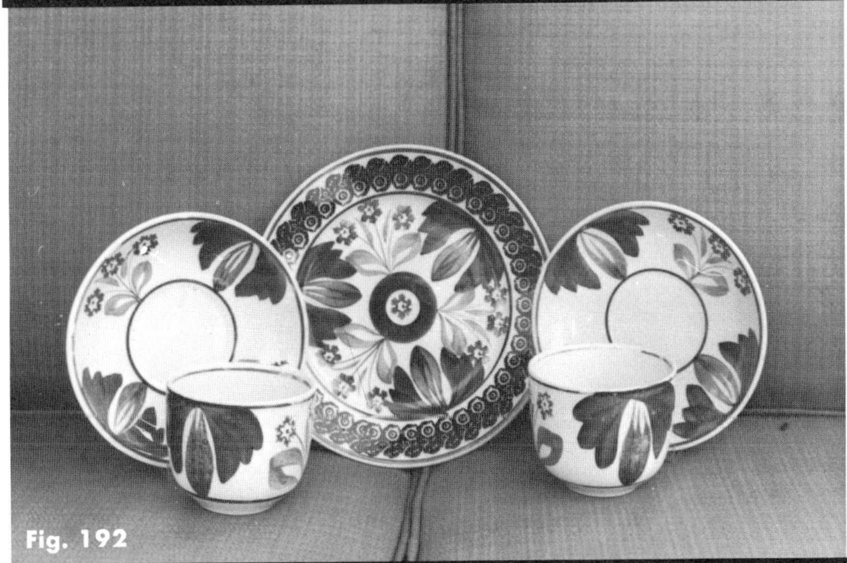

Fig. 192

Fig. 193

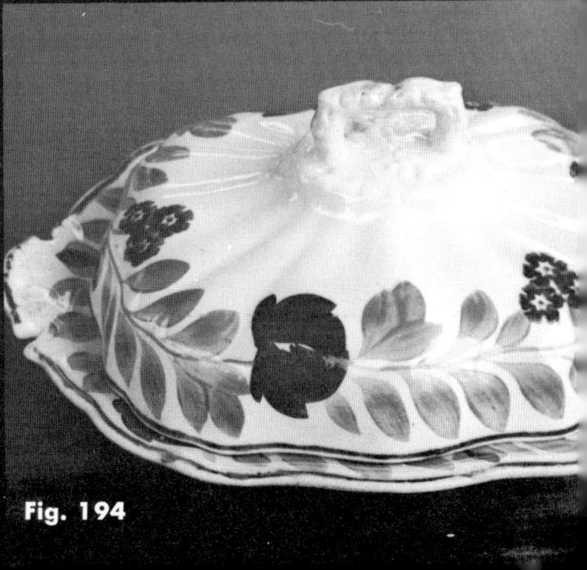

Fig. 194

FIGURE 195 plate of Design Spatterware made 1866 to 1870 by J F Wileman at the Foley Potteries. The border and the flower are a brick Red but there are two shades of Red used as well as one shade of blue and one of green.

FIGURE 196 is an assortment of wild colors, quite similar to FIGURE 195 and quite possibly made by J F Wileman as well.

FIGURE 197 plate Design Spatter—The Fruit is Red, the flowers are blue, and the leaves are two shades of green.

FIGURE 198 bowl with Red Design Spatter flowers and blue Spatter rim.

FIGURE 199 all green Design Spatter leaves and a Red rim.

FIGURE 200 Mixing Dish in Stoneware Sponged in a Brown color on a tan background.

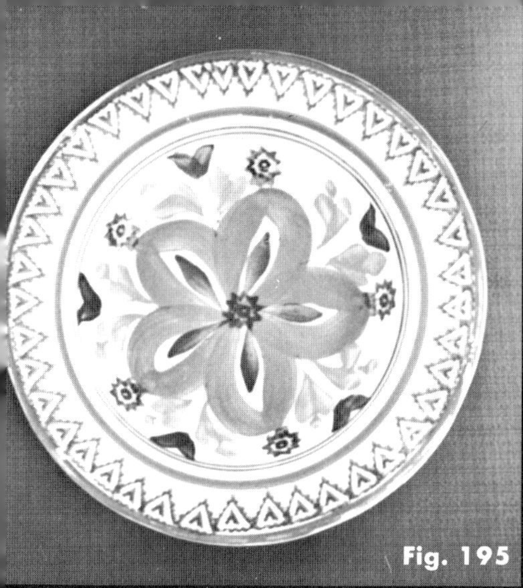

Fig. 195

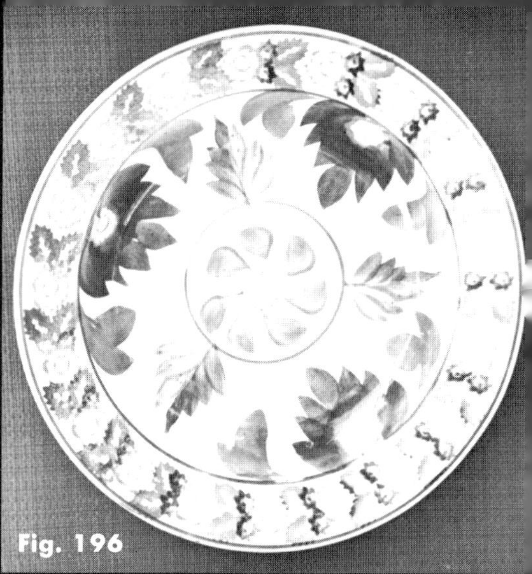

Fig. 196

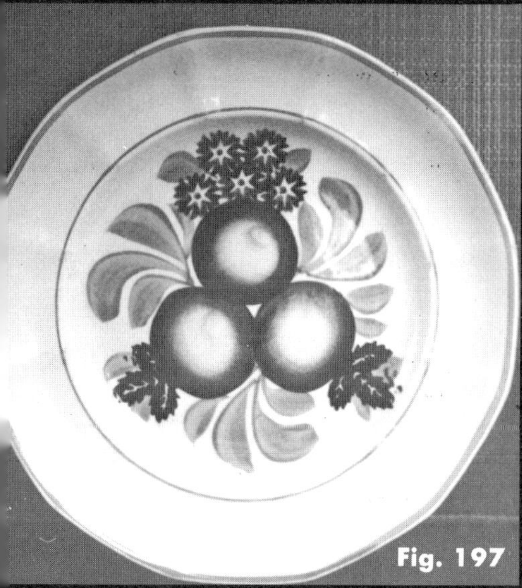

Fig. 197

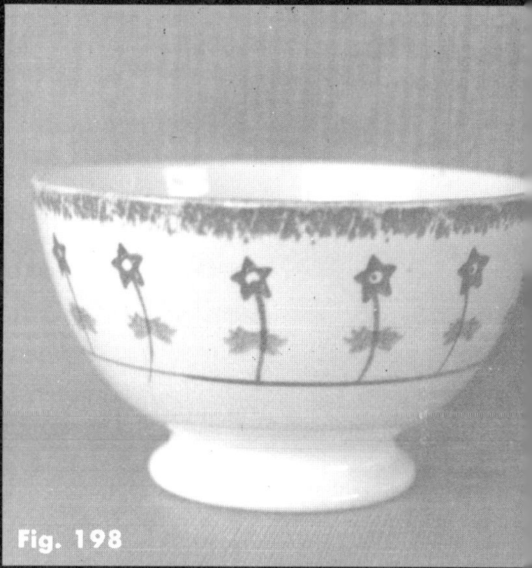

Fig. 198

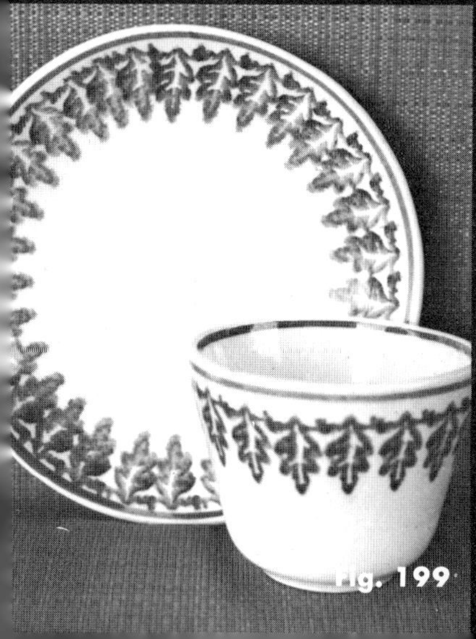

Fig. 199

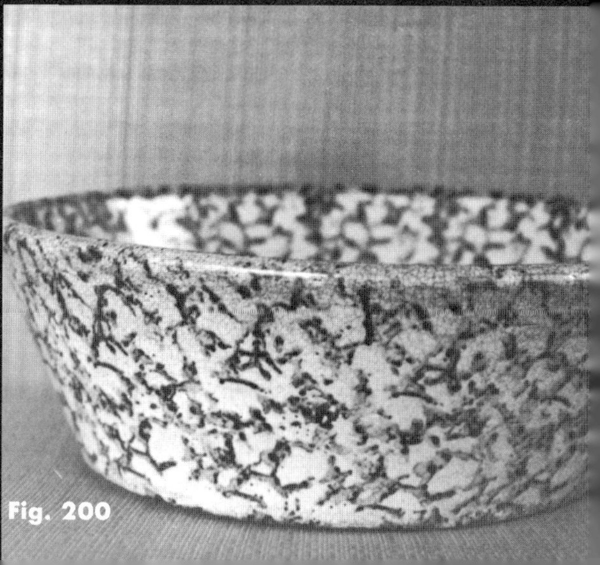

Fig. 200

FIGURE 201 Red Roses, Blue Star Flowers, Green and Yellow leaves, and a Red line at rim. Plate is marked "Guaranteed Leadless Glaze". (Possibly the John Rose Borax method.)

FIGURE 202 Rose flower in center, Rose and light Blue Design Spatter flowers or symbols at rim, green leaves and blue buds, with a red line at rim. Seems to be of a similar composition to 201.

FIGURE 203 Adam's Design Spatterware plate with identical marking to 190 but observe the round and round loops between the Roses among the foliage as done with a brush and in a manner as usually associated with the wrist movement recommended in penmanship classes.

FIGURE 204 bowl with flower and Design Spatter similar to Adam's FIGURE 203 and with the same round and round loops as in the foregoing example but printed Baker & Co.,

FIGURE 205 plate with similar characteristics to the previous 2 items and with the same exercises but made in Holland and marked as 206.

FIGURE 206 marking on back of plate #205—Petrus Regout & Co.-Maastricht-Holland.

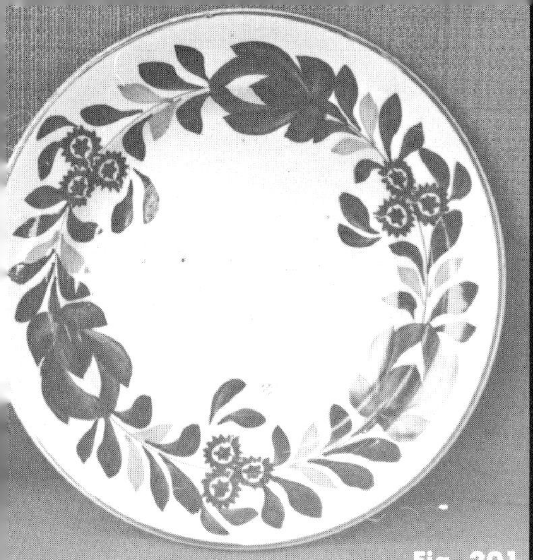

Fig. 201

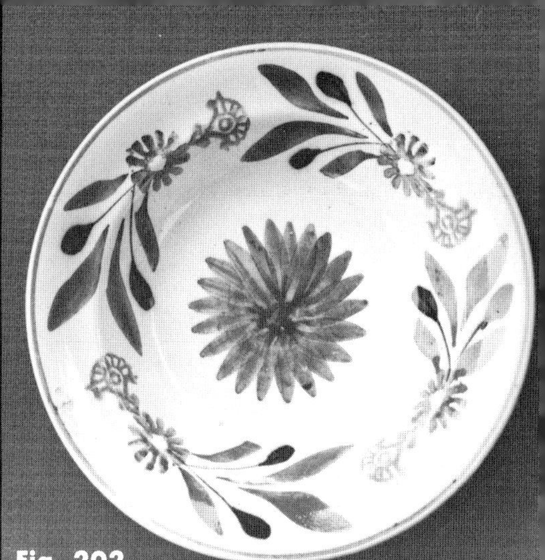

Fig. 202

Fig. 203

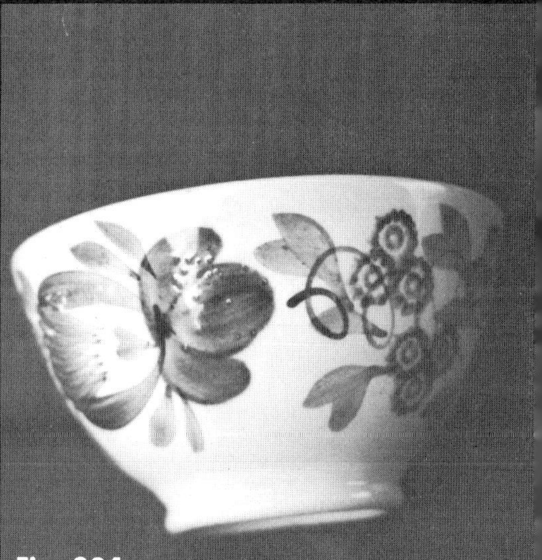

Fig. 204

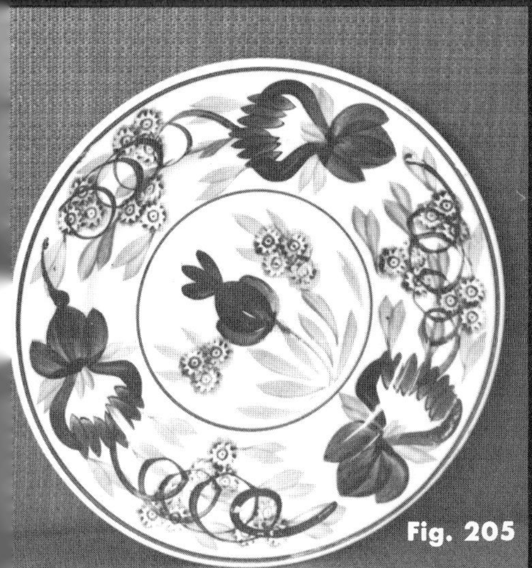

Fig. 205

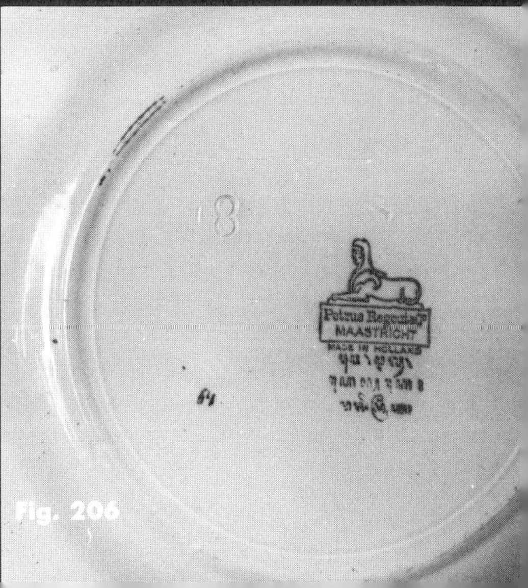


Fig. 206

FIGURE 207 two color Rainbow plate 8 inch diameter with a 3¼ inch diameter black circle enclosing a plain undecorated center and red and blue spattered bands radiating to edge from circle.

FIGURE 208 another variation of Spray design with two flowers formed by 7 blue dots each and one flower formed by 6 red rots enclosing a blue center dot. This cup and saucer are miniature with a 4½ inch diameter saucer and a 3 inch diameter cup 2 inches high.

FIGURE 209 A Childs Necessary—Blue Spattered top rim and handle—Rim 6½ inches outside diameter and 5 inches inside diameter—overall 3½ inches high, with a different nursery rhyme on either side and a completely unnecessary warning humorously on bottom. (This is one side).

FIGURE 209-A other side and bottom of 209. Transfer in blue and trees Spattered.

FIGURE 210 part of a plain overall blue Spatter miniature set with 2¾ inch diameter scalloped edge plates—3½ inch diameter plates and 4¼ inch diameter plates all with similarly scalloped edges, and a 2 piece gravy boat 1½ inch overall height by 2½ inches length.

FIGURE 211 additional pieces from 210 miniature set of blue Spatter—three piece Soup tureen 3¼ inches overall height including the 4¼ inch diameter round tray on which it stands—(Note Acorn and leaf finial)—2 piece covered Vegetable dish 2¼ inches high by 4¼ inch diameter, similar finial and scalloped edges.

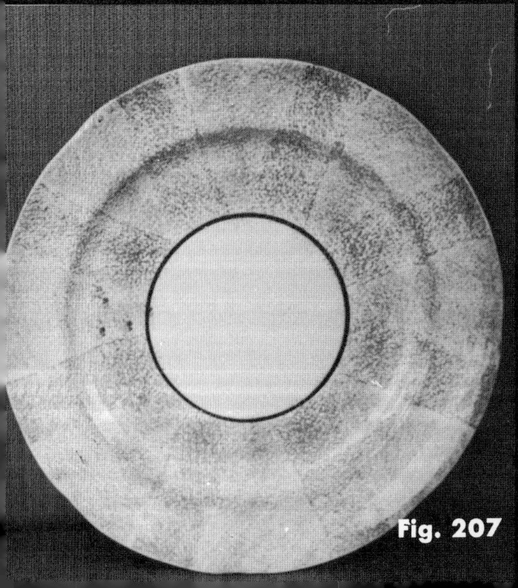
Fig. 207

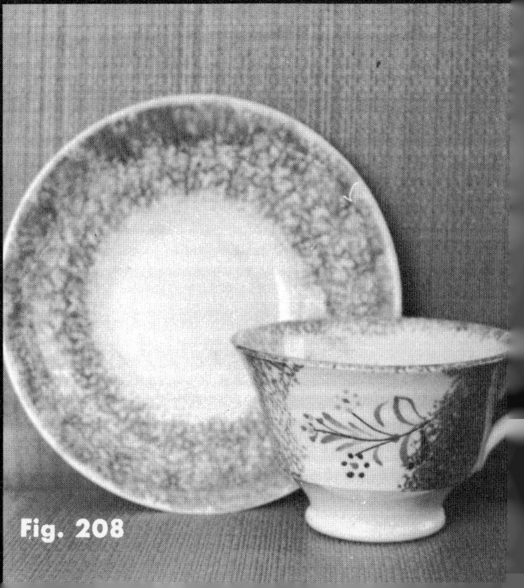
Fig. 208

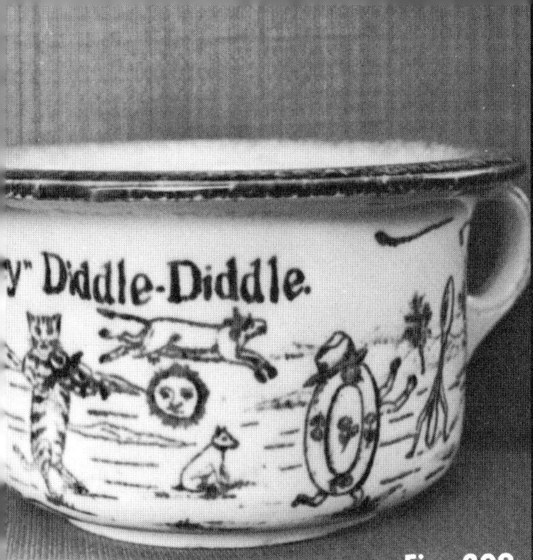


Fig. 209

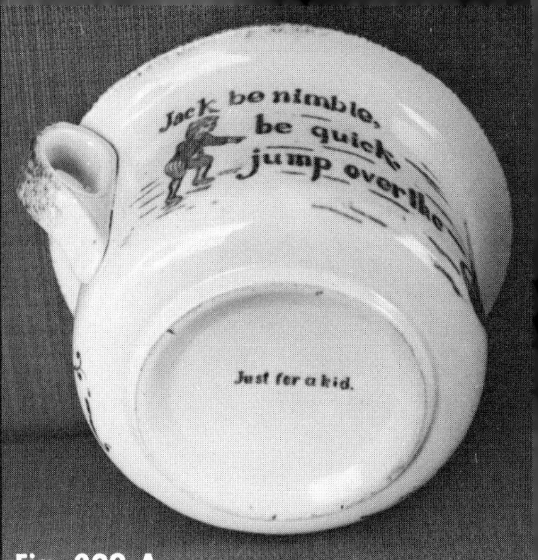


Fig. 209-A

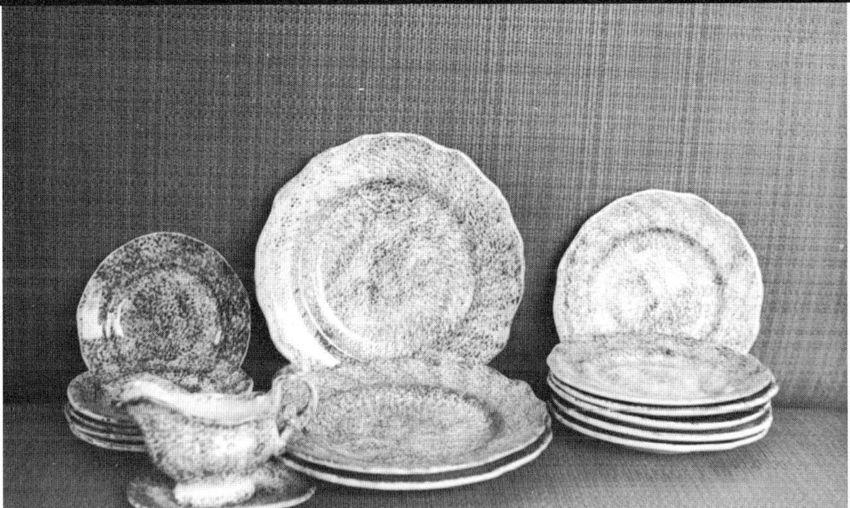

Fig. 210

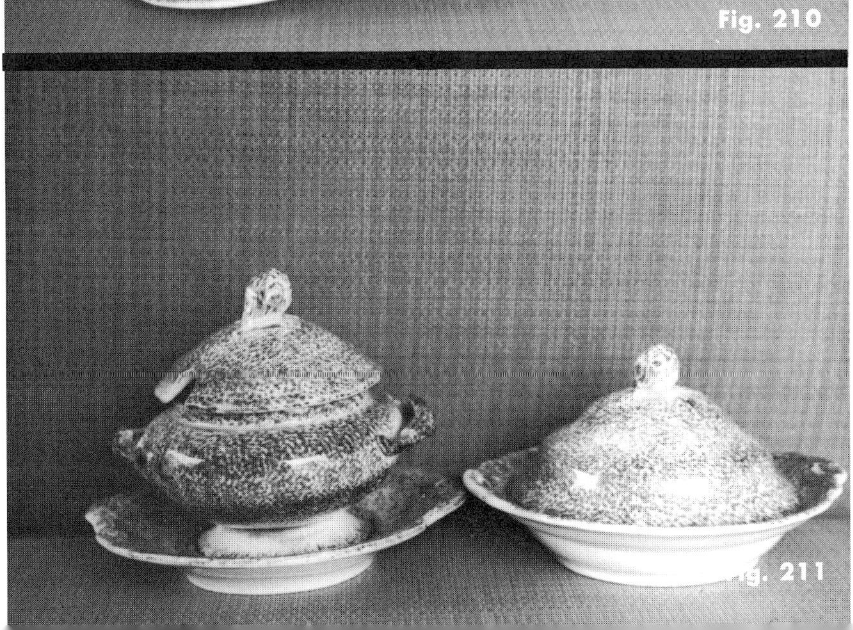

Fig. 211

FIGURE 212 additional pieces from 210—Blue Spattered well and tree platter with scalloped edge, 5 inches long by 3¾ inches wide—a 4 inch by 3 inch platter—two 4 inch by 3 inch open vegetables and a 3 inch by 2¼ inch open vegetable dish, all with similar scalloped edges.

FIGURE 213 a Spongeware miniature set in blue with 4 inch plates—3½ inch diameter saucers—3 inch diameter cups 1½ inches high—3½ inch Teapot and similarly proportioned sugar and creamer.

FIGURE 214 Crystal Palace Tea Pot. This Palace built in 1851 in Hyde Park, London, so captured the imagination of all that it was reproduced in Prints by N Currier, in transfers as on this Tea Pot, etc. The crystal semi-circular roof, 104 feet high, designed to retain several of the trees which stood at this location in their identical position, made it a dramatic feature of the exhibition and gave the building its name.

FIGURE 215 Arabian Horse, trainer with lance—blue Spattered border and blue transfer—7½ inch plate with a seemingly jousting scene.

FIGURE 216 9½ inch plate—3 red circles—black sponged designs on border—brown and blue flowered center—3 brown flowers on outer circle with red flowers.

FIGURE 217 9½ inch plate—bold black designs on border—3 blue and red flowers and 3 lavender and blue flowers and leaves on outer circle—one blue flower and green leaves in center circle.

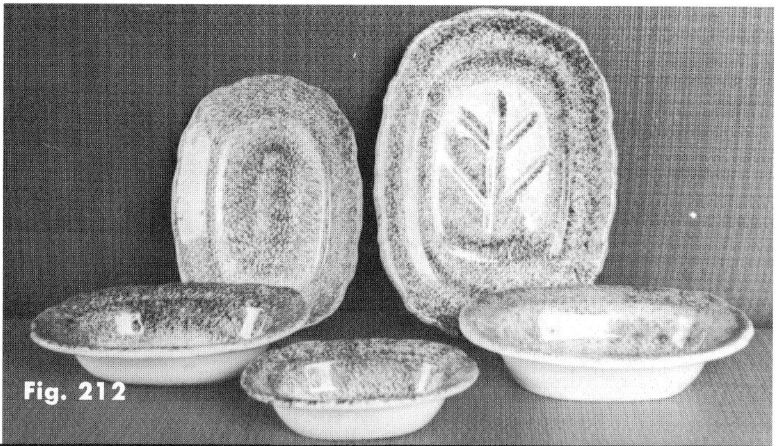

Fig. 212

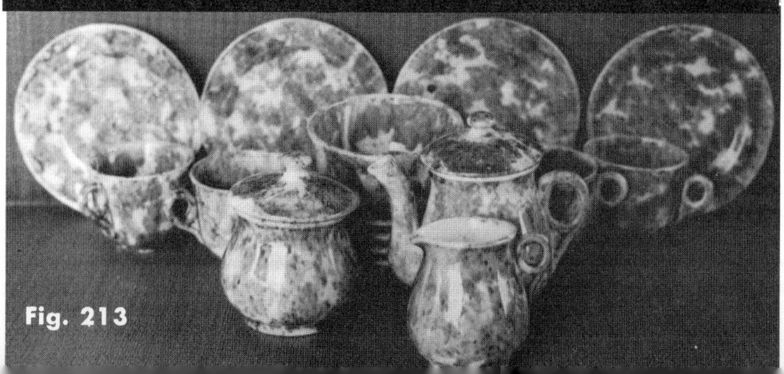

Fig. 213

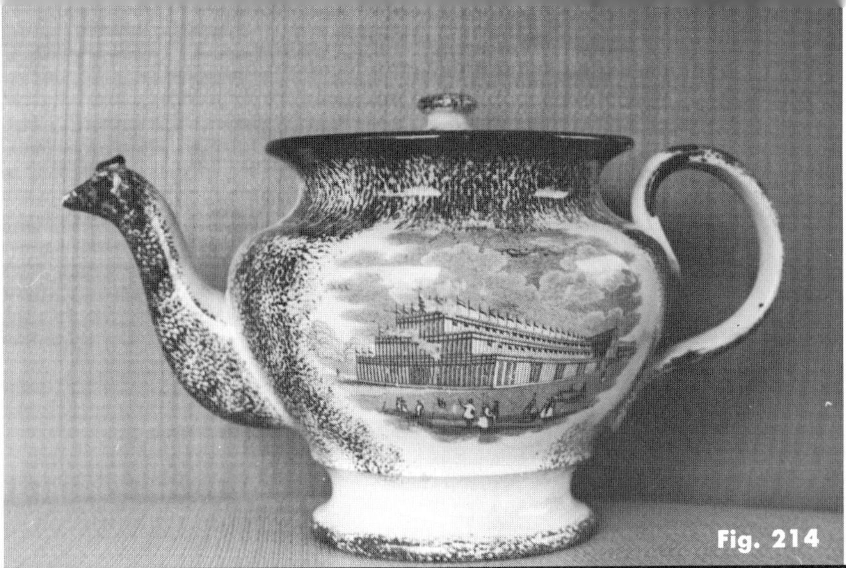
Fig. 214

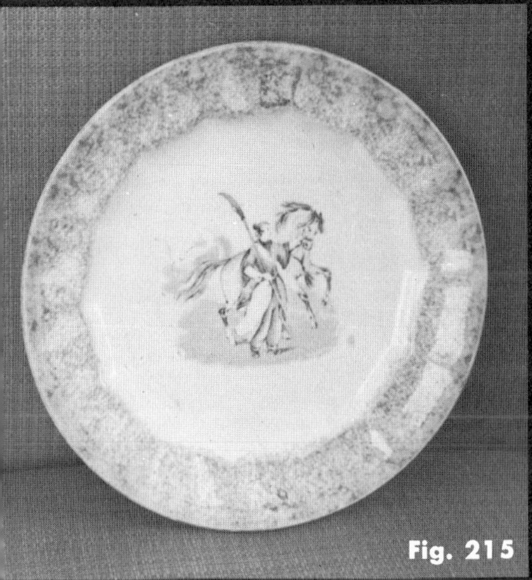
Fig. 215

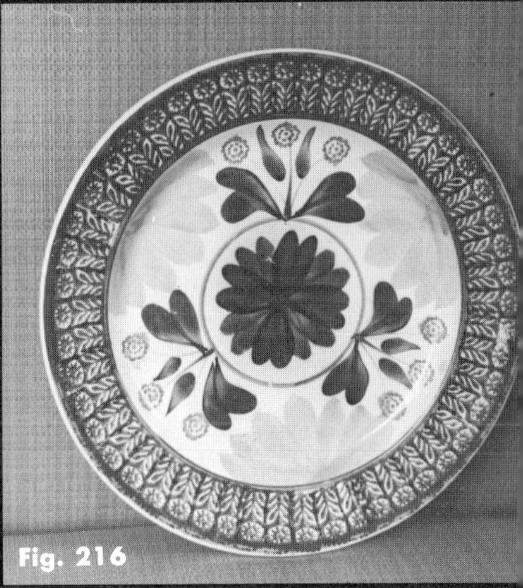
Fig. 216

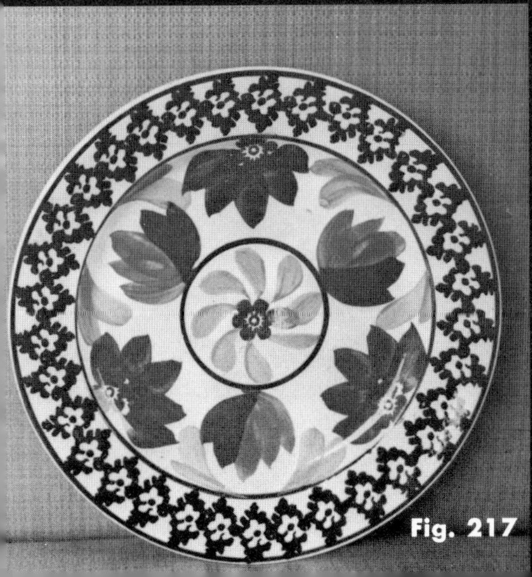
Fig. 217

FIGURE 218 19 inch charger Flow Blue and multiple types and kinds of red cut sponge designs.

FIGURE 219 9½ inch plate red line at rim—green design (presumably leaves) on rim—red garland on star shaped flowers in center of plate—very heavy—Ironstone type—impressed—"Clemson Brothers—Hanley."

FIGURE 220 8 inch plate, blue designs closely grouped around border—Mayer Pottery Mfg. Co.—Beaver Falls, Penna.—1881.

FIGURE 221 8 inch plate—brown designs around rim and with blue flowers and brown leaves in inside design—Mayer Pottery Mfg. Co.—Beaver Falls, Penna.—1881.

FIGURE 222 a 17 inch by 13 inch platter with a green line at edge and with red butterfly border-Stoke-On-Trent.

FIGURE 223 Cottage Ware with a Design Spatter decoration produced with cut Sponges.

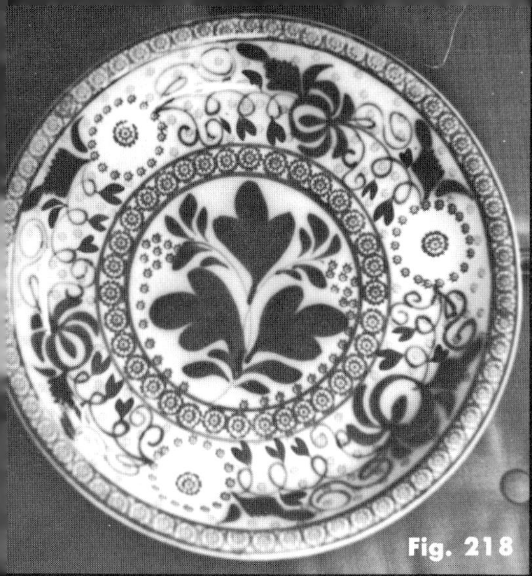
Fig. 218

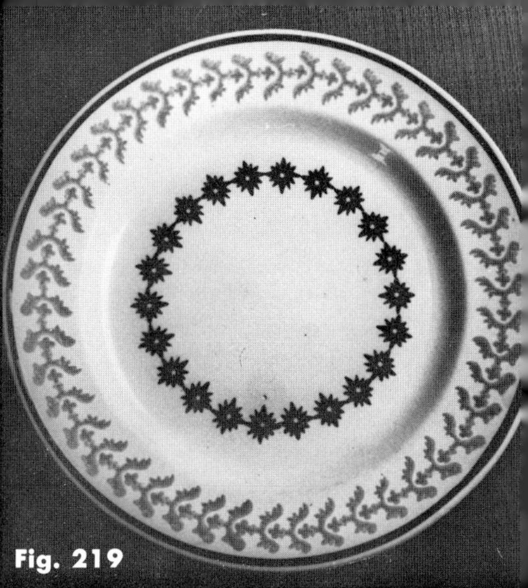
Fig. 219

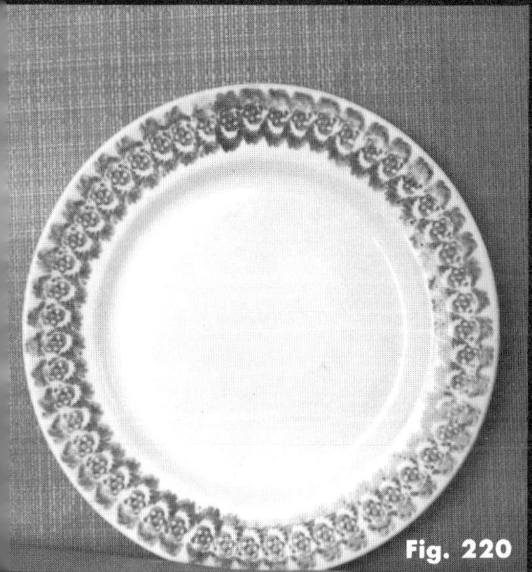
Fig. 220

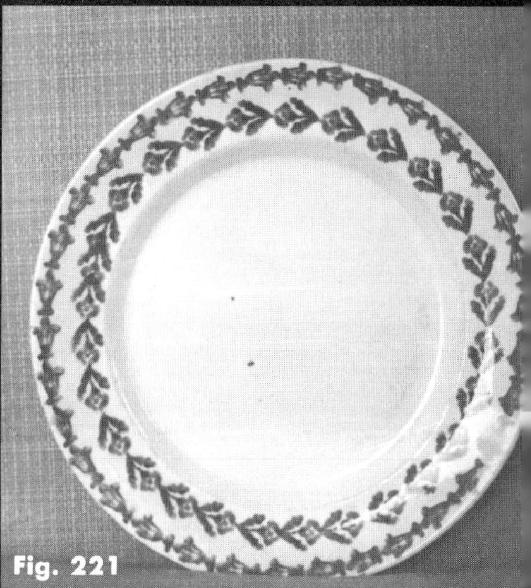
Fig. 221

Fig. 222

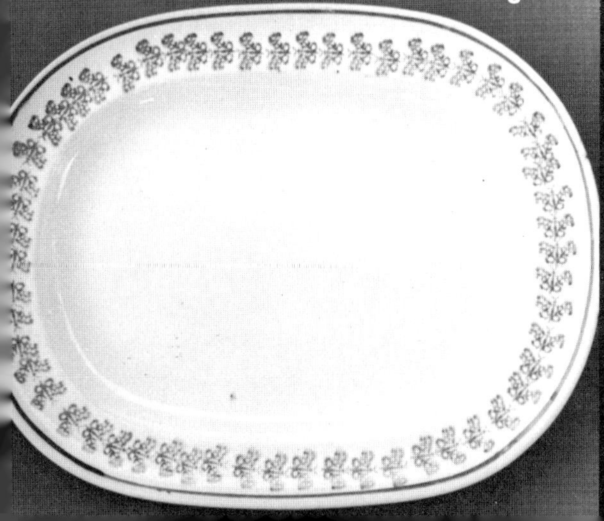

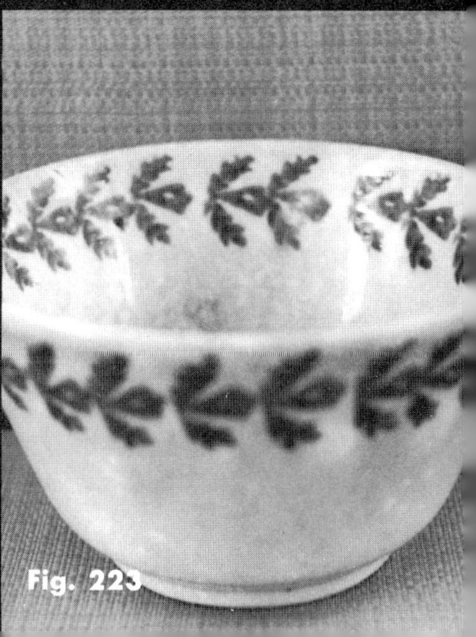
Fig. 223

FIGURE 224 9 inch plate with an outer and an inner circle in green—the leaves on rim between these two circles are red and the leaves inside of rim are green—the flowers were formed by the use of a sponge using 6 spots and using a blue color.

FIGURE 225 an open vegetable dish, unmarked, Graniteware, blue Design Spatterware very cleanly and carefully done, a soft glaze, no doubt Staffordshire origin.

FIGURE 226 9 inch plate with an outer and an inner circle in red—the rabbits and frogs are in brown transfer with the frogs and the cabbage filled in later in green—center star in blue surrounded by stars in red inside inner circle—green stars between this small circle and inner rim circle blue flowers and red leaves—Staffordshire, in fact the stars are so nearly the size, the shape and the color of the smaller stars on FIGURE 218—charger—as to almost indicate that they could have been made in the same pottery and at about the same time. Based on a comparison of color and relative size of the animals to surroundings it would appear that these are the brown hare of Britain rather than the Irish variety described in "Manual of British Vertebrate Animals"—1835 by Jengens or the Scottish variety, known, we believe, as the blue hare.

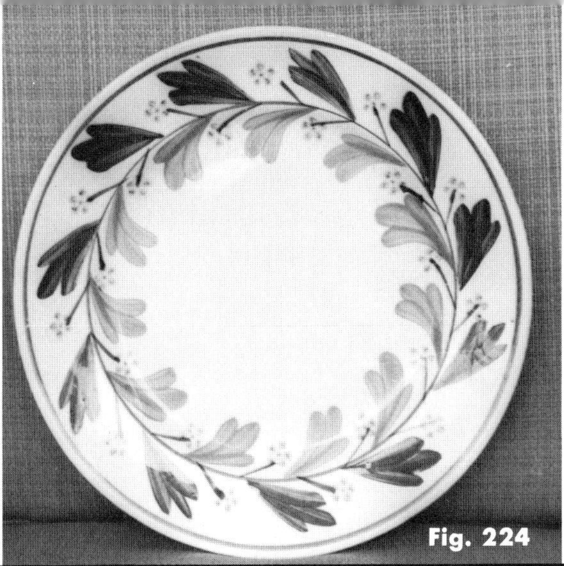

Fig. 224

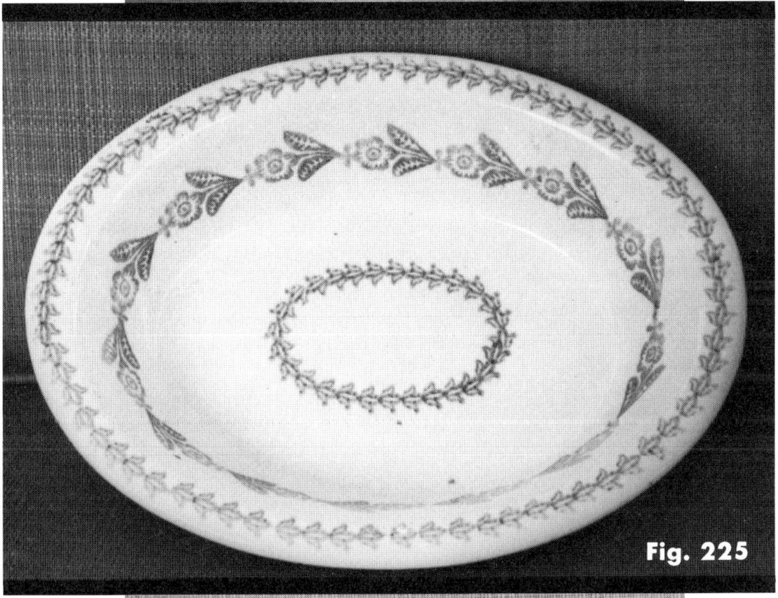

Fig. 225

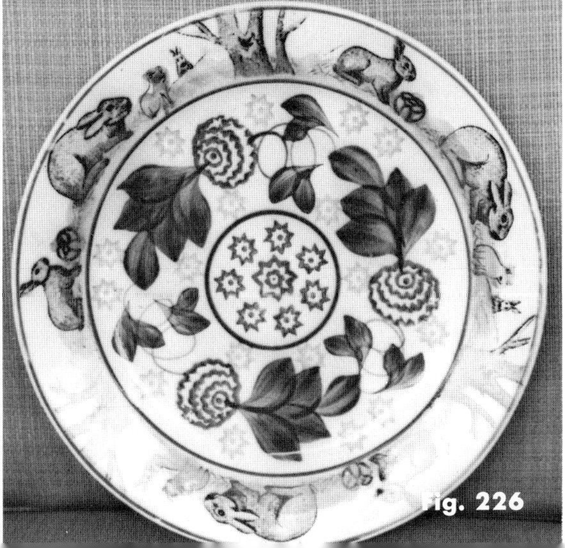

Fig. 226

FIGURE 227 9¼ inch plate Rabbit design similar to 226 on border but the center decoration is roses leaning more toward the Adams rose type. Heavy Ironstone type—unmarked.

FIGURE 228 9¼ inch plate—large red flowers with green leaves and blue starflowers on rim and with a 4¾ inch diameter sepia picture in center with a fence and four rabbits at play.

FIGURE 229 9¼ inch plate border identical to 228 but the center picture in sepia has no fence and only three rabbits but a green frog has been added —Ironstone type no marking.

FIGURE 230 9¼ inch plate—red line at rim—green stars—red double leaves and blue flowers and larger seven edged leaves—heavy but not as heavy as the above three examples—sepia picture in center has three rabbits at rest—only marking is three lines side by side in blue. The center one is the larger one and the top and bottom lines are slightly smaller.

FIGURE 231 9 inch plate—red line at rim—red flower, green leaves, blue five edged leaves and smaller blue star flowers—Heavy Ironstone type—stamped "Made in Great Britain" and inside of the circle where this appears is an anchor otherwise undecipherable.

FIGURE 232 9½ inch plate—red design border resembling berries and leaves—a red line is inside this border and four small brown star flowers on brown stems are separated by green leaves and four five edged leaves three of the edges in red and two in blue—an unmarked lighter type Ironstone.

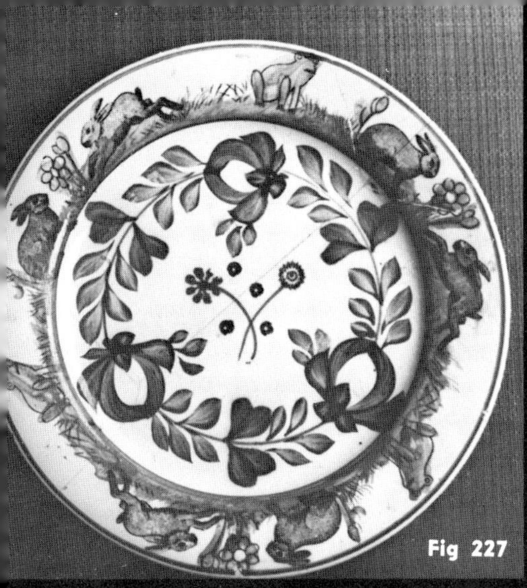
Fig 227

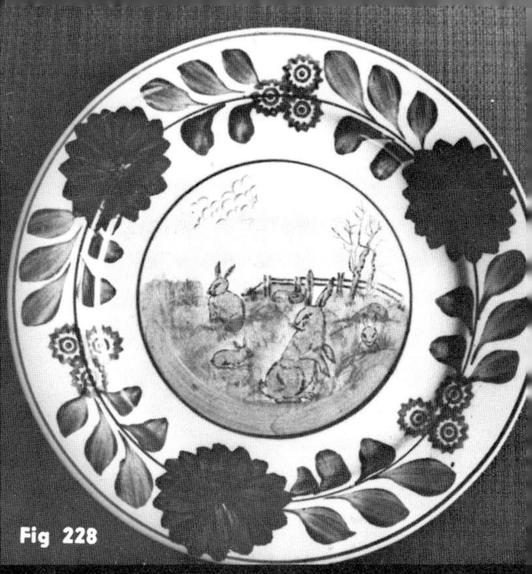
Fig 228

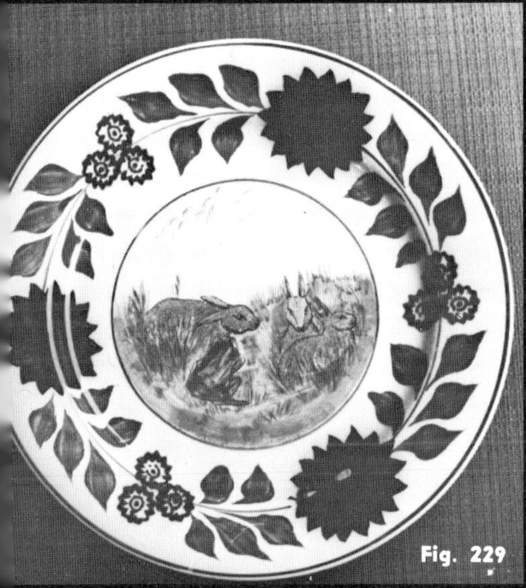
Fig. 229

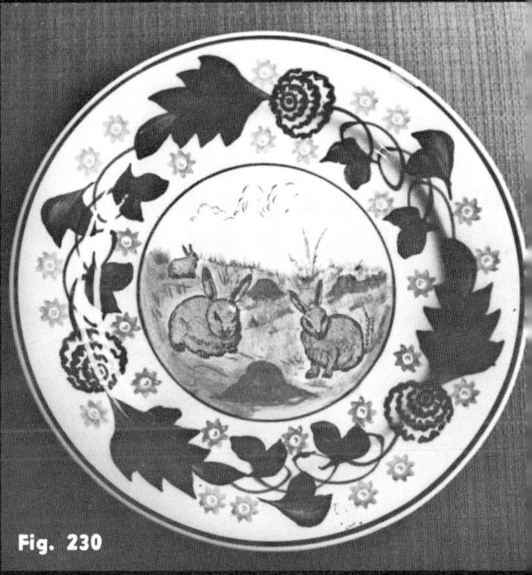
Fig. 230

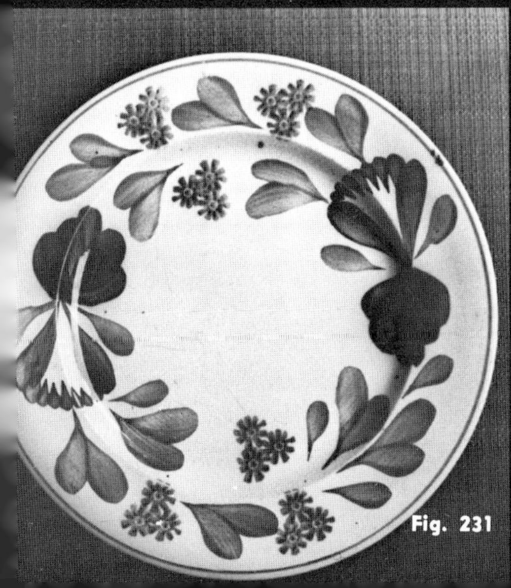
Fig. 231

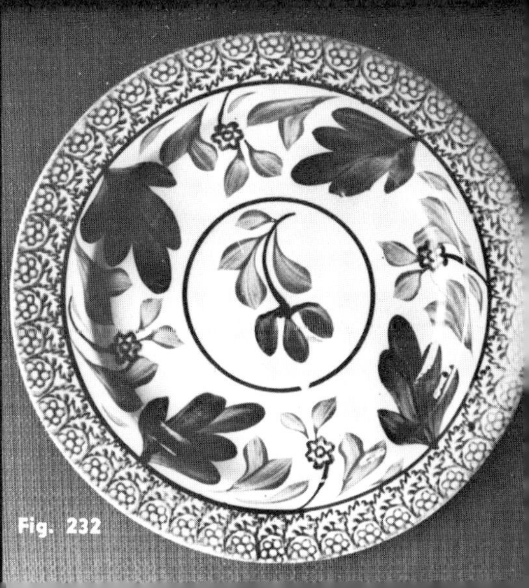
Fig. 232

FIGURE 233 8½ inch plate with a yellow and purple tulip as FIGURE 50 but with a red line rim and inner line in red and the design border in green of an entirely different pattern—unmarked.

FIGURE 234 8⅞ inch plate—line at rim—star flowers—and the seven drapes well as the center circle in red—the presumed leaves in green and the three edged leaves in blue; a clean design and colorful—Impressed "Edge, Malkin & Co." Not otherwise marked, presumably 1871-1890.

FIGURE 235 8¾ inch plate—4 red circles—on edge are 28 green stars each one circled by a blue circle. Not marked—medium heavy.

FIGURE 236 A necessity having a flat rim, red flowers—a red line through the center and green leaves—the center loops seem to be leaves meeting at top and bottom to form a design but these are a much darker green than the balance of the leaves. Unmarked.

FIGURE 237 Miniature cup and saucer with a red line at top edge inside and outside and a green chain design—a very early example—inside on bottom rim has a very heavy bluish appearance from the excess accumulation of glaze. Not marked.

FIGURE 238 Cup and saucer with red open roses—blue starflowers and green leaves—not marked.

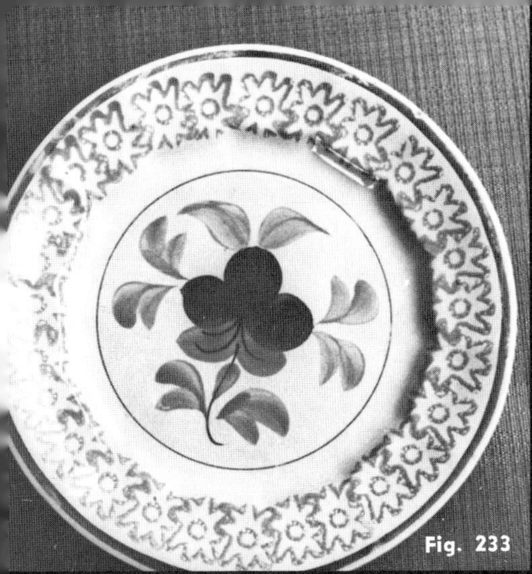
Fig. 233

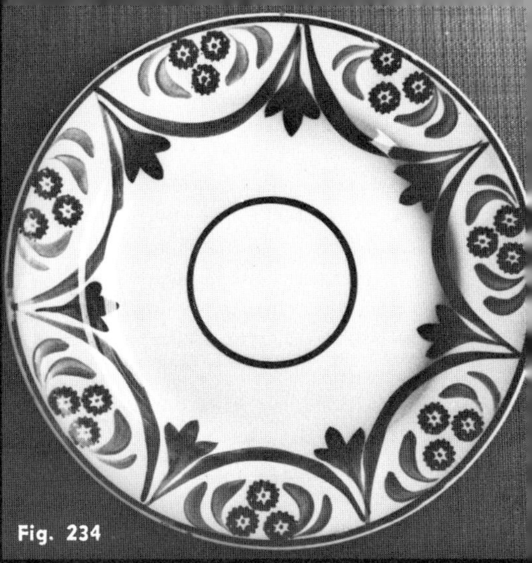
Fig. 234

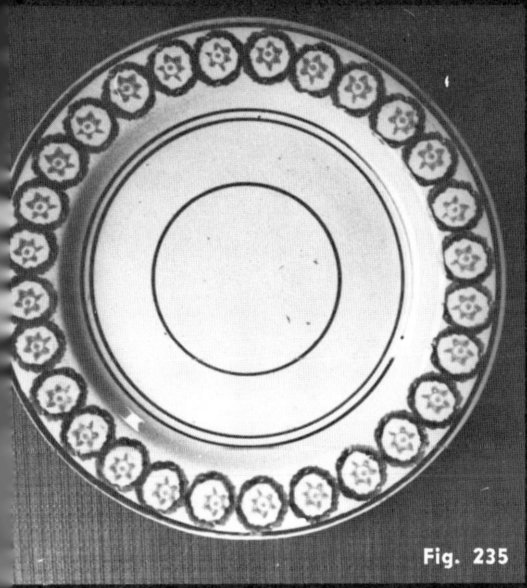
Fig. 235

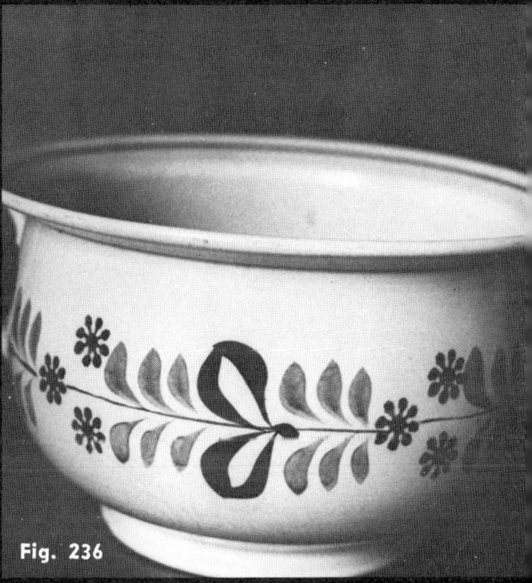
Fig. 236

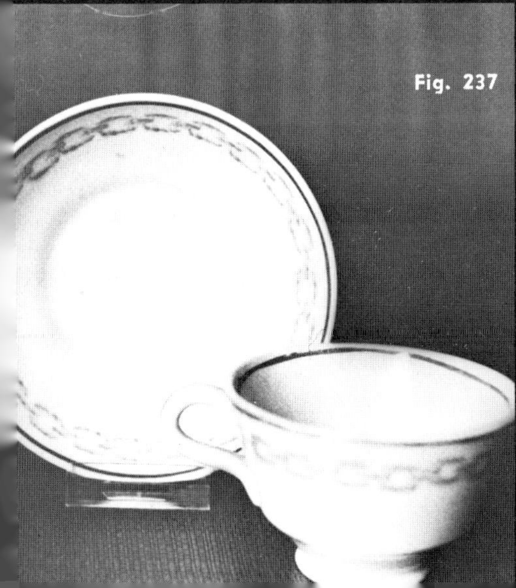
Fig. 237

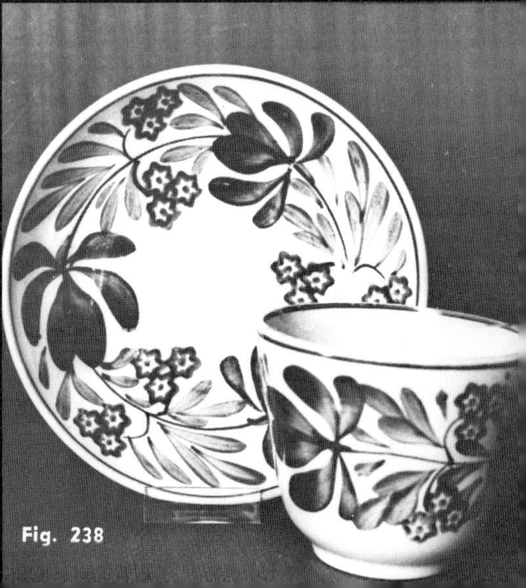
Fig. 238

FIGURE 239 Cup and saucer—red starflowers and blue starflowers alternating around the center of the cup and the rim of the saucer—all linked together by a blue line and separated by green leaves. An impressed design poorly done and undecipherable.

FIGURE 240 Cup and saucer—green line at edge with two rows of hearts facing one another around the circumference of the cup and the saucer in black and a red sprig between each of the upper hearts and a yellow sprig between each of the lower hearts.

FIGURE 241 Miniature cup and saucer—blue spattered edge and a blue tulip with brown shadings and brown cornflower shaped leaves—green leaves.

FIGURE 242 4 inch toddy plate—10 sides—star pattern in a sunburst spattered border.

FIGURE 243 7 inch 18th century soft paste octagon shaped plate—brown spattered border surrounding a brown line border—with a brown and a blue tulip—small brown flowers and green leaves.

FIGURE 244 3 inch diameter ball used in the English game as a Carpet Ball—completely covered by star flowered design spatter markings.

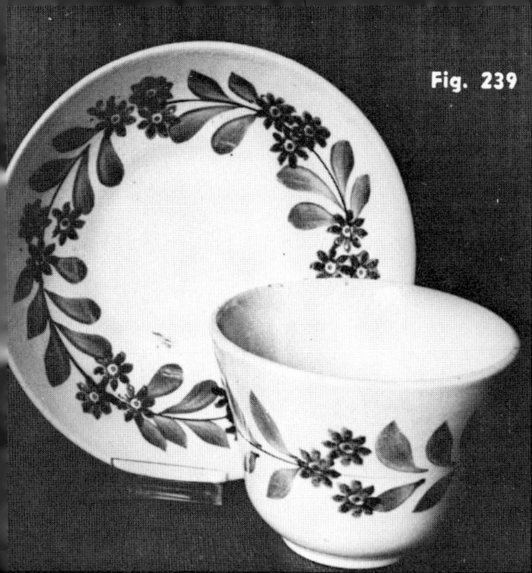
Fig. 239

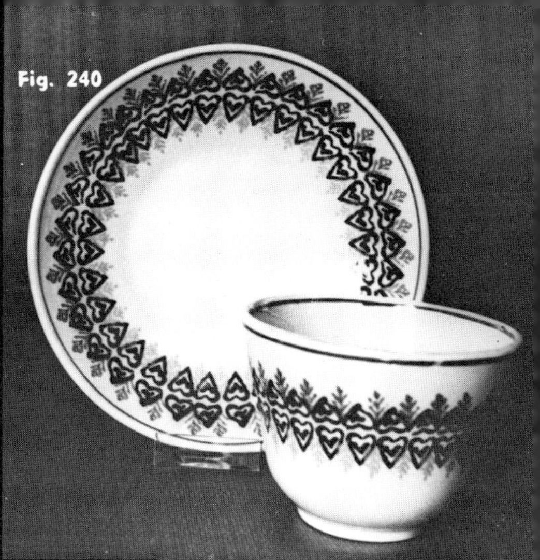
Fig. 240

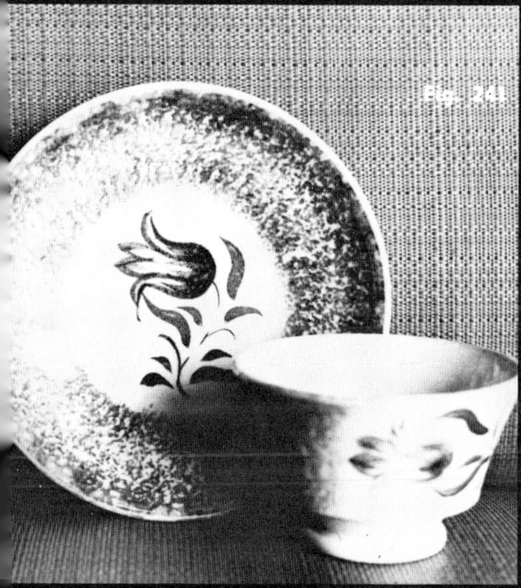
Fig. 241

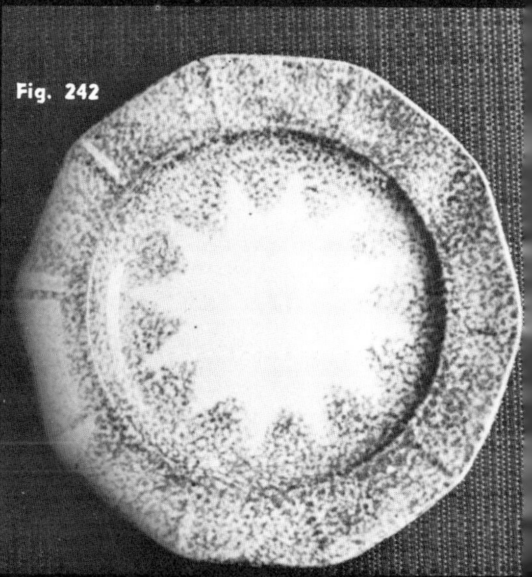
Fig. 242

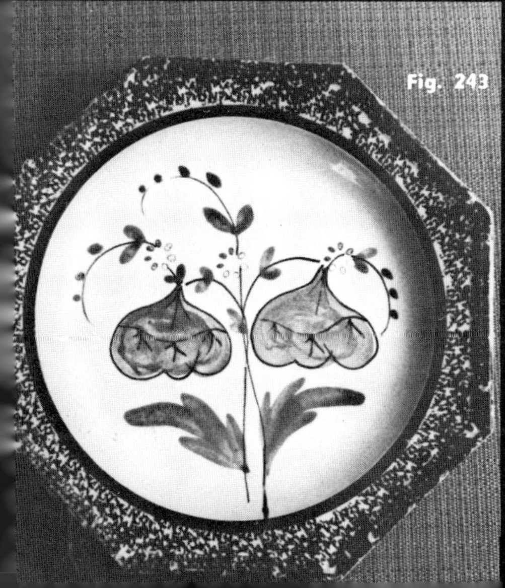
Fig. 243

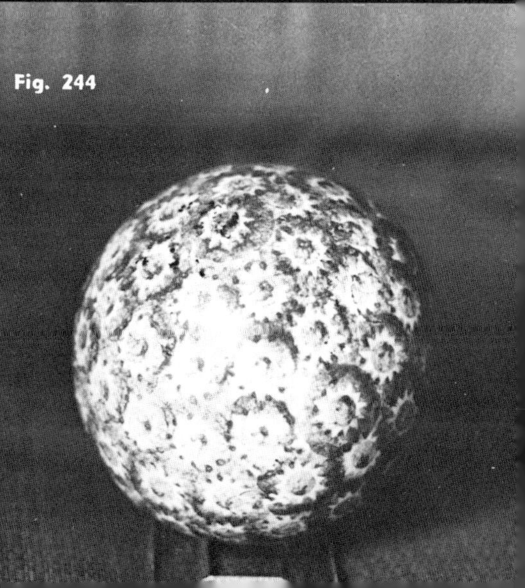
Fig. 244

Having decided to study this subject for our own gratification only, and to add to our own fund of knowledge we soon found that we had, of necessity, to discuss it with other collectors and dealers to secure their views to augment our own, and with few exceptions found that the above views were generally held. One collector and dealer asked if we would put these views in book or pamphlet form, giving our references for her guidance and pictures for her reference and we must have had about 30 or more similar requests.

One of the Curators we interviewed in regard to the Creamware examples asked that we put it in printed form in one manner or another after we had several opinions besides her own to settle it for all time and to have it in the files for later reference. Having it settled and a matter of record they would have the answers for their own reference in the future and for others to build on, to gain more and better knowledge of Antiques and to continue the ever continuing search for facts. A true example of an open mind policy and a credit to the Museum where she operates.

We then feel that we have an obligation to them for their kind guidance and assistance and are listing our findings and our opinions gained from this assistance and from our studies.

It may also be of assistance to that museum who has a large exhibition of this ceramic with a sign—At present, as in the past, there is more or less mystery concerning this type of ceramic. One point that is generally accepted is that it was made in the Staffordshire District of England and principally for the Pennsylvania Dutch trade—It is indeed a pathetic condition when only one fact is conceded regarding any subject and one that needs examining and study. We do not have all the answers and do not profess to do so, but we have advanced our opinion for the examination of those who have a far greater knowledge of the subject than we do and for their foundation to more and better knowledge of what we believe will prove to be one of the most outstanding and important of all ceramics on the antique market.

We suggest, that you study other hand-decorated items such as, for instance, Gaudy Dutch and you will find that while there may be a slight variance they are almost identical—almost over a pattern by comparison. Such a condition will not be found in Spatterware and strangely on Leed's or Leed's type ceramics the Peafowl will face right as often as left but on Spatterware the Peafowl, the Parrots, the Deer, many flowers all face left with but two exceptions, the Dove and the Gooney bird—if this is the result of having a right handed teacher we would not want to decide but it is an interesting fact.

For those who have read thus far and desire to continue the subject in more detail we will list a few of the facts and findings which prompted our opinion for their guidance, and consideration.

On page 26—Pennsylvania Dutch Art—World Publishing Co.—1950—Miss Ruth Adams, in describing Sgraffito advises us that the inscriptions, which are maxims, biblical quotations or moral sentiments should be studied in the framework of the times. While they came easily to the lips of the potter and his customers every day, they had many shades of meaning which from our period of history, we cannot fathom to the last rich ingredient.

While the maxims, quotations and sentiments are missing in Spatterware there is much to recommend in her suggestion of a cautious approach and her suggestion of a thoughtful study in the framework of the times.

On page 1058—Marks and Monograms on European and Oriental Pottery and Porcelain—William Chaffers—14th Edition—Borden Publishing Co. —1946—we find that we should not place too much reliance on the mark itself. Consider the mark not the evidence of genuineness but the confirmation of other evidence. If the specimen possesses all the characteristics of a certain factory-paste, glaze, form, color, quality—then if marked, so much the better; it will confirm our opinion, but the mark should come last —not first.

Since one in a hundred is marked with a name or mark this does not necessarily mean that these names give the potting date of the entire production of this ceramic, nor does it, if we place any credence in the admonition above, particularly mean that the owner of the mark or name was responsible for the decoration or even of the body on which it appears and it becomes our obligation to study the subject carefully and in complete detail.

We have been advised, reliably we are certain, that potters names and marks have been found on Spatterware as follows—

| | | |
|---|---|---|
| Charles and W K Harvey | Carver | J & G Heath |
| Mellor & Venables | Barker & Till | Davenport |
| Samuel Alcock & Co. | Cotton & Barlow | Elsmore & Fisher |
| P. W. & Co-Stoneware | Podmore, Walker | Wedgwood |
| Swan Bank Works | B T Troutbeck Tunst | Schramberg |
| J Pratt & Co | Mayer | Holden |
| Powell & Bishop | J or T. Walker | Meigh |
| E Challinor | G. Adams & Sons | Meakin |
| Adams | | |

We found, however, on page 563 "Ceramic Art" by Llewellynn Jewitt, that Podmore Walker & Co. decorations are characterized by pure taste, artistic feeling, and precision of execution—so that we can hardly credit to this potter a cereamic which does not fit this description simply because it bears their name.

On page 498—Powell & Bishop—we find that the decorations, whether simple or complicated, are characterized by the purest taste and the most artistic feeling. We regret that once more, studying this crude ceramic in the framework of the times, does not permit us to credit it to this potter, even though it may bear his name.

As early as 1876 John Haslam in "The Old Derby China Factory"—page 219—told us that in nothing do authors, who write on ceramic art, appear so apt to be lead astray as on the subject of marks, to which they often attach undue importance. He continues, on page 231, to tell us that forgery for the purpose of deceiving collectors of old china is by no means limited to marks, but is extensively applied to the body, the decorations, and the indications of age which highly prized old porcelain presents.

On page 239 "The Art of the Old English Potter"—Mr. Solon tells us that artistic property was in no way protected, perhaps not even acknowledged; as soon as a model enjoyed a run of success, it was at once taken up by a crowd of imitations. Pirating other's ideas and shapes was considered almost legitimate. The poor struggling potter, who could not keep a modeller, depended for his forms upon the assistance of his wealthier brethren, and took his best models, with or without his permission.

A study of these potters and their workmanship will confirm, we believe, that we cannot blame on them the production of this ceramic, merely because it bears their name or mark, since there is no comparison in decorating type to productions known to be their work, and the subject matter, variety and application are not, as far as we can determine, within the scope of the balance of their designs or workmanship.

One writer told us that the Schoolhouse is one of the crudest Spatterware designs. Undoubtedly, they continued, this design was made by unskilled workmen, in fact, the work could even have been done by a child and we find that a study of all of the designs and their variety, their poor execution, their crudeness, their fantasies, their change in plan, or design between start and completion in many examples, points to only one conclusion. This decoration must indeed have been done by children in schools established for the purpose of teaching them a trade.

Among the factors to be considered is the shape, but we must bear in mind the caution urged by Prof. F. H. Garner—page 27—English Delftware—Pitman Publishing Corporation when he tells us that shapes often give a clue to origin which is of value *if taken in conjunction with other factors.*

His caution is well advised, it appears, since on page 275, Ceramic Art, Mr. Jewitt tells us that about 1800 black ware was introduced at Leed's and that up to 1812-13 probably from ninety to a hundred distinct patterns and sizes of teapots alone were produced in black at these works. The patterns of the teapots were very varied both in form, in style of ornamentation, and in size. In form, they were round, oval, octagonal, and other shapes, including some of twelve sides. The lids were of every variety, both inward and outward fitting, sliding, and attached with hinges. This report of the variety to be found, in one area and in teapots alone gives one a good idea of the need of care and study necessary.

We should likewise bear in mind the comments on page 26—Anglo-American Pottery—Edwin Atlee Barber—1901—where he tells us that the printing of American Scenery on crockery in the Staffordshire potteries for sale in the United States used the deep color in such profusion because the ware was made to sell at a moderate price, was of an inferior grade, frequently blistered, warped and otherwise imperfect in body and *always showing the cockspur marks* used to separate the pieces in the kiln. Since there seems to be a somewhat similar condition in Spatterware it would therefore seem that the same conditions and reasons apply here also.

One writer told us that our familiar Spatterware presented nothing new in technique, only an exceptionally liberal and somewhat ingenious utilization of a process long in vogue, and perfectly familiar to the veriest tyro among ceramic painters.

A careful study of this subject is necessary to determine manner of decoration so that we do not get confused between references to Spatterware and Spongeware, which are entirely different in appearance, are made in a different manner and many times by completely different potters.

It must, for instance, be realized that a sponge is the soft, light, porous, and easily compressible framework which remains after the living matter has been removed from various species of porifers. It is a tough elastic skeleton of interlaced fibres, it is porous and resembles somewhat an irregularly shaped honeycomb, in that, if dipped in paint or color and applied to a surface it would leave a series of apertures or openings of, however, varying sizes and shapes on the surface to which it had been applied in conformity with the construction of the sponge used as in examples FIGURES 149 and 163.

Any attempt to apply a sponge to such a surface, whether smooth or curved, as at a rim, and then remove it must of necessity result in a blurred effect. Either a fast or a slow application with a sponge will give a blurred fuzzy result since sufficient pressure must be applied with this soft, pliable, easily compressed framework to a firm object to secure the desired strong effect and one writer tells us that after the tree trunks and branches were drawn, only a few dabs with a color-saturated sponge were required to clothe the forest skeletons with a *satisfyingly fuzzy verdure.*

While American Rockingham was accomplished, we are told, by striking the paddle on the edge of the vat and *spattering* the glaze on the pottery, Bennington Pottery and Porcelain—Richard Carter Barret—Crown Publishers, Inc.—1958—the term Spatterware is applied to a ceramic where it is covered with spattered effect as done by a brush, from the dots, the sprinkled, speckled or splashed effect which gives it its name, and since the dots frequently number as many as 250 to 300 dots per square inch it seems reasonable to assume that it could hardly have been done by means of a sponge. In fact Bernard Rackham and Herbert Read—"English Pottery"—Ernest Benn, Limited—1924—page 58 describe a method of decoration often adopted at Bristol where the ground is speckled by splashing the pigment from a heavily charged brush. This was also practiced at Liverpool and was a common practice at both places they proceed to advise us. It is also, no doubt, the method used by Whieldon to spatter the decorative effect on the animals he produced in the latter part of the 18th century.

Mr. Pountney on page 84—"Old Bristol Potteries"—tells us that the painter took his brush, containing a moderate supply of the liquid color, which he tapped on his mahlstick, thus causing a *sprinkling* to go over that part of the dish not covered with paper. This he then repeated until he got an *evenly sprinkled* surface. He would then remove the paper covering the surfaces he protected and paint upon these vacant spaces the design he desired.

To make further comparisons we referred to "Ceramic Art" page 565 and found that the Swan Bank Works, when operated by Beech & Hancock and later by James Beech, made ordinary classes of earthenware and stoneware for the *home trade,* in which all the usual services are largely made in *"sponged,"* printed, painted, enamelled, gilt, and lustred styles. These were not, you will observe, for export, not for the East but for the home trade and the designation was "sponged"—not spattered and the word "sponged" was in quotation marks—he was quoting another individual.

While continued search produced no reference to spattered ware, Mr. Jewitt again referring to "Sponged Wares" advises that they were produced by Guest and Duesbury at Llanelly in South Wales in 1877—by Clyde Pottery in Greenock in 1862—by E & C Challinor of the Fenton Pottery (Successors to E Challinor, of Sandyford and Tunstall)—by W T Copeland and Sons at Stoke-upon-Trent in 1867—by William Powe at St. Gregory's Pottery in 1864—by Lowe, Ratcliffe & Co. at the Gold Street Works—by Fell or Fell & Co. at St. Peter's Pottery after 1869—by Dixon, Austin, Phillips & Co. at the Sunderland Pottery or the Garrison Pottery—by G. F. Smith and Co. at Church Gresley Pottery in 1871, and, of course, William & Thomas Adams at the Greenfield Works.

Mr. Jewitt then proceeds to tell us, regarding William & Thomas Adams, that—page 564—their earthenware is noted for the richness and variety of its coloured and *sponged patterns* which is much admired in the foreign markets of the world to which it was entirely confined and he then proceeds to name these markets as the Brazils, Cuba, Central America, Java, Manilla, Singapore, The United States, etc., the first six of which he tells us, are the special trade of this firm. Transfer-printing, he continues, is much used, and is judiciously combined with "sponged" patterns with good effect.

Mr. Jewitt was a contemporary of these potters, and he required, we understand, 20 years to accumulate the information necessary and to write

"Ceramic Art of Great Britain." In doing so he had frequent communication with the potters referred to and since the book was first published in November, 1877, he had from 1857 to 1877 to secure the facts and information required for its completion. His second edition was published in 1883 and must be assumed to be correct since there was an interval of 6 years for errors or corrections to be called to his attention. This is indeed fortunate since William Turner—"William Adams—An Old English Potter"—page 17 tells us that in 1879-1880 many of the account books were destroyed at Greengates and on page 146 he refers to the account books, still extant at Greenfield, indicating that there were some missing at this pottery also.

Kindly observe that Mr. Jewitt continues to put the word "sponged" in quotation marks. Printed, painted, enamelled, gilt and lustred appear in just this manner, but the word "sponged" is in quotation marks to call to our attention that he is quoting the name or word applied to this process by another and apparently that he did not desire to be known as the author thereof. The fact that he continues to refer to "sponged patterns" helps to clear the situation somewhat but does not identify the ceramic and when he tells that transfer-printing is judiciously combined with "sponged" *patterns* we realize that this is indeed a ceramic with which we have no knowledge, which is understandable since few of them apparently reached the United States, the last and seventh area named above.

Since we desired accurate and first hand knowledge and information we turned next to "William Adams—An Old English Potter"—by William Turner and found that—page 149—in 1845-50 Adams, at Greenfield, produced sponged and painted goods for the East and that William Hancock, the manager of the department at Greenfield, kept it under his control for a long time, and that he was allowed a premium for so doing.

This gives us continued assurance that this was not our Spatterware since he tells very plainly sponged (not spattered) but above all Mr. Turner, an English author, tells us that this ceramic was produced for the *East* and the United States is to the west from England. Mr. Turner tells us that much of this painted ware (not the sponged ware) was done by means of cut sponges and in order to introduce it Adams procured persons from Scotland who understood the process.

Since Mr. Hancock, the manager, produced this unidentified product from 1845-50 at Greenfield, since he kept it under his control for a long time it would be at least 1850 or later before the process would have been known to other potters or other individuals, therefore it would have been difficult for potters such as John Holden, Burslem—1846, Mellor & Venables, Burslem—1834-51, Barker & Till, Burslem—1846-50, Charles Meigh, Hanley—1835-49 and similar potters whose name appears, we are told, on Spatterware as we are studying, if this were the same process, to have copied this secret process but it would have been no problem for those potters listed as manufacturers of "sponged" items in 1862, 1864, 1867, 1869, 1871 and 1877 by Mr. Jewitt to have done so.

It is an acknowledged fact that Whieldon and some of his contemporaries used spatterwork in their decorative processes in the last half of the 18th century. It is likewise well known that spongework was produced in Bristol in the latter part of the 17th century. It therefore, does not seem that an alert potter as Adams proved to be, and one who learned of a secret process in Scotland, about 200 miles to the North, would send for, or would have to send for persons to produce a product that was being done in their area and which had been done by these neighbors for one or two centuries past if it was the same process. It would likewise be foolhardy to try to keep secret a process which his grandfather and all of his neighbors had known of and had practiced for a century or more previously. This process, we feel more certain, was not Spatterware as we are studying it.

Mr. Turner solves our problem by telling us, very simply, that the earlier hand painted ware is, however, the most sought after in America and since our ceramic is hand painted it removes it completely from the above referred to realm of possible consideration.

Mr. Turner tells us—page 127—that a complete list of the Adams designs is not given, for all the old books are not in existence and, we are referred by him to Professor Edwin Atlee Barber and his works for further study of Scenic Views, particularly his "Anglo-American Pottery" advising us that the professor has every opportunity for writing upon the subject of these rick dark blue plates, page 119, with authority, for America, he tells us, possesses by far the greatest number that were ever produced. He likewise refers us to Mayer, and his "History of the Art of Potting in Liverpool" regarding the art of transfer printing.

It is unfortunate that there was no similar specialized study of either Spatterware or Spongeware in 1904 for Mr. Turner to refer us to as he had done on Scenic Views since a similar condition existed and here we also had the greatest number that were ever produced, but fortunately his references are sufficiently clear and conclusive to determine that this is not our ceramic to which he was referring and that there was no similarity.

Since examples, as FIGURE 9 and 152, have a design as featured on Spatterware, they are included in this classification as a matter of course, even though the work is unmistakably spongework. The sponge never having made the pretense of resting for even an instant, the result is but a number of continuing blurs, sometimes referred to as Flowing Spatter and similarly the few, as 149 and 163, are similarly included automatically because there are too few of this type for a separate classification.

Frequently the question is asked as to whether the Schoolhouse design might not have been intended for the Harrison Log Cabin so much exploited in the Presidential campaign of 1840. We attach FIGURE B, a Delft plate, circa 1710, with a Schoolhouse and suggest that the reader compare with FIGURES M and N of the Log Cabin design of the Harrison campaign.

The one is a Log Cabin design on an Adams sugar bowl and the other is the same design on a Sandwich type cup plate. The Log Cabin is a one story building whereas the Schoolhouse usually has an upper story window. The Log Cabin is ribbed to denote logs rather graphically whereas the Schoolhouse artistry has never attained such detailed illustration. The Log Cabin, being a symbol in a Presidential campaign rated a flag on the roof, a display never found, to the best of our knowledge, on the lowly Schoolhouse but even more outstanding was the fact that the "Hard Cider" barrel, another symbol of the Presidential campaign, was never found on the Schoolhouse, only on the Log Cabin. These are the variations apparent from a picture and, of course, the ceramic, glaze and other details will each tell their own story. In our opinion this design does not tell potting date or supply any other data except the best possible evidence of authorship—children—and an index of the era whose style of architecture was copied.

If a potter had a reputation for doing excellent workmanship, if his decorations are characterized by pure taste, artistic feeling and precision of execution it is, we believe, reasonable to expect that he did not permit any shoddy work to be done by his workmen or in his pottery.

When he sold his seconds or rejects, as explained above, he had no reason or need to remove his name, if embossed, since his work was known to his friends and customers as well as we know the signature or handwriting of our friends. He therefore had nothing to be worried or concerned about.

While these potters had limited materials, they had unlimited resourcefulness, unbounded enthusiasm, a native ability and the knowledge of a craft in which they were making tremendously rapid strides. We are certain that the potters, whose names appear in connection with Spatterware, would have taken no pride in the production of such a product, in fact they took no credit in their catalogues or lists and we believe that a study of potting personalities in this era is essential for additional clarification.

In "Old Derby China Factory"—1876—John Haslem tells us that William Duesbury, the founder of the Derby China manufacture, was a native of Longton, in the Staffordshire Potteries, where, in early life he had acquired knowledge of enamelling and of the manufacture of earthenware, etc.

We realize that he is not credited with the production of any of the foregoing products but more detailed information is available about his pottery than is the case in most of those in question that it should assist us in determining the capabilities of the potters, and the type of production we should expect, during this era.

We learn, for instance, that in 1773 King George III visited the pottery, that the works were patronized not only by the best families, but by numbers of the Nobility, that the patterns were neat and plain and characteristic of the good King. In 1811 the plant was sold to Robert Bloor who made a marked change in production but still, while his patterns were more showy, produced items possessed of much artistic excellence and at no time did the Derby works stand higher for the production of its celebrated figures.

In 1832 he employed a manager,a traveler or salesman, 2 clerks, a body mixer, an overlooker and 12 potters, an overlooker and 5 figure makers or ornamental repairers, 9 painters (3 landscape, 4 flowers, 1 birds and 1 ground-layer and birds), an overlooker and 40 gilders, 9 paintresses, an overlooker and 31 burnishers, 7 kilnmen (2 biscuit, 2 glaze, 2 enamel and a glaze dipper), 2 slipmen, 1 packer, 1 bricklayer, 1 lodgeman, 1 bonewasher and 1 ware sorter.

These potters were keen businessmen, plenty of supervision, specialization so that all were expert in their respective fields and a good index of the type of work being done at the time.

He employed, for instance, Thomas Steele, whose fruit painting on china, he tells, has never been surpassed, who was a native of the Staffordshire potteries, where he first learned his art and worked at Derby from 1815 until about 1840, shortly before its close.

His fruit painting, the peaches, plums, grapes, and flowers, were done with the hand and eye of one who had looked at the originals, and whose brush could reproduce every feature and detail. He could turn a defect into an advantage, and thus almost turn it into a beauty.

His roses were not as good as those of Billingsley, but his leaves could hardly be surpassed. His roses were sometimes left too white in the lights, the outline cutting hard against a dark background, which was never the case with his fruit. On fruit, we find, he had no superior, if, indeed, he had an equal in his day. His color is remarkably pleasing, being rich and transparent, and his large fruit pieces are painted with great force. His groupings are harmonious, the light and the dark shades being well managed, each piece of fruit is well rounded, the outline softened and blended into the one next to it, each partaking of the reflected colour from the other, etc.

His sons, Edwin and Horatio Steele were chiefly employed in the Staffordshire Potteries after leaving Derby.

William Wheeldon was a flower painter, 1801 to 1823, at Derby having received his instruction from his uncle, William Billingsley, the most eminent of the Derby painters.

Zachariah Boreman, one of the most celebrated of the Chelsea hands, worked at the Derby factory eleven years, 1783 to 1794. As a painter of landscapes and birds he was considered unrivalled, etc.

William Pegg was one of the best flower painters, we learn, employed at Derby.

This then supplies an idea, an insight into the type of work done in and about the era which we are studying by former and future residents and pupils of Staffordshire. It indicates the type of reporting done by the writers and their attention to detail and their knowledge of the subject. When, therefore, we learn of production of a pottery as being of pure taste, artistic feeling and precision of execution we feel that the writers knew their subject and the potters their craft. We do not think that they should be sold short or their labors underestimated.

It is difficult for us to envision these potters doing such crude work, but it is next to impossible for us to conceive of these writers overlooking such crude efforts on the part of the potters and not referring to it in no uncertain terms. In fact, in their constant search of patterns, and sometimes locating in this manner, otherwise unknown artists, it would seem that they would have reported on these crude patterns as well.

These writers, it is true, tell us that young lads were invited to learn the art of pottery and that children of either sex may be learned to draw and paint by persons appointed for that purpose. They tell us that there were two or three drawing schools established in Birmingham, about 1759, for the instructing of youth in the arts of designing and drawing. They know, and expect that we will, without referring thereto, that this work will not be perfect, in fact, rather crude. They know that to learn the art of pottery or pottery decoration will require that the work be done on a ceramic and expect, with no further comment, that we know the method employed in securing these bodies, since it was, at that time, such a common and accepted procedure.

They may have, from our period of history, confused the issues by their lack of complete detail but the expected, the obvious certainly has never needed comment or clarification, it needs only study and understanding and Josiah C. Wedgwood, page 13, supplied this information.

The student will then understand, we believe, that it is going to be difficult to belatedly study and probe a subject which, while known familiarly to our grandparents was practically unknown to us prior to three or four decades ago, when the first article concerning it was written.

He will, likewise, understand that we have given only a partial listing, for his guidance, of some of the more important factors in forming our opinion and that this subject is endless. We trust that our listing of previously unlisted designs may assist in establishing a pattern, that we have helped the reader form an opinion as to the starting date and decorators who created these delightful ceramics, that we may continue to study it in the framework of the times, that we continue to compare with other examples, that we consider the aggressiveness of the potters and the general economic condition of the country, as a whole, consider their method of depicting buildings and the era which the Spatterware decorators followed, consider carefully the meaning of their references, as well as all of the other advices given us above, thoughtfully and carefully.

In Pottery—by Charles King—1966—Blackie & Son Ltd., Bishopbriggs, Glasgow, we find on page 8 a reference to the fact that nowadays the main reason pottery is made in Stoke-on-Trent is that some 60,000 pottery workers are employed in 200 factories and that nowhere else can all the necessary skills be found, not to mention all the service industries—kiln builders, transfer makers, glaze manufacturers, etc.

He continues, indicating that pots have been made in Stoke since medieval and even Roman times.

In "The Concise Encyclopedia of English Pottery and Porcelain" by Wolf Mankowitz & Reginald G. Haggar-Hawthorn Books, Inc.-1957 we found a very helpful listing in Appendix 2—Engravers for pottery and porcelain. We found that there were about 15 engravers in the latter part of the 18th century—about 125 in the first half of the 19th century—about 110 in the last half of the 19th century—and about 31 since 1900, who were centered in and around this area.

In so far as transfer engraving is concerned, it seems that there was the larger number in this area from 1801 to 1850, than is found at other periods.

It seems that William Brookes, the younger, engraved the Ferrara pattern transfer in 1832 that Wedgwood used in 1845 at Etruria in decorating Queen's Ware as well as many other patterns, but it seems that he did engraving for Ward's Stoke-on-Trent as well.

William Brookes, the elder, did designing for New Hall as well as for William Adams of Greengate, Tunstall.

Some like Lewis Hackwood worked for Wedgwood 1799, William Hales worked for Wedgwood 1806-1808, Isaac Keeling was a designer and engraver for Wedgwood, and seemingly no other, but generally engravers secured employment when and where they could, on a free lance basis, since few potters could provide full time employment.

The Flying Eagle pattern plate—FIGURE 95 is marked T Walker—a potter who, we believe, was at the Lion Works, Tunstall from 1845 to 1851—and since the other specimens we have of this identical pattern have the same paste, the same glaze, the same shape and appearance as our other Staffordshire ceramics we believe that they are unquestionably Staffordshire. Any potter could have, we believe, purchased transfers and produced a similar product but this practice was, so far as we have been able to learn, limited to the Staffordshire area.

In referring to a chocolate jug stamped American Pottery Co., Jersey City, N.J., Mr. Homer Eaton Keyes, Editor in 1930 of Antiques magazine in the April 1930 issue, page 335 tells us that possibly Daniel Greatbach, the English Potter, who had become associated with the American Pottery Co., had imparted the secret of sponging to the workmen in this plant. But he tells us, even if unmarked this American specimen could hardly be mistaken for English ware. Its glaze, he tells us, seems somewhat colder, harder, and more forbidding than that of the Staffordshire ware, etc. and he reminds us that it (the chocolate Jug) was only stippled, no attempt at ornamentation is visible. Our examples and those in some of our National shrines and museums are, so far as we have been able to determine, English.

The Eagle and Shield pattern seems to have been engraved by the same individual and seemingly the same statements apply to this pattern, even though efforts have been made to claim it as American.

We, however, would like to point to some very interesting facts in regard to transfer patterns.

Kindly examine FIGURE 214—Crystal Palace—and compare with the N. Currier picture—FIGURE R—and you will find that apparently these engravers used current events frequently in their work.

Examine FIGURE 150 and it will immediately become apparent that this Sugar Bowl, named "Mule Train" should have been named either "Gold Rush" or "Prospector" and that the inspiration was, no doubt, "Gold Rush of 1849."

Examine FIGURE 215 of an Arabian Horse and Trainer with lance and compare it with FIGURE W and W A and we believe that you will find by study of Jousting that there was an application of local or national interest which prompted this transfer being produced.

Number 91 can no doubt be traced to some eventful ceremony or interest since if there was no interest they could not have been sold and there would have been no incentive to make or to stock them.

The same thing, no doubt applies to 92-93-94-95 and all of the other transfer patterns and could be a very rewarding and interesting study.

Constantly new patterns appear and we feel sure that the surface has not been scratched in this branch of the Spatterware field.

For the student who wants further to study the type of decoration referred to by William Turner, when (page 11) he told us that much of this painted ware was done by means of cut sponges and in order to introduce it Adams procured persons from Scotland who understood the process, we refer you to page 65—Scottish Pottery—by J. Arnold Fleming, O.B.E.—Maclehose, Jackson & Co.—Glasgow—1923. He tells us in detail of an interesting process of decoration on biscuit ware by means of portions cut out of the smooth root of a sponge, which are dipped in moistened color and then brought into contact with the ware. It is, he tells us, a rapid and cheap method and is effective in coloring "Cottage Pottery."

It is, he adds, usually forceful in *design* and executed on plain but good—(not seconds)—forms evidently destined for the rank and file of working folks.

This then is the "Design Spatterware" done with cut sponges according to the taste or decorative ideas of the artist. These were indeed on good bodies, with artistically executed designs and commercially uniform. These were indeed done by the potters and the references to sponge work which we found are in connection with potters who were doing business after 1845-50, and therefore referred to cut sponge work producing a "design" Spatterware.

On page 195 Mr. Fleming adds that Andrew Ramsay Young, who had been with the "Methvens" at "Kirkcaldy Pottery" from boyhood is credited with being the first to develop the art of *decorating ware with designs cut out of the roots of sponges,* in connection with underglaze colors.

This practice was usual in almost every pottery in Scotland during the 19th century and one of the potters is said to have remarked that this type of ware was about 50% of his total production.

We understand that Mr. R. Heron of "Kirkcaldy" (Fife) was advertising this ware in 1845, before Young's time, so that while the credit may possibly be slightly misplaced, the facts are not, nor is the timing. This practice of decorating ware with designs cut out of the roots of sponges was sometimes of a simple type and frequently quite intricate as we have tried, by our examples, to indicate and was, we are advised, actually begun in the early part of the 19th century, in Scotland.

The English language is ever changing—hundreds of words in common use in the 17th and the 18th centuries are, we understand, meaningless today. When Llewellyn Jewitt referred to a "suspender" in connection with the product of a potter we know full well that it was in reference to a suspended bowl and quite possibly for hanging flowers from the ceiling rather than the usage commonly known to us today.

When we hear an individual refer to razing a building we need more information and must make inquiry since he just could be raising the building, and so to those who have observed the reference of Mr. Jewitt to "Sponged Patterns" there can be very little doubt that the patterns were the designs referred to by Mr. Fleming and that they were made by means of cut sponges—cut artistically to render the desired effect of Stars, Circles, Butterflies, Eagles, etc.

Who can read, for instance, that these designs were executed "on plain but good bodies" without questioning why he made a point of the bodies being good—why was it not taken for granted that the finished product was a good and entirely satisfactory ceramic.

He apparently did not want it to get into the same category as a somewhat similar product previously unnamed, poorly done, often decorated overglaze, but made with sponges (uncut) on some occasions.

Mr. Fleming tells us of Trade Processions, page 259, of how these generations when keen and friendly rivalry existed as to which factory would turn out the finest display on the great day. During the march Lorries were requisitioned, horses all caparisoned with colored ribbons and the Lorries carried a "thrower" at the wheel making vases, in the procession, and various other potters also at work, or the lorry may have contained a huge teapot, the spout of which alone held over a gallon, to the astonishment and amusement of everyone. Would these potters, taking such pride in their products and their skilled workers turn out work that was not in conformity to their general and well published lines?

# OTHER EXAMPLES FOR GUIDANCE AND STUDY

The idea, advanced by one writer, of selecting a sequence of English Wares from early Delft to ultimate Spatter appealed to us for many reasons, that may now seem apparent, over and above our desire to secure examples of buildings and Schoolhouses to study the subject and the origin of some of these designs more fully. We attach several of the more outstanding examples for comparison and further study.

FIGURE A illustrates a building with two trees and some bushes on a Robin's Egg Blue Delft body, circa 1690. The Green trees and bushes are blurred and indicate clearly the use of a sponge, which is, of course, more pronounced since the Lavender on the building, the ground and the smoke are merely smears.

FIGURE B is a Delft plate, circa 1710, and the trees, bushes, windows and ground follow the same description as A above, except that the color is an odd shade of Brown. A careful study of this plate will indicate that it is the forerunner and inspiration for the Spatter Schoolhouse plates that we are studying.

FIGURE C is a Delft plate, circa 1750, showing Sponged trees, bushes and ground. The Peacock is a Blue wing and neck creation with a Yellow body and Red decorative and outline markings.

FIGURE D is a Delft Jug with no Spatter, circa 1750, having Rust, Lavender, Yellow, Green decorative treatment outlined in a Dark Brown.

FIGURE E is a Whieldon Bowl—an early use of Design Spatter.

FIGURE F a Leed's type bowl—a colorful subject using Orange, Yellow, Blue and Green in a Schoolhouse pattern. Kindly observe square top of doorway, and beauty of execution and detail, also minute spongework in trees.

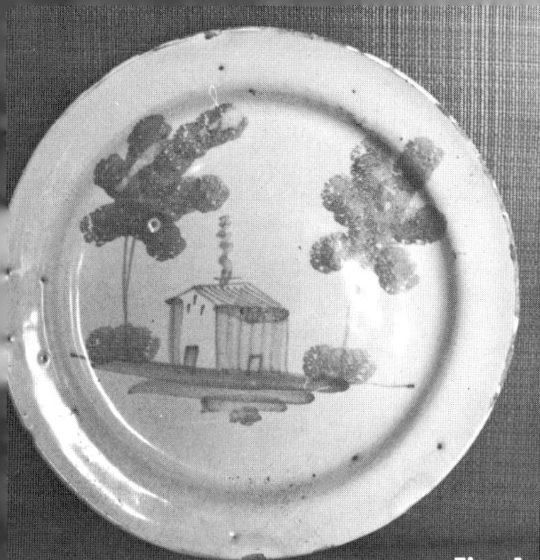
Fig. A

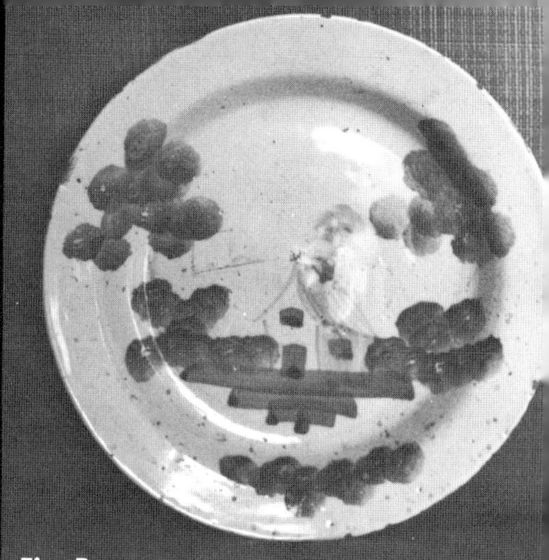
Fig. B

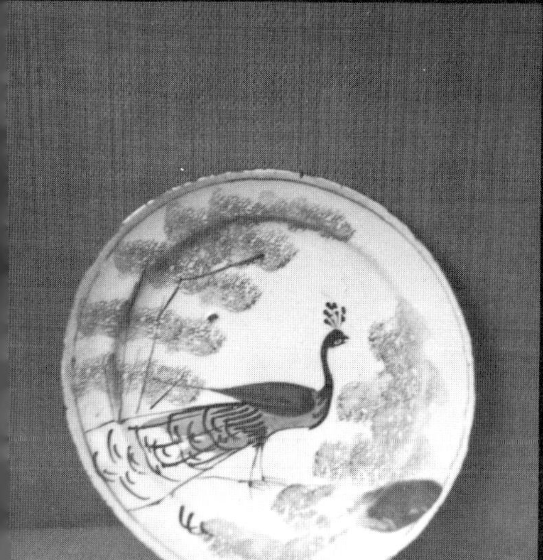
Fig. C

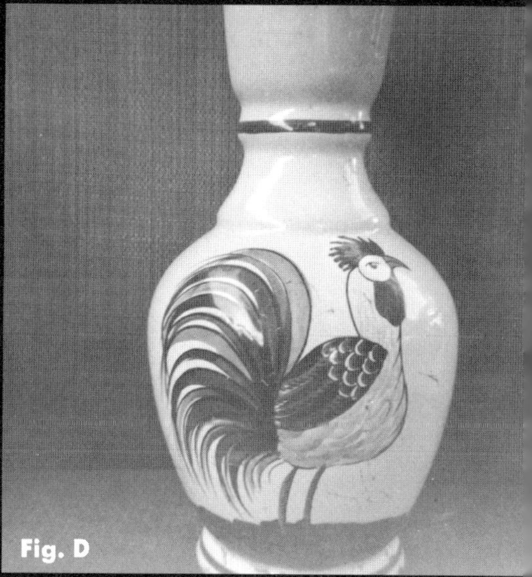
Fig. D

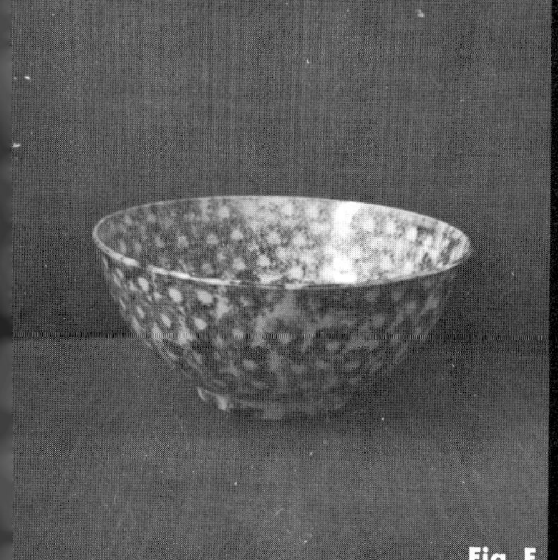
Fig. E

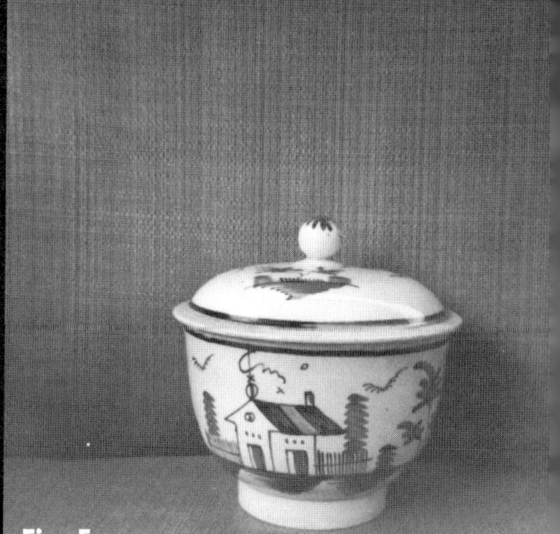
Fig. F

FIGURE G illustrates a Leed's type cup and saucer with a church pattern—The clouds and part of the foreground is a Lavender shade, the fence, the side of the church, the door and the window, as well as part of the foreground is a Rust shade, the roof is Lavender, Rust and Yellow, and the trees, bushes and part of the foreground is Green. While the colors are all a smudged or smeared effect, the whole execution is once more complete, detailed and beautiful and is enhanced by having minute Brown dashes side by side to give shadings to the trees and bushes. Kindly observe cross on roof and curved top of doorway.

FIGURE H is a Leed's type plate with a Church design—The colors and treatment are very similar to FIGURE G above except on the trees and bushes there is a long wavy line drawn on as many as 22 to 27 widths on each tree for instance and then these same Brown dashes are drawn from this line down to indicate branches and boughs. Kindly observe as above the curved top of doorway and the elongated windows used on many early churches for illumination of both the first floor and the balcony.

FIGURE I is an unusual example of a bowl with Spatterwork, a House design and an Acorn finial.

FIGURE J is an early Flask-pottery in the shape of a potato, with Red eyes and neck, overall Blue Spattered.

FIGURE K is an unusual plate with Brown circles, Yellow inside, two-center circular hoops, Lavender sponged festoons and Sage Green leaflike markings. Identified as German lettering, early potting, otherwise unidentified.

FIGURE K A a bottom view of plate FIGURE K for study.

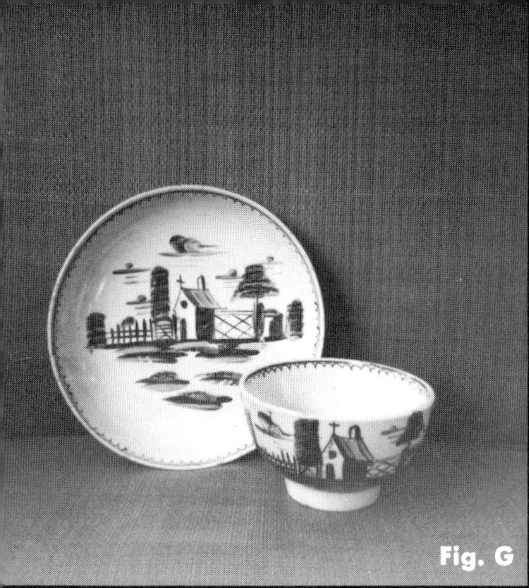

Fig. G

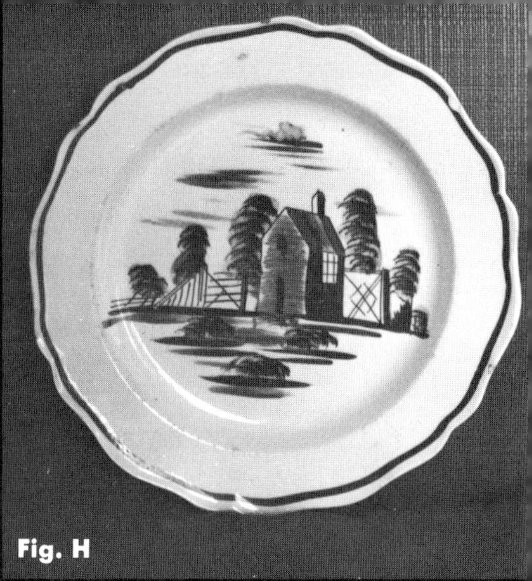

Fig. H

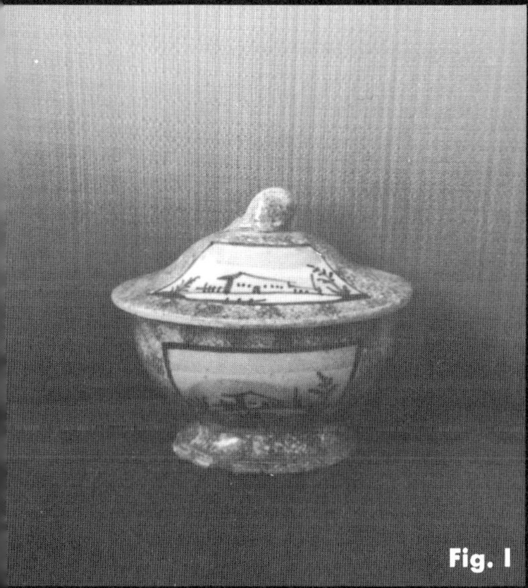

Fig. I

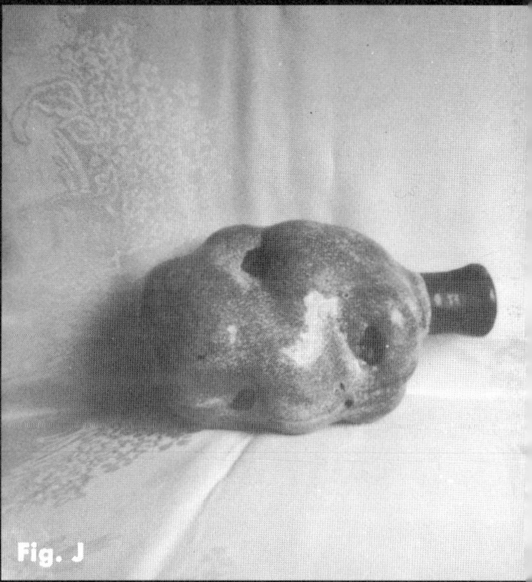

Fig. J

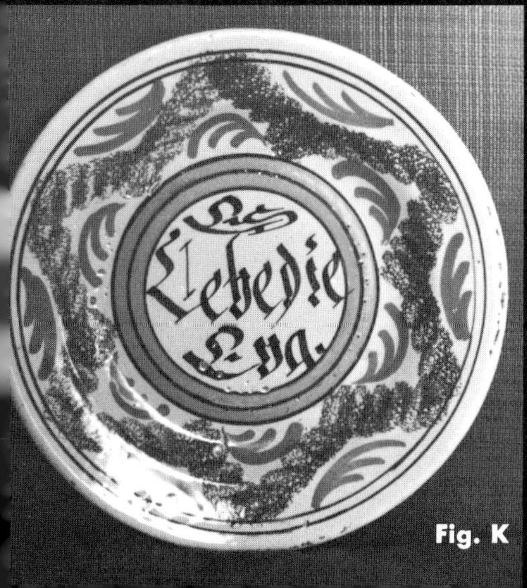

Fig. K

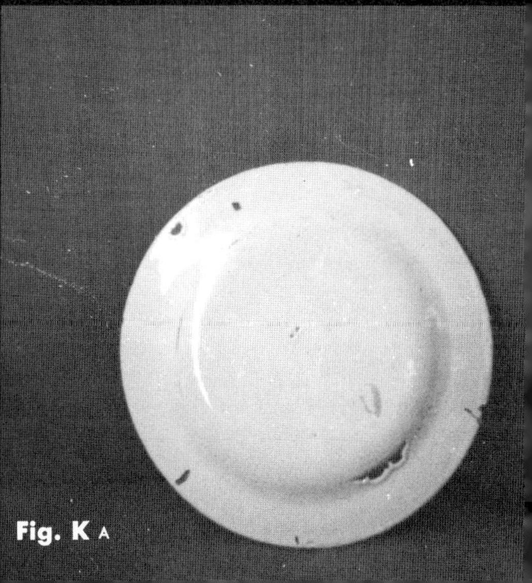

Fig. K A

FIGURE L Whieldon Lion circa 1775 spattered in Yellow and Blue, an early and representative example of workmanship.

FIGURE M Log Cabin design in Pink on an Adams sugar bowl. Note the ribbed log effect on walls and roof, one window at end and one door in side, one floor only, patriotic note added by flag on roof and the "Hard Cider" barrel in foreground, a prominent feature of the campaign.

FIGURE N Log Cabin in a Sandwich type Cup Plate—kindly note the window and door placement as well as the other points as FIGURE M.

FIGURE O Whieldon Cow Creamer with Milkmaid—Early example of Spatterware.

FIGURE P Cottage Spongeware—An American product late 19th century and becoming increasingly collectable.

FIGURES QA-QB-QC are three views of a mug apparently distributed circa 1831 by J. WHITTAKER-FRUIT PRESERVER-SUNDERLAND to commemorate the valor of JOHN CRAWFORD, a native of SUNDERLAND, for his heroic deed on October 11, 1797. This soft paste, lead glazed mug is not Spattered but the Black, White, Red and Blue transfer design with the dots forming the background carefully spaced by the engraver—approximately 2400 to 2800 per square inch—make a very interesting study and the occupation of Mr. Whittaker in that area and in that period were, we felt, unusual but the alertness and the approach to a public relations effort of this type at that time, over 130 years ago, seems to us to be remarkable.

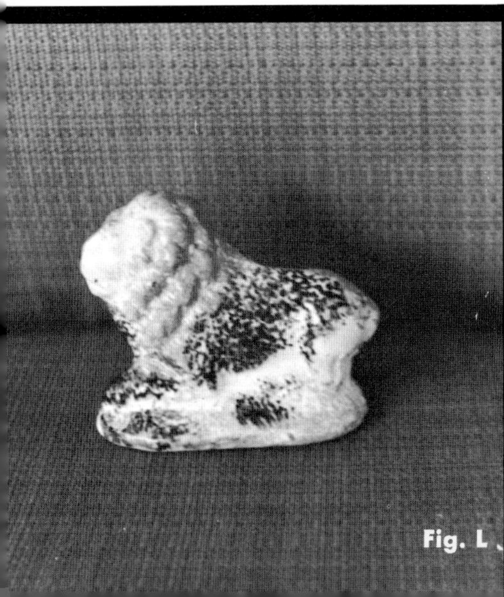

Fig. L

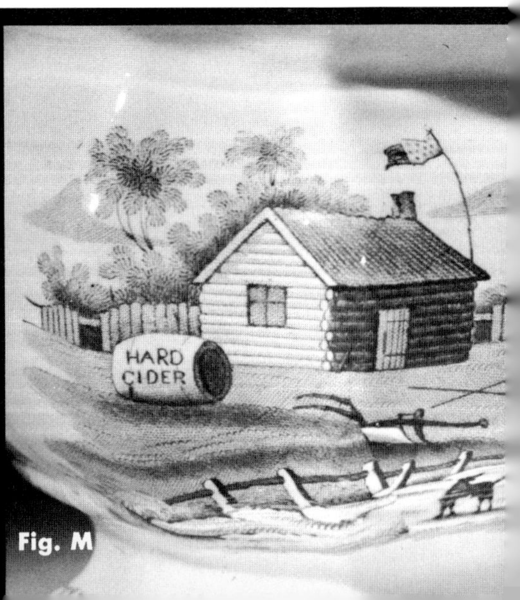


Fig. M

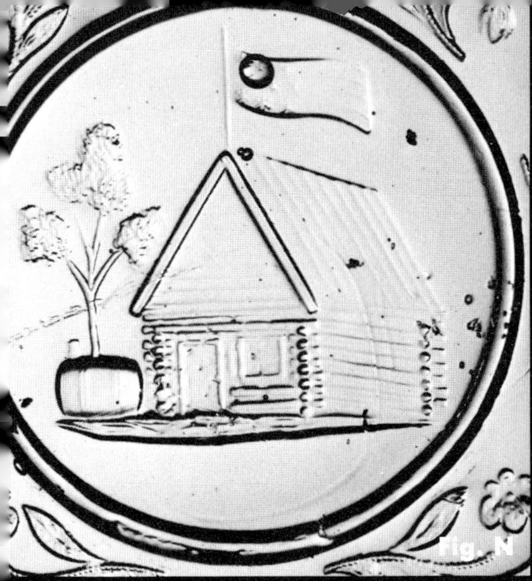

Fig. N

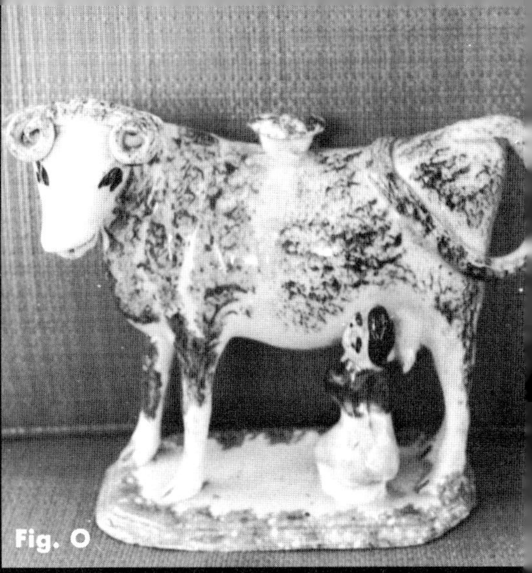

Fig. O

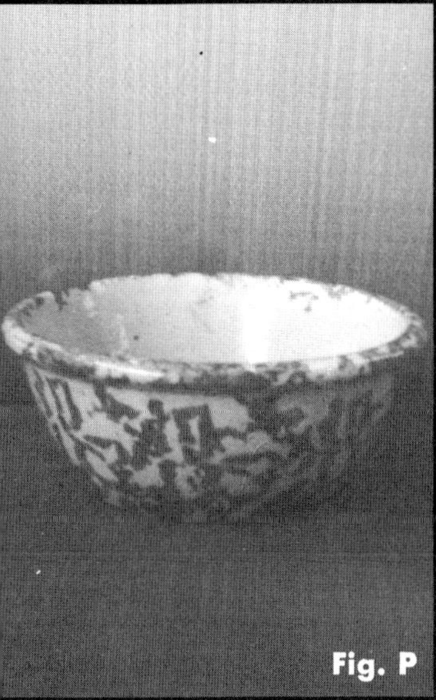

Fig. P

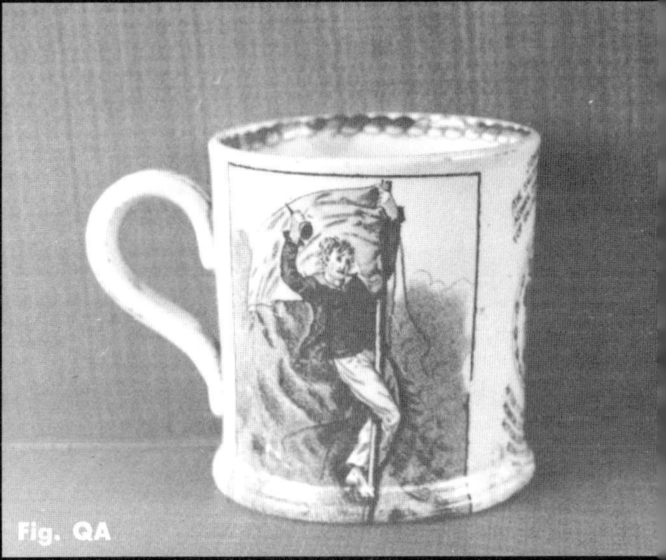

Fig. QA

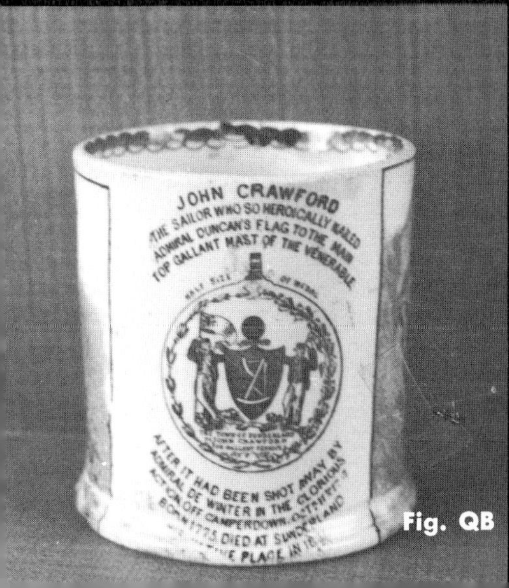


Fig. QB

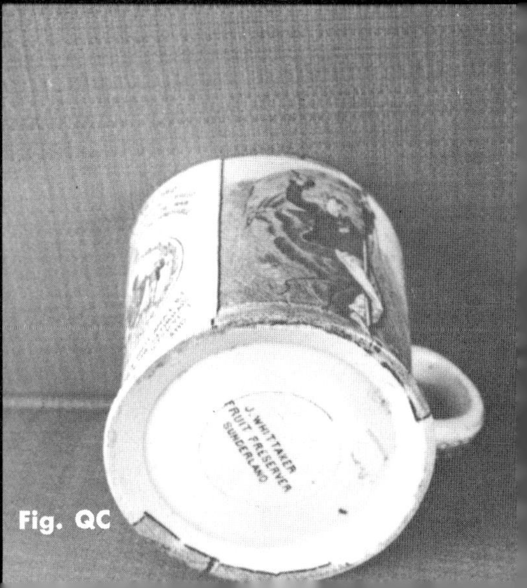


Fig. QC

To add the following supporting exhibits without explanation may cause some misunderstanding and confusion and we trust that the student will consider the following additional facts and findings.

FIGURES A-B-C-D-F-G-H are examples of Delft and of Leed's type ceramics where the center motif is large and dominant.

John Niglett (1714-1754) has been frequently given credit for having been a caricaturist of English pottery and with possibly having developed that curious creature referred to on Spatterware as Peafowl as well as other Farm series including the Rooster, the Parrot, and the house designs where he has, as is so frequently done on Spatterware, taken "artistic license" to accentuate some part of the picture or the entire picture if it suited his fancy.

He caricatured everything that he copied. Even fences, trees, and boats would be shown in impossible places and positions.

While we agree that much credit must be given Niglett we believe that E. Ward, Senior and some of the other artists who worked on Delft in a bold manner must also be given credit for having supplied examples although the practice of Niglett to add boats, fences, trees, etc. of impossible shapes and in impossible places and positions was taken advantage of simultaneously.

If you examine examples in "English Delft Pottery" by Major R. G. Mundy in his School House pattern (plate 3) and his Windmills (plate V) and his House pattern (plate V 1) you will find them approximating our examples B-F-G.

A study of our FIGURE 188 and a comparison with Ward's FIGURE V—left —will indicate a duplication of this very unusual effect being carried out under very similar circumstances except—the Niglett influence is being evidenced with no supporting foundation under the Windmill, a ladder with a man coming down supporting a large object on his head with both arms, his boats defy description, the X on the Windmill is similar to FIGURE V—right, and the Apple Tree again adds a Farm atmosphere to the scene.

Again, you may desire to refer to our FIGURE 116 and to our FIGURE 171 and compare with the interior view of bowl—(FIGURE SA). This bowl on which Mr. Archer tells us the painting is much less skilled than that of Liverpool artists is said to have been used at "Saracen's Head," the chief Glasgow Inn and was one of the examples he used in his interesting article in the September 1966 American Edition of "The Connoisseur".

The point he makes particularly is that the interior was painted with a free interpretation of the arms of the City of Glasgow, and while we show—FIGURE T—the arms adopted October 5, 1866 there were varied interpretations prior to that date and the artist took liberties with each and every one known to and shown by Mr. A. MacGeorge in his inquiry and presentation to John Blackie, Jun., Lord Provost, November 1, 1866 and through Mr. Blackie to the Magistrates and Town Council of the City of Glasgow. —W. G. Blackie and Co.,—Printers.

The tree, the bird, the fish and the bell appeared in the artists picture but not in conformity with any prior use. The fish did not have the customary ring in its mouth and the bell was oversize by comparison. Each of these items, having special significance had appeared infrequently on the seal of bishops and while sometimes they all might appear on a seal, sometimes only some of them appear, and sometimes none of them would occur at all (page 21).

It is therefore understandable when the artist in producing our #116 and 171 desired to do just this in the manner customary prior to 1866, and we believe that the subject material is so unusual that the reader will have no difficulty in determining that this was indeed the inspirational source of these subjects.

If these Spatterware ceramics were copied from Delft as has been held and as we are inclined to agree, where were they displayed for the artist to study and copy them if the ceramics were made at all of the varying potteries that have been given credit for their production.

How is it that the same pattern was made on bodies of different potters if the few marks found are to be relied upon?

Examine the designs of, for instance, Adams and learn of the sharpness, clarity, and artistic modelling of his Stoneware—look at his Jasper ware including Jasper cameos—look at his blue printed ware, his basalts, his mocha and his enamelled wares, as well as the later and professionally produced Design Spatterware done as Mr. Turner has explained, with cut sponges and where the painting is uniformly and superbly done.

Examine the craftsmanship of his potters and his artists and then attempt to compare with Spatterware and see if these artists could have produced so inferior and so poorly decorated a product.

If throwers and pressers were paid only for those items that came from the oven in good condition and if some potters were said to have refused to pay for those items which they themselves afterwards sold as seconds, who would purchase these seconds and for what purpose? Those sold as seconds undoubtedly in many cases had the potters name impressed and so the final spattered product was not his handicraft and should not therefore be his handicap.

Kindly observe FIGURES 191 and 192 of the sponged and painted goods referred to above, and described by William Turner as having been produced by means of cut sponges in the 1845-50 period by Adams, at Greenfield, and for which he had to procure persons from Scotland who understood the process. They bear the mark as FIGURE 190 used by Adams on his Graniteware after 1840. Note the uniformity of design and of decoration. They have the quality and decorative control to enhance the Adams name and reputation and due to this uniformity sets could be filled in as required.

The same applies to FIGURES 193 and 194.

If, by chance, you were checking on the Dish, Plate, and Cup picture #393 —(our FIGURE U) which William Turner marked "sponged and painted underglaze" and which he says is "mark impressed" and which he attributes to "Mrs. Haynes" you may have been confused, as we were.

In specimen #393 he credits an example to "Mrs. Haynes"—in #348 he credits it to "Mrs. N. M. Haynes"—in #330 he credits it to "Mrs. W. M. Haynes"—and in #316 the credit is to "Mrs. W. M. Haines, Sherman, U.S.A.

In other words Mrs. W. M. Haynes—(correct spelling) who was in 1904 a resident of Sherman, New York, U.S.A. and later of Ithaca, New York—and who was an avid collector of ceramics learned in some manner that in England an author or a potter was looking for examples to illustrate his planned book and she submitted several pictures to assist him with examples he could not secure in his home area. In the preface he states that "he desires to thank collectors who have permitted him to see their specimens and obtain illustrations. Some were good enough to supply photographs of their own taking".

Mr. Turner did not have the ceramic to personally inspect it, he tells us that it had an impressed mark, and through possibly allowing someone to do his proofreading several inaccuracies crept in.

They should have noticed that FIGURE #393 was not an illustration of ceramics as produced by means of cut sponges as he was referring to and since no designs appeared to show the manner in which the sponges were cut it should have been clear even from a picture that this was an incorrect item being shown and it is regretable since it has, in the past, proven to be quite confusing.

We should probably mention, for the record, that in Staffordshire Pots & Potters—by G. Wooliscroft Rhead, R. E. and Frederick Alfred Rhead-Hutchinson and Co., London—1906 on page facing #240 is an identical picture to Turner's #393 and our FIGURE U—which they credit to Tunstall Museum.

The picture includes the Dish, Plate and Cup identically—they are placed in identically the same positions and with the same spacing—although variations must and do exist in such decorated items there is no variance here—there are two dark spots above the head of the Peafowl on the plate in both pictures—the light source is to the right and slightly above in both pictures casting identical shadows—the cup in both pictures show very plainly a crack and this crack is in the same relative position and place on both.

It is therefore our opinion that both pictures were made from the same negative.

Tunstall, Burslem, Hanley, Stoke, Fenton and Longton each had its own museum prior to 1910 but at that time they were combined in one City Museum which is situated in the center of the Potteries, in Hanley.

All collections from the six museums are since 1910 under one roof and a recent check indicates that the three specimens shown in this picture are not now in the museum and therefore were not there so that this was an error also.

Mrs. Haynes, therefore, for the record seems to have been the owner of the Spatterware items shown in Turner's notations, and having none available for comparison he or his proofreader must have assumed it was correct even though it did not fit his own description.

The Design Spatter ceramics were apparently available from early in the 19th century from sources in Scotland where it was widely practiced but when it was advertised in 1845 Mr. Adams immediately sought the secret and started manufacturing as well and it seems that they must have surpassed Scottish potters since most of the marked specimens are of Staffordshire potters, both by Adams and other potters who later learned the process.

The earlier, regular Spatterware first introduced to collectors by Prof. Cornelius Weygandt in 1929, and never previously having been referred to as far as we have been able to determine, seems to have been made from 1785 to about 1860. It started to taper off in favor of the newer type highly decorative and possibly more elaborate Design Spatterware shortly after its large scale introduction on or about 1845-50.

We have made an honest effort to collect in one area the pertinent facts pertaining to this ceramic, to isolate cause and effect, which have strangely been intermingled, and confused, and feel that the student should experience little difficulty in coming to an early conclusion, and be able to continue the study in a clearer atmosphere.

FIGURE R—Published by N. Currier. "The Magnificent Building, For The World's Fair of 1851; Built of Iron and Glass, In Hyde Park, London.—Covers 21 acres, is 1848 feet long, by 408 ft. wide, with addition on north side 936 ft. long & 48 ft. wide, height 66 ft., cubic contents 33,000,000 ft., 3,230 columns for supporting roof, 34 miles of gutters, 202 miles of sash bars & 900,000 superficial ft. of glass, cost $399,000, but if permanently retained $750,000." It is interesting to find that while not completely finished it was opened at the appointed time of May 1, 1851 and that from May to October inclusive, there were in the building 6,170,000 persons for a daily average of 43,536.

FIGURE S—Outer View of bowl said to have come from the "Saracen's Head" in Gallowgate, Glasgow and presently in the People's Palace Museum, Glasgow (No. 10-1879). This is the bowl that was so interestingly presented by Mr. Michael Archer in his article—"Delftware made at the Glasgow pottery of Delftfield" in the September 1966 American Edition of "The Connoisseur" pages 16 through 22.

FIGURE S A—Interior view of bowl (FIGURE S) to enable the reader to compare with arms of the City of Glasgow (FIGURE T) to view what Mr. Archer had in mind when he said that it had been "painted with a free interpretation of the arms of the City of Glasgow". (That deviation from strict fact, form or rule in which an artist or writer indulges, assuming that it will be permitted for the sake of the advantage or effect gained; as, poetic license or artistic license.)

FIGURE T—Arms of the City of Glasgow, Scotland, adopted October 5, 1866.

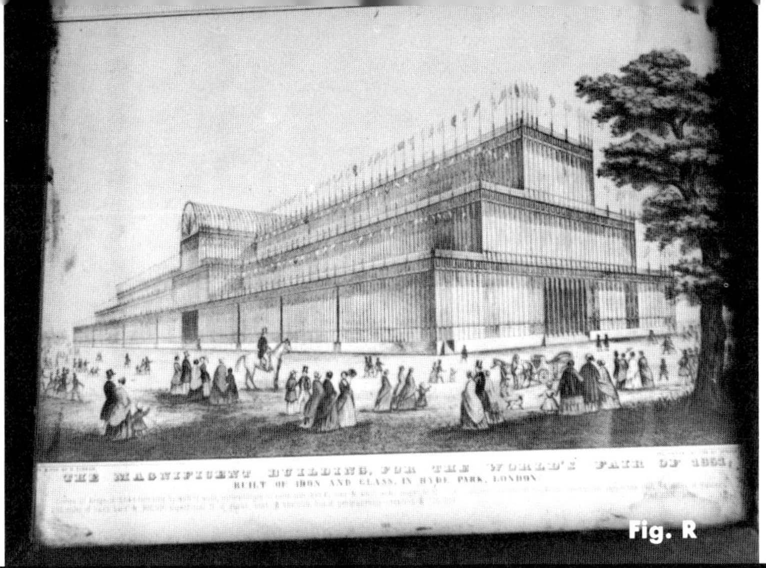

Fig. R

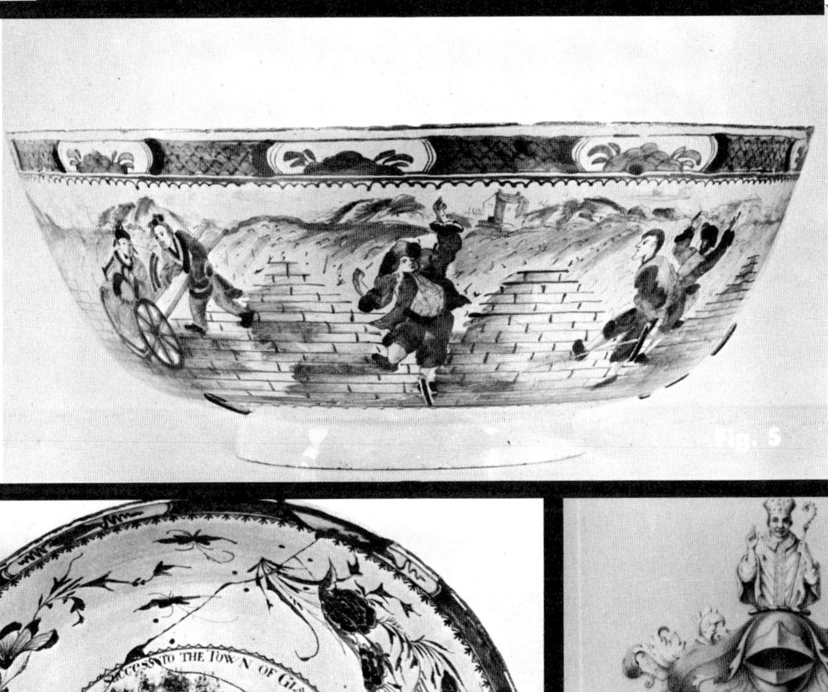
Fig. S

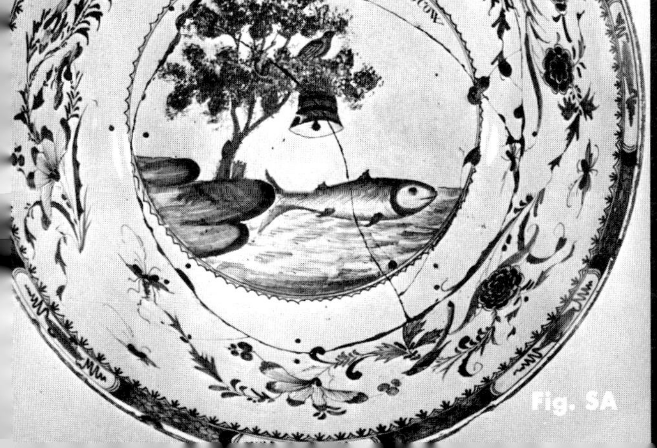

Fig. SA

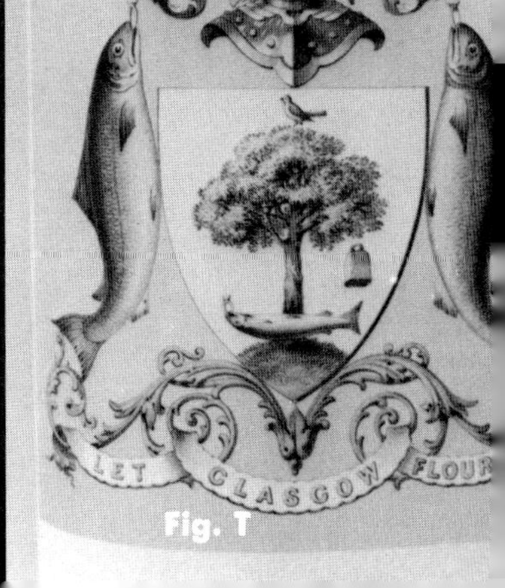

Fig. T

FIGURE U—Dish, plate, and cup as pictured by William Turner, list 393, opposite page 144, William Adams, An Old English Potter and described as dark blue dappled ground; bird with green body, tail red, neck bright blue—name "ADAMS" impressed and the owner is identified as "MRS. HAYNES".

FIGURE V—2 plates very early Delft, attributed to E. Ward, Senior and dated about 1680—note the elevated windmills, the unusual ladder effect at right of windmill on plate to the left.

FIGURE W—Unmarked Creamer—transfer with a jousting scene—one rider unhorsed.

FIGURE W A—other side of FIGURE W—new horse for downed rider.

FIGURE X—6¾ inch diameter plate, circa 1770, the foliage supplied with uncut sponge—the bird with the similar feeling as used on Spatterware, mechanically mottled border similar to tortoise shell decoration—and the border has impressed border moulded in relief with four plain panels enclosed by flower and scroll design. The four moulded panels have a flower and scroll design on the trelliswork background. An early attempt to follow Niglett in a Spatterware effort.

## BOOKS FOR REFERENCE AND STUDY

*Pictorial History of the American Circus*—John and Alice Durant—1957—A. S. Barnes and Company, Inc.

*September 1966 American Edition of "The Connoisseur"*

*Pottery*—Charles King—1966—Blackie & Son Ltd., Bishopbriggs, Glasgow.

*"The Concise Encyclopedia of English Pottery and Porcelain"*—Wolf Mankowitz & Reginald G. Haggar—1957—Hawthorn Books, Inc.

*Antiques Magazine*—April 1930

*Scottish Pottery*—J. Arnold Fleming, O.B.E.—1923—Maclehose, Jackson & Co.,—Glasgow.

*Staffordshire Pots & Potters*—G. Wooliscroft Rhead, R. E. and Frederick Alfred Rhead—1906—Hutchinson and Co., London.

*The Armorial Insignia of The City of Glasgow*—A. Macgeorge—1866—W. G. Blackie and Co.,—Glasgow.

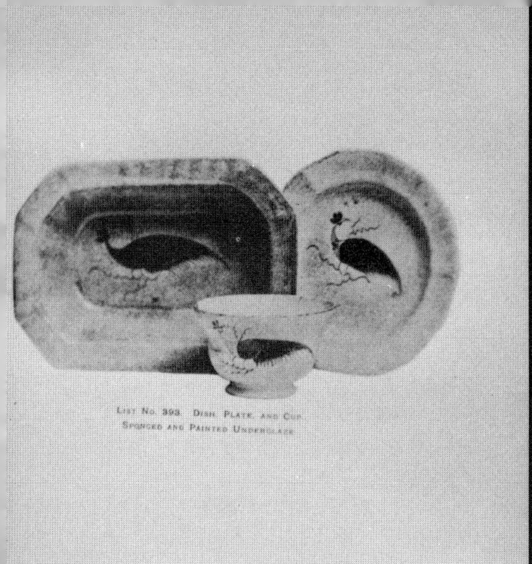


Fig. U

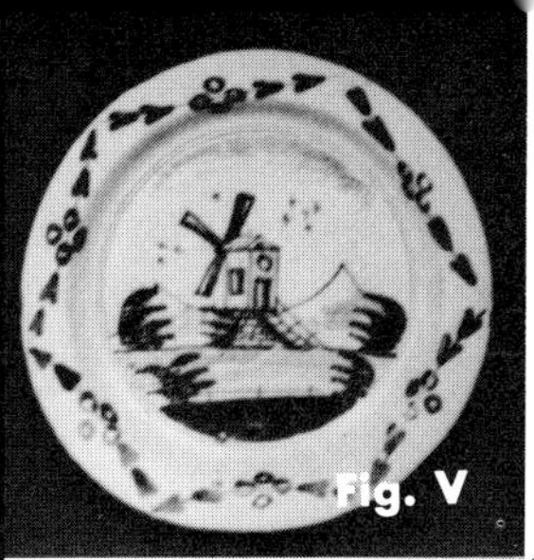

Fig. V

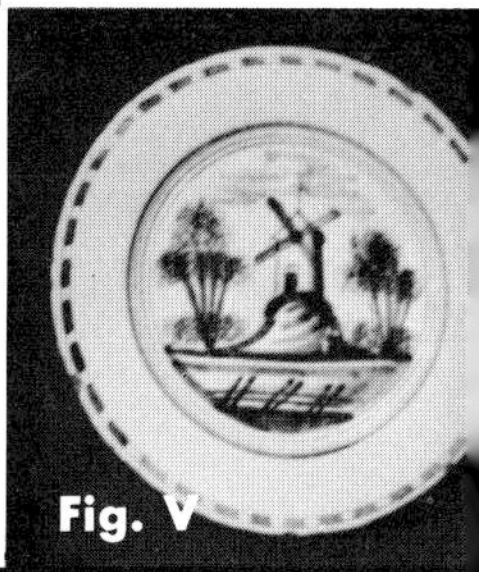

Fig. V

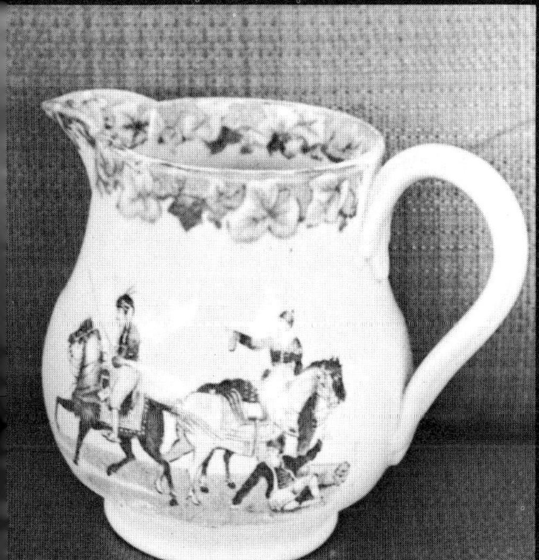

Fig. W

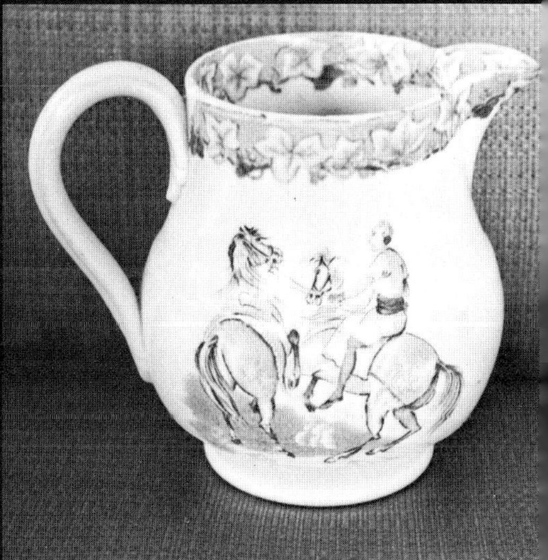

Fig. WA

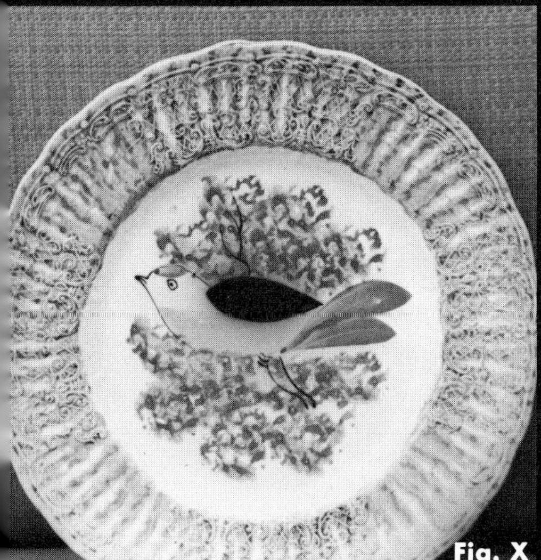

Fig. X

# BOOKS FOR REFERENCE AND STUDY

*The Old China Book*—N. Hudson Moore—1903—Frederick A Stokes Co.

*The Art of the Old English Potter*—L. M. Solon—1906—John Francis Co.

*The Connoisseur's Handbook of Antique Collecting*—Helena Hayward—1960—The Connoisseur.

*Handbook of Old Pottery and Porcelain Marks*—C. Jordan Thorn—1962—Tudor Publishing Co.

*Tulip Ware of the Pennsylvania-German Potters*—Edwin Atlee Barber—1903—Pennsylvania Museum and School of Industrial Art.

*Chats on Old Earthenware*—Arthur Hayden—1909—Frederick A. Stokes Co.

*Ten Generations of a Potting Family*—William Turner—1931—Percy Lund, Humphries & Co. Ltd.

*A Pride of Potters*—Derek Peel—1957—Morrison and Gibb Ltd.

*A Handbook of Popular Antiques*—Katharine Morrison McClinton—1946—Random House.

*Ceramics for the Artist Potter*—F. H. Norton—1956—Addison-Wesley Publishing Co., Inc.

*An Encyclopedia of Antiques*—Harold Lewis Bond—1947—Tudor Publishing Co.

*Early American Pottery and China*—John Spargo—1926—Garden City Publishing Co.

*Ceramic Art of Great Britain*—Llewellynn Jewitt—1883—J. S. Virtue & Co.

*A.B.C. of Collecting Old English Pottery*—J. F. Blacker—N. D.—Stanley Paul & Co.

*English Pottery and Porcelain*—The English Ceramic Circle—1949—Routledge and Kegan Paul Ltd.

*English Pottery*—The Burnap Collection—1953—Nelson-Atkins Gallery of Art.

*Pennsylvania Dutch Stuff*—Earl F. Robacker—1961—University of Pennsylvania Press.

*English Porcelain and Bone China*—Bernard & Therle Hughes—1960—Lutterworth Press.

*The Old Derby China Factory*—John Haslem—1876—George Bell and Sons.

*Concise Encyclopedia of Antiques*—Volumes 1, 2, 3, 4—The Connoisseur—1954—Hawthorn Books.

*Bennington Pottery and Porcelain*—Richard Carter Barret—1958—Crown Publishers.

*William Adams, An Old English Potter*—William Turner—1904—Keramic Studio Publishing Co.

*Marks and Monograms on European and Oriental Pottery and Porcelain*—William Chaffers—1946—Borden Publishing Co.

*Pennsylvania Dutch, American Folk Art*—Henry Kauffman—1946—American Studio Books.

*The Chemistry of Pottery*—Karl Langenbeck—1895—Chemical Publishing Co.

*The Collecting of Antiques*—Esther Singleton—1926—Macmillan Co.

*Tin Enamelled Pottery*—Edwin Atlee Barber—1907—Doubleday, Page & Co.

*Pennsylvania Folk Art*—John Joseph Stoudt—1948—Schlechter's.

*The Index of American Design*—Edwin O. Christensen—1950—Macmillan Co.

*Catalogue of the Collection of English Pottery in the Department of British and Medieval Antiquities and Ethnography of the British Museum*—R. L. Hobson—1903—Bemrose and Sons, Ltd.

*English Delft Pottery*—Major R. G. Mundy—1927—Herbert Jenkins Ltd.

*Catalogue of Lowestoft China in the possession of Frederick Arthur Crisp*—1907—privately printed—Grove Park Press.

*English Painted Enamels*—Therle and Bernard Hughes—1951—Charles Scribner's Sons.

*Dictionary of Antiques and the Decorative Arts*—Louise Ade Boger and H. Batterson Boger—1957—Charles Scribner's Sons.

*A New Guide to Old Pottery*—Reginald Haggar—1950—Medill McBride Co.

*The New Keramic Gallery*—2 Volumes—William Chaffers—1926—Reeves and Turner.

*English Delftware*—F. H. Garner—N.D.—Pitman Publishing Corp.

*Staffordshire Pottery and its History*—Josiah C. Wedgwood—1913—McBride, Nast & Co.

*Old Bristol Potteries*—W. J. Pountney—1920—E. P. Dutton & Co.

*Anglo-American Pottery*—Edwin Atlee Barber—1901—Patterson & White Co.

*English Blue and White Porcelain of the 18th Century*—Stanley W. Fisher—1947—B. T. Batsford Ltd.

*Wedgwood and Artists*—Harry M. Buten—1960—Buten Museum of Wedgwood.

*The Red Hills*—Cornelius Weygandt—1929—University of Pennsylvania Press.

*The Story of Wedgwood*—Alison Kelly—1962—Viking Press.

*Wedgwood, A Living Tradition*—John Meredith Graham II and Hensleigh Cecil Wedgwood—1948—Brooklyn Institute of Arts and Sciences—Brooklyn Museum—John B. Watkins Co.

*America's Arts and Skills*—Editors of Life—1957—E. P. Dutton & Co.

*English Pottery*—Bernard Rackham and Herbert Read—1924—Ernest Benn, Limited.

*Pennsylvania Dutch Art*—Ruth Adams—1950—World Publishing Co.

*Anglo-American China*—Sam Laidacker—1954.

*American Antique Collector*—Sam Laidacker—October-November, 1939.

*American Antiques Collector*—Sam Laidacker—March, 1940.

*American Antiques Collector*—Sam Laidacker—Volume 111 #8—1952.

*Dictionary of Marks—Pottery and Porcelain*—Ralph M. and Terry H. Kovel—1964—Crown Publishers, Inc.

*Oxford Universal Dictionary*—1955—Rand McNally & Co.—Conkey Division.

*European Ceramic Art*—W. B. Honey—N. D.—Book Collectors Society.

*Old English Lustre Pottery*—W. D. John and Warren Baker—1962—Ceramic Book Co.

*French Faience*—Jeanne Giacomotti—1963—Universe Books.

*1851 and the Crystal Palace*—Christopher Hobhouse—1937—E. P. Dutton & Co., Inc.